THIS INCREDIBLE LONGING

*Finding My Self
in a Near-Cult Experience*

BLAIR GLASER

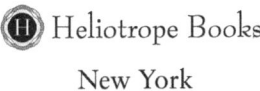

Heliotrope Books
New York

Copyright © 2026 Blair Glaser

All rights reserved. No part of this book may be reproduced or transmitted in any form or by any means, electronic or mechanical, including photocopying, recording or by an information storage or retrieval system now known or hereafter invented—except by a reviewer who may quote brief passages in a review to be printed in a magazine or newspaper—without permission in writing from the publisher.

Heliotrope Books, LLC
heliotropebooks@gmail.com

ISBN 978-1-956474-74-9
ISBN 978-1-956474-75-6 eBook

Cover design by Rick Simner
Designed and typeset by Naomi Rosenblatt with AJ&J Design

Praise for *This Incredible Longing*

"For anyone who's ever questioned their path, their faith, or themselves, *This Incredible Longing* is a companion for the in-between. This isn't a story about finding the light. It's about walking through the dark and learning how to see."
—Kaitlyn Herman, ICF Certified Life Coach / Wellness Influencer

"A wise and emotionally generous account of a period of transformational growth by an author who is well-equipped to carry the dialectic truth that even an imperfect environment can give birth to a life-changing experience. Written with admirable self-awareness and deep compassion, Blair held me captivated on her journey from the naivety of her early adulthood through to her own unique version of spiritual enlightenment."
—Oliver Radclyffe, author *Frighten the Horses*

"It's easy to write about the harmful aspects of having submitted to life in a religious cult. In *This Incredible Longing*, Blair Glaser pulls off a more difficult and nuanced trick, unsentimentally excavating the twentysomething of herself and the tendencies that made her vulnerable, while also acknowledging what good she took away from the experience. This memoir will resonate strongly with anyone who had a quarter-life crisis that led them to make questionable choices as young adults; anyone who rejected the faith they were programmed to grow up in, in order to find their true spiritual nature; and anyone who ever longed to feel as if they belonged, which is everyone."
—Sari Botton, Oldster Magazine editor, author *And You May Find Yourself*

"*This Incredible Longing* is Blair Glaser's memoir of how a smart, skeptical New Yorker got pulled into the glow of a near-cult—and why she's grateful for what she found there. Equal parts funny, heartbreaking, and uncomfortably familiar, it's the story of how longing can make us vulnerable, how gurus thrive on our hunger, and how you can walk away carrying both scars and gifts."
—Daniella Mestyanek Young, author *Uncultured* and *The Culting of America*

"Glaser's writing is evocative, relatable, and humorous. It's a relief to read a book that does not take a hard line for or against a place, but rather explores the greater longing in human beings, and how places and institutions can both serve and exploit at once. Nothing is easy—Glaser demonstrates this in her heartfelt examination and tender exploration."
—Anna Rollins, author *Famished: On Food, Sex, and Growing Up as a Good Girl*

"What draws us to spiritual communities, and where is the line between devotion and delusion? *This Incredible Longing* chronicles Blair Glaser's search for transcendence within an organization that promises enlightenment but unravels in scandal. With wit and candor, Glaser reveals the tensions between belonging and autonomy, leaving seekers of all kinds with a nuanced take on faith, power, and personal transformation."
—Jeffrey Davis, author *Tracking Wonder*

"For anyone who has gotten lured into something you are not quite sure about, but you felt the need to follow your impulse to explore it. Blair Glaser's *This Incredible Longing* takes us inside the relatable journey of getting drawn into a cult (or something that might be a cult?) with the wisdom and self-awareness of a tale brilliantly told 30 years after it happened. If you are a searcher with longings of your own, you will love this book."
—Sasha Cagen, author *Quirkyalone: A Manifesto for Uncompromising Romantics*

To my teachers

Contents

Author's Note	8
Prologue: Lost and Found	9
1: Tapasaya	15
2: The Nameless Ache	23
3: Loaves & Fishy	34
4: Equipoise	44
5: Knots of the Heart	52
6: A Real Guru	59
7: Tested	66
8: Longing	77
9: Bridge	85
10: Recognition	97
11: The Orange Flag	105
12: A New Nurse	113
13: Absolute Faith	125
14: Quarantine	132
15: Blazing	140
16: Wannabe-ananda	148
17: The Guru's Hat	156
18: Correspondence	167
19: Righteousness	176
20: Invitation	190
21: The Doctors	198
22: *The New Yorker*	205
23: Velvet Air	212
24: A Trail of Equipoise	224
Epilogue: Reckoning	229
Author Bio	234
Acknowledgments	235

Author's Note

This is a work of creative nonfiction. I relied heavily on my journals to create the narrative. Most names and some identifying features of many characters have been changed, and a minor character became a composite. On rare occasions, the timeline of events has been altered for better storytelling, but all the contents are true. This story is from my point of view, as my memory serves. But memory, as we have learned, is totally subjective. Others may tell it differently.

Prologue: Lost and Found, 2003

I'm not exactly sure how one manages to get lost in Tompkins Square Park. It's only four blocks wide and one block long. Yet, on an early spring day, en route to the hair salon, I looked up from the half-moon path that winds its way through the park's belly and didn't know where I was. Was I facing Avenue B, where I was headed, or was that Seventh Street? Had I walked far enough around the semi-circle that I was now facing back uptown?

I entered the park at Ninth and A, completely absorbed in an elaborate fantasy about moving to Los Angeles. So absorbed, I barely noticed the twisted hypodermic needles beneath the benches, or the stream of passing New Yorkers I habitually checked out to determine whether or not they were a threat, sexually desirable, or enviably fashionable.

My life in New York City had taken a turn for the worse. My best friend had started dating my recent ex, and needless to say, she wasn't my best friend anymore. My car had just been rear-ended by a huge truck at a traffic light in Bed-Stuy. I was fine, but a passerby summed up the damage nicely: "That *wuz* a Jetta." My landlord was selling my lovely little one-bedroom Park Slope apartment, and I was in no position to buy it. I had to be out of the apartment by the end of the month.

LA, a city I'd lived in for one year after college, suddenly seemed like the answer. My remaining best friend lived there, as did my cousin and the sexy screenwriter I met on my last visit. I imagined an instant community to replace the one falling apart in New York, a community very different from the one I found the first time I'd moved to LA. I cringed in remembrance: moving to LA to be an actress, sinking into depression and then falling for a guru and the golden carrot of "enlightenment" — a concept which as a therapist I now viewed as a ruse to keep people spinning in the web of their own inadequacies.

But that was then. *Leaving New York wouldn't be running away from life now,* I told myself. *It would be running towards it.* I wanted to pack up my private practice which had taken five years to establish, and transport it to the other coast, as if LA clients would simply line up to work with me.

I had ten minutes before I was due at the salon, but I had no idea where I was. How on earth had I gotten so spun around? I prided myself on knowing my way around the city I had grown up in, and I was mortified. I just needed to find Avenue B. I scanned the perimeter, trying to locate a landmark, a street sign, anything familiar through the gray-green veil of burgeoning tree blossoms. A colorful awning sporting graffiti became my compass point. As I approached what I eventually recognized as Seventh Street, the bubble letters emerged into the words *Soul Dog*.

I didn't know what Soul Dog had in store, but maybe I could get my bearings and find something to nosh.

Soul Dog could have been a drug front. It had white office ceiling tiles and depressing, fluorescent lights. A small glass food heater stood on one side of the countertop, spinning glistening hot dogs. A CD boombox sat on the other.

"They're tofu," said the man behind the counter, of the dogs behind the glass. "The regular ones are in the steamer." He wore a stylish t-shirt and his dyed-black hair was firm with gel. He unpacked and folded up boxes. "Sorry, we're just getting up and running here. I plan to have a variety of options once we get set up."

"Cool," I said, eyeing the drinks in a fridge behind the counter.

The boombox released a quiet sound that caused my eyes to widen, searching to place it. It was the hum of a tamboura, an Indian instrument that makes a meditative twang. But it wasn't just any tamboura. *I know that particular twang*, I thought, as I contemplated a diet soda and Tofu Pup. And then the flute came in, the flute that sang a melody I knew so well, and it struck me to the core: it was the version of the *Pasayadan* — a devotional poem by the 13th-century King Jnaneshwar — that had played in the Siddha Yoga ashram where I lived, after LA, for over a year.

I stood there, fingers tingling, breath deepening. That gorgeous, lilting melody was only played during *darshan*, a time when you knelt before the spiritual teacher and placed your head at her feet to receive blessings, ask questions, and get direction.

In the middle of the East Village, in a barren hot dog shop with bad lighting, I stood listening to the music that I'd associated with the most sacred of experiences. Minutes before, I'd lost my bearings. Now, I was deep in a *Twilight Zone* episode, experiencing a conditioned response of receptivity to blessings. Maybe, in Soul Dog, I was being found.

"Gurumayi?!" I asked the friendly young man, saying my old guru's name in disbelief. I had never heard the *Pasayadan* played outside the ashram. You couldn't buy it at Tower Records. Although recordings of some of the other chants could be heard in little dosa shops from Amagansett to Prince Street and the Upper West Side, you really had to be in the know to own or play them.

"Yes! You know her?!" he asked, raising his eyebrows.

"Yes. Yes, I do."

"I love Gurumayi," he said, looking down at a box crease and shaking his head. "She tried to save my life ... But I didn't listen."

He looked up at me to see if I was following. I was.

"Basically, I asked her if I should move to LA." He returned to breaking down boxes and folding them. "She told me not to, and, you know — when the guru tells you to do something, it's a sacred command. But I went anyway. It was a complete disaster. I mean, the worst experience of my life. Now I'm back. I'm living with my mother while I get this business off the ground."

I stood motionless as the confluence of information hit me. I felt like someone far away was tickling me with the end of a peacock feather — one of the materials the Siddha Yoga gurus used during *darshan* to transmit blessings. I started to giggle.

Am I really in an East Village hot dog shop called Soul Dog, *with the* Pasayadan *playing, hearing a story in which Gurumayi told someone not to go to LA after seriously fantasizing about moving there?* This experience, one of having "powers that be" send me a psychic telegraph with a broad-toothed smile and an exaggerated wink, was very familiar. It was a hallmark of the relationship with my spiritual teacher, Gurumayi, whose playful persona apparently transcended time and space to freely dole out slaps upside the head, inspiring epiphany and awe.

I spent the walk to the salon — and the better part of the day — shaking my head and muttering to myself, marveling at the coincidences. I felt as if the whole little play, or *lila*, as it is called in Sanskrit, was orchestrated just for me. Friends would come and go, break the girl code, deal in half-truths, do the thing you never thought they would. But in Soul Dog, I was powerfully reminded that, whether or not I believed in enlightenment, I had loyal "friends" in spirit, a lineage of teachers rooting for me. Friends who were a part of so many serendipitous moments like this one that seemed beyond explanation, which pointed to a mysterious truth: even when I abandoned my faith, it didn't abandon me. Friends who drew me to a place inside myself that I hadn't known existed, a fountain of awareness beyond my personality. Friends who, even when I lost touch, forgot their birthdays, or looked back upon our relationship with embarrassment, still showed up to let me know when I was on the brink of making a really bad decision.

I didn't move to LA. I didn't go back to the ashram, or even start meditating again with any regularity. But I was compelled to revisit my uncanny story — which sometimes looked like I'd gotten sucked into a crazy cult — to recoup the many gifts within it that could help me move forward, including the ability to trust that, when least expected, love would find me when I lost my way.

PART I:
OH, MOTHER, WHERE ART THOU?

"I am quite used to skeptics, they generally turn out to be the most vulnerable and receptive in the long run."
—Noel Coward, *Blithe Spirit*

1: Tapasya

South Fallsburg, NY; 1992

In the echo of the car door slam, I knew exactly what I wanted to do: grab a bite, shower off the travel anxiety of the past twenty-four hours, and collapse into bed. But as we made our way from the parking lot to the registration building, my agenda slipped away. Crowds of people clustered around the entrance.

"Ah, a line!" Gabby said as we made our way inside. Her green eyes opened wider and she wore a tentative smile. "I forgot to tell you about them."

She led the way to what we thought was the back. We turned a corner and stood there. A man behind us holding a peacoat pointed it at us and then towards a row of people behind him, shooing us further back.

"Wow," I sighed. The line snaked through several layers of tape rope into another room.

"Welcome to *tapasya*," Gabby said, using the Sanskrit term for austerity, also known as the "burning" of karma or impurities while on the spiritual path. "I can't believe you're *here*!"

"Me neither," I said, trying to project excitement. This was not what I imagined my first visit to The Ashram would be like. In fact, all the pictures I'd had in my mind of this peaceful, powerful place clashed with the chaotic scene before me. My first time, and instead of peace, all I felt was irritation and impatience. Clearly, I was in the right place: I had a lot of spiritual work to do.

The ashram smelled like the LA and Chicago centers I'd been to: vaguely of nag champa, a sweet, sandalwood-y incense. And the ashram, too, was decorated with large framed photos, mostly of Gurumayi dressed in various shades of red, gazing intensely or laughing ecstatically as though someone was tickling her. But at its core, the registration lobby, with its floor-to-ceiling windows, looked like a hotel that forgot to dim its indoor lights and piped Sanskrit chanting instead of Muzak through the sound system.

"Can you tell it was a hotel?" Gabby asked as we settled into the mile-long queue of devotees. "All the ashram buildings were once Catskill summer resorts — *for Jews*. Crazy. Like, our parents probably stayed here."

I shook my head and looked around, trying to imagine my parents here, wincing at the thought. The loudspeaker chant failed to soothe my mounting agitation. Upon our arrival, a misty rain was evaporating crusty old snow, and a chill worked its way into my now West Coast bones. The gray sky was morphing into the royal blue of dusk.

Though she no longer lived at the ashram, Gabby looked at home in the environment. She'd cut her hair shorter, let it go from dyed blond to her natural brown, and wore a long cotton pullover called a *punjab* over an ankle-length skirt. Skirts and dresses were the preferred ashram attire for women. I had on black leggings that still smelled of airplane. Gabby had pressed a circle of red turmeric known as *kumkum* into the space between her eyebrows to form a *bindi*. I wanted to reach out and push it with my index finger. The clock and the line stood still. I sank beneath the weight of my backpack.

The only thing that would make this moment more bearable would be if Gurumayi walked in. I heard she sometimes breezed through the ashram, uplifting everyone as she did. What I wouldn't give to see her graceful form sauntering through the lobby and feel the elevated vibe that came with it — the crackling energy I had experienced once in a powerful dream when she showed up. The thought of it made my heart beat faster.

"Hi Prita!" An official *sevite* — as noted by the green STAFF sticker on her nametag — stopped by the line. Gabby turned away from me to greet her. I unzipped my parka.

"Sundara, hi!" They shared a light embrace.

Gabby had a new name: *Prita* — dearest — given to her from the guru herself. Various people I'd met at the LA Center — clearly not of South Asian descent — had Sanskrit names like Kamuda, Parvani, Mandala, which had been given to them by the guru as spiritual names. But I couldn't call Gabby *Prita*. To me, she was and would always be Gab or Gabby.

"Are you coming to Amrit *seva*?" Sundara, who actually was of Indian descent and wore a fancy silk *punjab*, asked in a lilting voice.

"Yes! I'll be there tomorrow." Gabby said. "Tonight I'm helping my friend Blair get settled in. It's her first time."

"Ohhhh. Welcome!" Sundara's eyes sparkled with her smile. "Going to the Intensive?"

I nodded. My brow moistened.

"It is sure to be a *maha* intensive," she said, using the Sanskrit word for grand. "Oh, and tonight's vegetable biryani is sublime. See you!"

I took off my parka. I felt like a tourist, not knowing the land, the layout, the language. Gabby leaned in. "Sundara's the head of the Main Building Amrit. I report to her for *seva* there. They're going to be busy this weekend."

The Amrit was the name for Siddha Yoga restaurants and snack bars worldwide and meant *nectar* in Sanskrit. Gabby's current *seva* — selfless service — of cleaning in Amrit seemed a step up from her summer *seva* of riding around on an ashram garbage truck in an orange jumpsuit picking up trash.

I took off my pack and put it on the floor in front of me, kicking it along as we inched closer to the registration desk. The smell of that biryani — stronger than my airplane BO — wafted over from the dining hall, and my stomach responded with a pining gurgle.

There was a large Indian family speaking a dialect of Hindi. There were a number of kids running around the line — alternately irksome and refreshing to see that people included their families. There were hip, smart-looking New Yorkers with expensive plastic glasses, flowy-clothed spiritual types, and a couple speaking Spanish at the registration desk, which appeared to be more than 100 people away. They all seemed so calm. After forty-five minutes, we shuffled two feet closer to the desk.

"The dining hall closes at 6:30. I hope we make it," Gab said. The big hand on the clock was close to five past. All the excitement that had been building since I'd heard about this Valentine's Day Intensive at the LA Center took a nosedive. After months of hearing her video talks and then hearing her voice inside of me, I wanted to meet Gurumayi more than anything. But being in the ashram made me panicky. In LA, I could pretend I was just occupying my free time with visits to the center, and I could just drive home after the program, even though I could feel my life changing with each practice I did. I'd been attending the Saturday night programs of chanting, meditation, and a video talk by Gurumayi — that had been recorded live in a hall on this very campus — in LA for three months. I felt calmer, more at ease, and notably not depressed. But since I knew so few people in LA, it was like I'd been leading a secret life. Nobody knew where I'd been spending my Saturday nights, or that I spent them doing spiritual practice. Being at the ashram was next level. *How did I even get here?*

In LA, whenever a devotee stood at the front of the hall and announced in soft, lush tones the details of an upcoming course, I would stop listening and look around the room at who was in it. The plugs for paid courses and classes interfered with my delight in the Center's free programs, which were lavish: in addition to videos of Gurumayi, they included live musicians and chanters in a beautiful carpeted hall. Then one January eve, when the emcee, a TV actress, announced that Gurumayi was going to be at the ashram in New York for a Valentine's Day Intensive, which had some sentimental title like *Living in Love*, I felt a click so strong it was as if it had a literal sound: *I would be going to this Intensive.*

Intensives were a two-day immersion in the *Shakti,* the meditative energy that guaranteed an experience of *Shaktipat* initiation: the transference of awakened spiritual energy from the master to the student. Gab had already taken two of them. Intensives weren't essential to spiritual progress, but the practices were, and Intensives were deep dives into practice, increasing your chances of having a profound and otherworldly spiritual experience. Plus, meeting Gurumayi in person was also guaranteed.

At the LA center that night, the pull to attend the Intensive in New York was more a feeling of destiny than choice. But then the actress quoted the price: $600. Even with the full-time job I'd gotten at a cutting-edge skincare company, it was too much. Even if I could pay for the Intensive, the plane tickets back east would push it over the edge. How could I make it work? As soon as I asked the question, the answer unfurled itself in a series of steps: I still had one more airline ticket voucher from American Express, which granted college students three free round-trip off-hour plane tickets when they signed up for the card. I would put the Intensive on the card, use my voucher to get there, and since the Intensive coincided with President's Day, I would miss only one day of work. I would stay in the cheap dorm, $25 a night, and ask Gab, who I knew would be thrilled at my decision to finally meet Gurumayi, to pick me up from the airport and drive us upstate. That way I would owe exactly $650 on the card — which would be easier to pay off now that I'd quit acting classes to focus full time on my *sadhana,* my spiritual growth. Done.

Back on the line there were ten people ahead of us. At five minutes each it might be fifty more minutes of standing. I'd protected myself by not buying into Siddha Yoga — at least not with money. But now I wondered — as I stood there supposedly burning up my impurities, with a raised body temperature to prove it — if I'd gotten snookered. *At least there are other people from all around the world who came here for this experience,* I thought. If I was in a cult, I wasn't alone.

I stared at the back of Gab's head and tried to calm myself. Gab was still, and her erect posture clashed with my slumping. If she was perturbed about waiting in line, it didn't show, but my irritation was unmasked, and this bothered me. She definitely had the upper hand in this situation, and my dependency on her made me vulnerable to her whims. Just before I'd left, she bowed out of picking me up at the airport, claiming, "It's too early!" So I had to spring for a cab to her house. Just a year ago, as seniors in college, when we were both actors in a short film together, I expressed doubt about my acting. She didn't do a thing to disabuse me of it. But then, and maybe reactively, I never complimented her acting, either. Now, as the less experienced disciple, I could feel her gloat scratching at me like a sharp-edged tag inside my T-shirt.

Our bond was competitive, but it was also made up of a common love of spiritual and psychological growth, and knowing intimately the pressures of growing up in New York City. During our senior year at Northwestern where we met, we were both brought to the Siddha Yoga Center of Chicago by different people within a span of two weeks. I was shocked when Gab traveled to New York to meet Gurumayi and see if she was the real deal, decided she was, and quickly moved to the ashram over spring break. *What's happened to my best friend?* I thought. But now, I envied her for her calm, how she knew her way around, knew all the lingo and most of all, for her personal connection with our teacher Gurumayi, which seemed to accelerate her spiritual growth.

"This is Atma Nidhi — where you'll come for meals," Gabby Prita said, describing the ashram campus to pass the time. In addition to the dining hall, Atma Nidhi also had accommodations for families. A partially modernized building in the throes of a full-scale renovation, some portion of it was always walled off with cloudy plastic sheets.

The line swung closer to the lobby doors and every time the door opened, a burst of cold air came in. I put my parka back on. Gab's verbal tour was soothing, and I was glad she resumed. "Anugraha is where you'll spend most of your time. It's also known as the Main Building. It's got the Intensive hall, the temple, the meditation cave, and the best Amrit. Plus, Gurumayi's house is there," Gab continued, "so she's more visible. We'll take the bus there tomorrow morning for the *Guru Gita*." I remembered seeing a big yellow school bus exiting the ashram grounds when we pulled in. It shuttled yogis between the three buildings all day.

"We'll be staying at Sadhana Kutir, the economical building," Gab said with raised eyebrows. Other than the airy, modern dorms, Sadhana Kutir was stuck in the 50s and pretty rundown. "Wait 'til you see the ornate carpet and dilapidated wood-paneled walls."

I couldn't wait. I wanted to go there immediately and plop my head on a pillow. Well, after eating something, anyway.

Nearly two hours after we'd arrived, registration was complete. My name tag had a little photo of me, the dates of my stay, and a sticker signifying I was a first-timer. We stuffed our square bundle of clean sheets and a measly white towel into our packs and shuffled over to a new line at the nearby dining hall, which thankfully was still open.

A stay at the ashram included three vegetarian meals per day, and everyone talked about how delicious they were and how it was impossible that meals cooked for so many could end up tasting so good. "It must be the blessings," people surmised. When we finally reached the long serving tables, welcoming devotees from behind them smiled and doled out dahl into plastic bowls, placing them on our sectioned trays, which were then piled high with biryani and other vegetables. The proximity to food helped the frenetic energy in my chest settle, although the food looked pretty sloppy and sad by the time we'd gotten to it. Gabby Prita found us a table with some people she knew from the city.

"It's Blair's first time at the ashram," she announced. "She came from LA where she's been attending programs at the Center."

"Ohhhhh," the diners responded, as if they knew a secret.

As I started eating, I stopped listening to the chatter — inside and out. The food *was* sublime. I couldn't then name the coriander, paprika, cumin, or ginger in the dahl, but each flavor erupted in little bursts over my tongue. And Sundara was right about the biryani.

A kind, red-headed woman jolted me out of my food trance. "So, Blair ... how did you get into Siddha Yoga?"

I wiped an errant piece of rice off my chin. The Siddha Yoga origin story: the stuff of legends. Everyone had one. Some were boring: *A friend introduced me, My sister got involved, and I tagged along one night and got Shaktipat.* Others were miraculous, like one I'd recently heard in LA: *I was in the ICU — heart attack — and asked the nurse what she was reading. She told me, "Play of Consciousness by this guru, Baba Swami Muktanada." The next night I had a dream in which Baba — Gurumayi's guru — told me I'd be fine, but I needed to heal my heart by loving. I bought the book as soon as I got out of the hospital, and the rest is history.*

What would I tell the lovely redhead whose name, I gleaned from her nametag, was Joan, about how I'd gotten involved? Would I tell her about feeling so lost and alone in LA that I almost took my own life but instead chanted the mantra and everything changed? No, that was too much for dinner. Should I tell her about the dream with Gurumayi or start from way back when I was little and loved God but hated Temple, wanting something I couldn't name? I looked at Gab for direction.

"Very slowly," she said. Everyone at the table laughed.

I decided on simple and true: "For a reason I couldn't understand, I was attracted to this set designer from a play I was in." A man nodded his head, as if he'd had an attraction, too. "I kept thinking about him, and when I learned a year later that his best friend and mine had started dating, they set us up. He brought me to a Center one night. We didn't work out, but the mantra did."

Before I could ask them for their stories, they pushed their chairs back and got up with their trays, bobbing their heads and wishing me a good Intensive. Gab and I sat for a moment in the silence that followed the clatter, and then we made our way to the bus stop to catch a ride to Sadhana Kutir.

2: The Nameless Ache
New York City; 1975-87

I remember the first time I felt it, though that doesn't mean I hadn't before. I was seven, my sister had just turned four, and the guests were leaving her birthday party. I was helping my mother crumple wrapping paper into a garbage bag, relieved to be done with the boisterous kiddos, constant nudges to "say cheese!" and overbearing oohs and ahhs that erupted when my sister's little hands opened her gifts. I couldn't wait to be alone with my diary, Broadway albums, and colored pastels. But when I finally closed the door to my room, it was as if another door had shut inside me: I couldn't find my way into my own company. I sat there, frozen, staring at my Victrola.

I had no name for this sensation. If I could have articulated it then, I might have said: "I want something, but I don't know what, and it hurts." My actor self would learn to call it "blocked." Later, in therapy, I called it "depression," and my therapist sometimes corrected me: "dissociation." Over the years, the sore spot turned into a gaping hole, the kind of demon that Buddhists call The Hungry Ghost. It sprouted into what the Diagnostics and Statistics Manual, the DSM-5, calls 307.51 (F50.8): a Binge Eating Disorder.

Eventually I would meet teachers who could name and help me sort through it, but back then, in trying to make sense of that numbing sensation, I settled on the word "bored."

I left my room to seek out my mother, who was in the dining room removing the Pin the Tail on the Donkey poster from the wall.

"Dammit, this tape wasn't supposed to leave a mark," she said, digging her polished nail into the linty spot.

"Mommy, I'm bored," I said.

"Go play with your sister, she just got a ton of new toys." Her gaze remained on the wall.

I didn't want to play with my sister or her toys. I knew how that would go. Any toy I played with, she'd suddenly want, and we'd fight. I didn't know that maybe I needed a hug, and, as the big sister, I certainly wouldn't have known how to ask for one — that was "baby" territory. The nameless ache was mine to manage alone.

Until I learned about God.

I only went to Sunday school because of my cousin Ricky. Anything he did, I wanted to do, too. We lived in the same apartment building, went to the same school, and because I always followed his lead, when our parents left us to our own devices, we caused trouble (once famously leaving my sister alone with the Art-o-matic, a paint spinner that ended up decorating her and her entire room).

Ricky was three years older and, as a boy, had to attend Sunday school to prepare for his Bar Mitzvah, the Jewish coming-into-adulthood ceremony. As a girl, it wasn't a requirement in my family, but I wouldn't be left behind. When we learned the story of Moses, I was amazed. God spoke to him through fire?! Was it a story, like Santa, or did God, who I pictured as a bearded white-robed man in the sky, really exist? And would He ever speak to *me*?

The question circled round and round in my head like the cars on Ricky's Hot Wheels race track. God. Does He know me? Does He know my parents? One night, I approached my father for answers. Daddy sometimes reminded me of the kind-hearted, children's TV show star, Mr. Rogers. He not only looked like him but he was sort of like the Mr. Rogers of Wall Street — a friendly, trustworthy money manager in a field riddled with corruption. He'd settled into a cushy armchair in the living room after work, ice cubes tinkling in his vodka. Paul McCartney was singing through the stereo, which meant the "Silly Love Songs" song — my favorite! — was coming up.

"Daddy, do you believe in God?" I asked, standing by his chair in my favorite Bugs Bunny footie PJs. I leaned my elbows on his armrest while my legs played hopscotch. He puckered his lips and took a sip.

"Yes, yes I do," he said, nodding.

I stopped hopping. I was sure he was going to say no. "But you don't go to temple that much."

"Well, I do go every year on the High Holidays. But you don't have to go to temple to believe in God."

Good, I thought. I hated temple. Everything about it was dreary: the inside of the Brooklyn-Battery Tunnel on the way there, the low-hanging clouds on the other side, the creeping silence in the car as we approached my grandfather's Orthodox schul in Manhattan Beach. My mother, aunt, and I sat on a hardwood bench on the women's side, separated from my father, uncle, and Ricky, and then we all stood, sat, and stood again for what seemed to be an eternal Yom Kippur service. I was always hungry. My sister got out of it on account of being a baby. Lucky her.

Daddy thought that believing in God meant "trying to be a good person and doing the right thing." That answer felt flat to me, because I wanted a relationship, someone to talk to. On the other hand, my mother didn't even believe in God. She only went to temple because my poppy would be mad if she didn't.

"I believe in reincarnation," Mommy told me one night after dinner, taking a drag of her True cigarette and releasing smoke clouds through her nose. "Nothing really dies. Everything comes back."

Everything comes back. My mommy was so smart. I fantasized about who we all might have been — maybe I was a princess! — and who we all would end up being. I knew that if I came back, I wanted to be Christian. Christians, like my best friend and next-door neighbor Marissa, had the best holidays with the best candy, presents, and decorations. But I knew I wouldn't be Christian in this life. As my mother liked to remind me throughout the years, "Judaism is both a religion *and* a race."

I asked our housekeeper, a short, sleek woman named May, whose squinting eyes made me think she knew what was really going on in our house.

"Do you believe in God?"

"Oh yes!" May replied. Her enthusiasm gave me hope and made me feel she had the most to offer on the subject. "God is everywhere, and He sees you."

May knew something about God that no one else around me did. I believed her.

He is everywhere, and He sees me.

That night the image of God morphed from a man into invisible space, all around. I thought about God seeing me in the bath. Did God mind my being naked? What about when I peed or pooped? Was God upset when I was mean to my little sister? On one hand, I didn't like the feeling I was being watched, but on the other hand, I felt like I had company. I really liked that part. I decided I believed in May's God and would try to make God proud, but I would keep it a secret. This included trying to like Sunday school and temple, and being a good girl.

But my devotion to God — even after writing a little book of poems about the mystery of life that lit up my second-grade teacher's face — was short-lived. Hebrew was hard to learn, and the synagogue classroom smelled like old, mildewed library books. Once I started having sleepover playdates, my dad had to pick me up early on Sundays to get to school, cutting the fun short. I quit.

And being good? Impossible. My mother was always angry because of me. I forgot to run the dishwasher. I forgot to bring the note to school. I lost my gloves. "If your head wasn't attached to your shoulders," she'd say through clenched teeth, "you'd lose it."

I knew she had to sell her accessories *and* take care of us *and* try to make her art, but I still talked back to her. Even when I knew it would be bad. She always asked me to fetch her cigarettes after dinner, and one night, about to dig into dessert, I'd had enough. "I'm not your slave," I told her.

"What did you say?" she shot back in her tone with the sharp darts, though I knew she heard me.

I looked at the apple slices on the little plate, wishing I could suck the words back in. "I saw on TV that cigarettes were bad for you," I said.

Then all hell broke loose, like when I told her *I hate you*, which also was a very bad thing to say. Her voice was a loud laser beam that sliced through me. She told me that I was selfish, and I'd better think about everything she does for me, and there was more, but what I remember most was feeling all shredded up inside, with hiccup tears.

But sometimes she came at me when I didn't talk back, when I didn't know I'd done anything wrong. Like when I'd thought I was helping a friend out by cutting her hair, or when my bike got stolen in the park. When Daddy was there, I would look to him for some back-up: *does she have to be so mean?* But he was mute. I did hate my mother sometimes. And Marissa and even Marissa's mom felt bad for me when they heard my mother yelling through the walls. When I'd go over after an episode, they asked if I was OK and looked at me with sad eyes.

If she loved me, would she rip me up the way she did? Here's what made sense: something in me was bad. Something I couldn't see, but my mother could.

God probably wasn't going to talk to me.

But when my parents, who both worshiped at the altar of Arts and Culture, took me to see *The Fantasticks*, the longest-running musical in New York, I forgot about God. The Sullivan Street Playhouse was a different kind of temple, one that had worn-out purple seat covers and smelled of musty old wood. It was so tiny and intimate. The actors, like the temple cantors, sang, but in English, and they were right in our faces. A young blonde lead stared into me and, with her beautiful voice, belted her heart out in total longing, begging me to help her escape her constricted world:

But I want much more ... Much more! Much more!

The beauty and power in her voice, the grace in her body as she reached her arms towards me ... I felt tingles, starting in my belly and moving up to my head, down to my toes, and back up again. I was entranced. Her character wanted something with every fiber of her being. I recognized that wanting feeling, the nameless ache in song. And I wanted more of the stirring I felt watching her. I wanted to be filled by it and create it in others.

It was my first religious experience. And, lucky for me, I discovered I could sing and act. This made me feel like I had some good in me. And it gave me a goal to work towards: to become a professional, to bury my badness so all anyone saw was a star. I belted my voice just like Andrea McCardle, the actress who played the lead in *Annie,* and could sing in a higher voice like Maria in *West Side Story,* too. I sang and danced along to Broadway albums in my room. I sang in the bath, I sang in plays, I sang at night in bed — sometimes so loud my father had to come to my room and tell me to shut up and go to sleep. I loved the feeling of my voice moving through my body and piercing the air, and how I felt after, as though my insides had gone through the washing machine and come out sparkling clean.

Singing melted the nameless ache, and praise did, too: when teachers and other parents told my mother, "She's so talented," I'd watch a smile come over her face, and warmth flushed mine. I could make her forget the parts of me she didn't love.

Theater became my religion, and I was devout. I spent my Saturdays in theater classes and eventually, summers in theaters. I managed to get into the "Fame" high school to study voice. But as I grew, the self-consciousness of adolescence started interfering with my ability to blow people away. My grade school acting teacher's feedback of *"Such good character work!"* turned into my high school teacher's *"You're too in your head, you need to be more in the moment."* In voice class, *"You have an incredible belt!"* turned into *"You have a lovely tone, but you're inconsistent."* Roles I used to get were handed off to more confident kids.

Even my mother, who liked to have me sing for her friends, pulled me aside one night and whispered, "What happened? You were so on key last time you sang that song!" It crushed me to lose my one trump card, the one thing I could rely on for praise. I rehearsed extra hard, and when I performed in class, it would go all wrong, as if I hadn't rehearsed at all. The nameless ache returned. It made me tired. It made me thirsty.

"You're drinking so much water!" my mother, and sometimes my father, would notice when we were out to dinner in some posh city eatery. I, too, was confused as to why I kept sipping, trying to extinguish some inner fire. If it wasn't water I was pumping in my mouth, it was food, and if it wasn't food, it was my thumb, which I sucked till I was sixteen, though you can still catch me lost in thought with its tip in my mouth. "You don't need to finish that brownie," my mother would say, but I had no clue how not to. When I tried to stop sipping the water, or slow down when the food came, or take a breath, the ache took the form of unbearable restlessness: yearning, mixed in with anxiety.

Three years into high school, I almost didn't get out of bed to meet my best friend Nina for breakfast. My limbs were so heavy, as if lined with the lead aprons they'd put over me during X-Rays at the dentist. I didn't understand why I was so tired, why I had this twisted hunger thrumming through me all the time. On the M11 bus to breakfast, near dozing, I leaned my head against the bus window and watched the multitude of riders enter and exit. A song called "Nothing" from *A Chorus Line*, my favorite one to belt out growing up, started playing in my head. As it did, I had a pathetic realization. The lyrics tell the story of a woman who can't wait to go to my high school — the High School of Performing Arts — to become an actress, but once in class, she feels nothing. She's bereft. As if the repetition of singing the song all those years had made it a reality, I felt nothing, too. Life at the High School of Performing Arts was meaningless. Studying classical voice was dry and boring. "Nothing" was excruciating.

I didn't know then that my unwavering devotion to theater was starting to lead me to a new place: back to God.

"So, how'd it go?" Nina asked about my new acting class.

A haggard waitress in a grungy diner on 9th Avenue filled our cups with coffee.

"I hate my new acting teacher," I confessed. I'd switched to a new Saturday morning acting class at Lee Strasberg Studios, the mecca of method acting in Manhattan. "He's so *actory*," I said of the gray-haired teacher with the chiseled face. "And he yelled at me for looking so old."

I fondled the ridges of an empty creamer while imitating his articulate, male theater voice. "*You look like you're twenty-five. Next week, come in here looking like you're sixteen. You're a young person. Don't try to be so old.*"

"Wow," Nina said, holding her cup to her chin. "He sounds harsh."

But he had a point: I and a pack of super sophisticated friends from my old private school wore heels, brand-name clothing, and too much iridescent make-up from pocket-sized pots I bought with my babysitting money at Bloomingdale's. We stole drugs from our parents and snuck out to dance at 80s clubs such as Studio 54, The Pyramid, The Peppermint Lounge, and Danceteria. In a way, we *were* old.

Nina lit up a cigarette and locked eyes with mine to increase the intensity of what she was about to say. "Male acting teachers will cut you down. You need to talk to Kate."

I reached for a drag, feeling rebellious. Our voice teachers repeatedly warned us about the dangers of cigarette smoke on the vocal cords.

Nina often referred to Kate, her mysterious arts camp acting teacher: *Kate taught me how to move my stuck energy. Kate taught me how to relax before sleep by breathing my energy down into my feet. Kate taught me how to really connect with an audience.* Kate received Nina's high-praise label of "deep," and I was curious.

Breakfast arrived, and I felt the relief from the familiar restless pit in my stomach. As I piled scrambled eggs on buttery toast, I wondered: *Could Nina's Kate help me fix what feels so broken?*

What I said: "Could Kate help me get my confidence back as a performer?"

"Definitely."

Outside the diner window, the traffic light changed and the cars on Ninth Avenue jolted to speed. I was full and wanted to put my head down on the table next to the scratched-up oval plates. But I had an entire day of school before I could collapse.

"I'll check her out," I said.

When I entered the bright Broadway studio of Kate's class, I spotted Nina, who smiled with her whole face, and took a seat next to other teens on the floor. Kate resembled the actress Sally Field in appearance, emotional expressiveness, and feistiness. Her petite 5'2" frame belied her huge presence and held her piercing, dark brown eyes. She nodded at me and began the class, pacing and talking about opposition.

I felt chills. It wasn't the subject. I'd learned about opposition in other acting classes — the notion that drama occurs in the opposing tension between what the characters want. It was the content. Kate did something I'd never seen an acting teacher or even an adult do. Way before social media and the norm of broadcasting your inner truth before large swaths of people, she told us about a big fight she'd had that morning with her husband, Bob. I don't remember the details, but I remember feeling floored that an adult was talking so casually and comfortably about marital conflict, talking about being immature with complete curiosity and composure as if it were the most normal thing in the world, as though she had mined the fight for talking points while it was happening. Then she linked her story to the dramatic components of the fight and why it would have made a good scene. I liked her instantly.

She introduced us to energy: "When energy is flowing within your body as an actor, you can make a connection with the audience. It's why performers like Liza Minnelli are so popular. You can feel her energy." Though she was a theater director, she instructed us to put our bodies in these positions she learned in her training as a mind/body therapist, positions like bending our knees and arching our back while standing, designed to get energy flowing from our heads to our feet, allowing us to be more in our bodies and the moment. It was all new and a little weird, and I wasn't sure I was getting it. But I knew my way around an improv, so when we started playing a theater game in which you'd tap someone out of a scene and change it, I volunteered. This improv morphed into younger kids on a playdate. My scene partner suggested we raid the cookie jar, and I begged her not to, imploring her to stop eating the cookies or I would get in big trouble. It seemed like a realistic, well-played scene with clear opposition, and when it ended, I sat down.

But the silence that followed when I did was ominous. Kate and Nina looked at each other, then at me, and said in unison with a sad knowing, " ... the cookie jar."

Um ... what was the big deal?

Kate saw my confusion and chimed in. "It must have been so hard to be in that much fear in your house. And around pleasure."

My brain scrambled to understand what was happening. And then I saw: she knew the scene had come from my real life. Of course it had. We act what we know. A sense of exposure flared. I felt tricked. Kate got, from one moment in one scene, how afraid I was of my mother and how connected to food it was. The mirroring was deeply embarrassing, but after a few minutes, I felt intensely liberated. I understood, on a whole new level, how revealing and how healing theater could be.

Nina was right. Kate was magical. I decided she was the one that could help me fix my acting problems. I decided to see her one-on-one.

In Kate's apartment, a small, ground-floor unit in a not-yet-gentrified part of the Upper East Side, for the third week in a row I recited the same monologue, trying to nail it for summer stock auditions. Each time I did, it fell flat. I tried to incorporate the directions Kate had given me: ground into your body, connect with your legs, make space for the impulses in you. Kate peered into me with her steady eyes and took a drag of her brown Nat Sherman cigarette.

"I think it's time we do some *work*, Sweetie," she said on the exhale. She wasn't referring to the work of improving the monologue I had come to see her about perfecting. She was talking about facing the personal issues that were getting in my way, blocking the talent I had so effortlessly accessed as a child.

I began my weekly journeys to see her as my therapist. We sat together on her mauve velvet couch, a gossamer curtain letting in light from the windows behind us, and often shared long silences with eye contact before she helped me figure out how to do therapy: I was supposed to speak. I loved the silent bathing in her gaze. I loved the coziness of her narrow living room with three cats perched in a variety of spots, snoozing. I didn't think of my work with Kate as spiritual, but in a way, it was. She actually gave me practices to do at home.

In an early session, Kate, barely able to make sense of the torrent of emotion that was spewing forth as I shared a recent argument with my mother, interrupted.

"You need to *ground*."

Kate stood up from the couch, got me on my feet, and had me bend at the waist, strands of my bushy, unbrushed curls dangling before my eyes. She had me bend and straighten my knees while hanging there, to the point of exhaustion. My thighs were burning, and I wanted to bolt or at least roll myself up and sit back down, at another point even vomit, but she coaxed me to breathe into it and held her hand gently on my back, loosened my neck, and began banging my calves where she sensed my energy was stuck. My legs began to shake as a torrent of energy released down them. Finally, she invited me to slowly roll up. The world looked different, brighter, clearer. I felt my feet. I felt space in my normally hardened shoulders, my own energy subtly coursing through my body, leaving me with two essential lessons: one, my energy was an invisible but tangible part of me, and two, freedom required discipline, the willingness to go through a portal of discomfort to access the other side.

So this is what it means to be grounded, I thought. *I could make decisions from this place.* I kinesthetically understood the word "grounded" as being connected to the earth instead of my usual state: a bumbling jumble of disembodied thoughts. Kate also taught me that even though I had friends and a family that loved me, I was emotionally isolated. My energy had gathered in thick knots of defensive armor around my shoulders and heart. My parents, due to their own unprocessed "stuff," weren't able to make space for my feelings, and I in turn wasn't making space for those feelings either. The nameless ache was those feelings trying to get my attention.

Working with Kate had unintentionally given my love for theater some serious competition, because now I also loved the process of unfolding the unconscious and reclaiming my personal freedom.

At the end of my last session with her before I left for college in Chicago, I stopped in the doorway and turned back to look at her.

"I still want to be an actress, but this ... this too, is my life's work."

"Yes." Her eyes met mine while closing the door. "Yes, it is."

3: Loaves and Fishy
Los Angeles; 1991

Alex was moving swiftly around the room, getting ready for work. I lay curled under the sheets, eyes shut, breath long and nasal. After fourteen years of acting training, sleep was a snap.

The bathroom door shut. Squeaky faucets gave way to running water. Foaming bristles clashed with teeth. The deep whir of the toilet faded to lighter, ethereal tones as the flush evaporated. The bathroom door opened. Keys jingled. Finally, the apartment's rickety screen door slammed, and the wood door behind it.

Ahhhh, quiet.

Alex was off to his job as a PA on a new TV show, and his three roommates were gone, too. An apartment to myself.

Get up, I thought.

I lay there, motionless.

The sun barged in through the edges of the floral shades — the insistent LA light — giving my closed lids a pinkish hue. I was parched. My tongue felt three times its size, rough and swollen like a beached whale inside my mouth. It was October, when I was used to cooler temperatures, sweaters, and scarves, but it seemed at every moment in this city, especially when I got in and out of the car — *ugh, the endless getting in and out of the car!* — the California heat cornered me.

I should get up, a part of me thought. *But what for?*

Moving to LA to live with Alex and be an actress after college seemed a ridiculous fantasy. Plus, the day before, I actually hadn't gotten up, and that made things worse on all fronts.

"You didn't get out of the house all day?" Alex asked. "How are you going to find a job?" He stared at my hair. I patted it, sensing it was extra poofy. I hadn't looked in the mirror. There might have been crud around my eyes.

"I'm still babysitting," I protested. Alex had gotten me a job watching a coworker's bratty kid three nights a week.

He sat down on the bed next to me. "You're not paying rent here. It's getting tense. Why don't we just live together as planned?"

I wished I had an answer.

Alex, my college boyfriend of three years — who for one month after college was actually my fiancé — was fighting for us. "I know you say you want to live alone," he pressed on, "but you're obviously not happy."

Obviously.

I opened my eyes and stared, frozen, at the cottage cheese ceiling. *I could just live with Alex,* I thought. *Maybe that would make things better.* But then Kate's face popped into my mind and I cringed, rolling over with embarrassment. How naive I'd been, marching into her office when I was back home after college graduation, thinking I'd finally gotten my life together.

"Guess what?" I'd said, thrilled to be in her live presence after talking on the phone during college. She had a summer tan and a new West Side apartment. The mauve couch was now red corduroy. Sun streamed into her living room, casting a slanted line across her torso like a pageant sash. I plopped down at the other end of the couch. She lit a cigarette. "Alex and I are getting married!"

He didn't exactly propose. I was in college finishing up finals and he, in his first year out, was starting another cool Hollywood job. We were on a long swampy phone call, circling a break-up: "With me here and you there, how will we ever make this work?" Even with our long-distance ups and downs, cutting things off felt impossible — almost as hard as getting a legitimate job after graduating college with a theater degree. So when he floated the idea, though I never imagined getting married right out of college, I said yes.

Kate did not congratulate me. She did not crack a smile. She took a long drag off her long cigarette and said, "Sounds fishy," on the exhale.

Two small words, and one big illusion smashed to pieces. I burst into tears because I knew exactly what she meant and how right she was. I'd walked into that hour thinking I was growing up, moving on from the paralyzing depression of my high school and college years, becoming an adult, that I didn't need her anymore. I walked out knowing I was nowhere near ready for marriage, the turbulent waters of my uncharted life still looming large before me.

Alex and I broke the engagement off, but living together was on. LA, despite my having no real training in film or TV, was an exciting new adventure — a ticket out of Chicago, which felt small, and out of New York, where my parents would be on top of me with every decision I made, and a ticket out of the state of *learning to be an adult by myself.*

But now, after just one month, it all smelled rotten. The whole move: fishy. Even when I arrived after the long cross-country drive, Alex welcomed me with a lame confession. I often replayed the scene in my head — me standing there, so excited to embrace him after six weeks of being apart and feeling the stiffness in his body during the reunion hug.

"I have to tell you something," he said, his luscious sandy curls framing his face.

My stomach rose into my throat as Alex led me by the hand into his room — our temporary room — with its stubby turquoise carpeting and floral shades. He sat me down on the edge of the bed, a duvet hastily thrown over wrinkled sheets.

"Okay," I said, stomach now in my knees. "Spill it."

"I kissed someone at the wrap party last Friday."

I kept my gaze on the floor, which seemed to double as a hamper. Dirty clothes lay haphazardly around the bed.

"We were all so happy to wrap the first episode, and she was hounding me, following me around like a puppy. We were drunk. I felt like I didn't know how to resist."

He followed my gaze to the wooden dresser, with its half-open drawers and more clothes spilling out.

"Sorry, I didn't have time to clean before you arrived. But I swear, it will not happen again. It was a crazy thing, a one-time fluke. I love you."

Though he swore, I didn't believe it was just a kiss. He wouldn't have felt so guilty — probably wouldn't have even told me — if that's all it was. We'd been here before, like the time we weren't technically on a break but he admitted to having slept with a junior agent at his first LA assistant job. And then, well, we did start dating when he was in a relationship with another woman — a close friend of mine — behind her back. That was my bad, and this was my karma. But underneath the sting of betrayal was a nudge from inside: *You can exit this relationship now. You made it to LA, and you have a legitimate excuse to break it off.*

I felt the nudge, but I could not act on it. Where would I go? I thought I loved Alex. But maybe I was in love with the *idea* of him — I mean, who wouldn't want a cute Hollywood mogul-in-training to marry?

Get up, I thought. *Get some water.*

But I couldn't. I lay there and made myself contemplate: *Should I break up with Alex?* There was no way I could live with him. Alex was driven. Alex was a player. If I wanted to be with him, I needed to see myself as one of the beautiful women who dotted every LA health food restaurant and every coffee shop with their silky highlighted hair, instead of hating how their presence made my curly brown mop seem so Roseanne Rosanna Danna, or how their long smooth legs brought my untanned, puckered thighs into bold relief. I needed to be someone more secure, like our friend Betsy who wore blazers with jeans and was already a producer, someone witty and biting like most of Alex's friends, who showed up at the apartment and launched into interesting stories, someone tough like his writer roommate who had zero interest in what anyone thought of her and swatted away my attempts at friendship like flies.

At least I needed to be the kind of person who could get out of bed, trek out into the wilds of Hollywood and hunt for a job and a decent studio apartment. But at the moment, I wasn't that person. I was a person who needed help.

Kate wasn't my only therapist. Because I had such a limited budget in college and talking to her on the phone in fits and starts was expensive, I started to see someone in Chicago when the suicidal thoughts intensified junior year. The level of depression was surprising because I was dating Alex, had a decent part in a MainStage show, and a circle of friends. That therapist helped, but Kate was the only therapist who rocked my world, and none other would ever compare. She would probably be able to help me out of this morass. But I couldn't call her. What would I say? *I wish I had stayed in New York and continued to do the work with you, since I'm still such a mess?* I feared my call would annoy her. If I'd only really listened to her, I wouldn't be here.

I couldn't call my parents. My freak-outs always evoked their oppressive concern and simple solutions like, "Why don't you just get a job?" as if I hadn't been trying. Even if I did manage to get out of the roommates' apartment and find one of my own, what would I really do with my life, other than sporadic babysitting gigs for high-level Hollywood people that Alex managed to get for me? Lying there, I had no illusions about who I was: a talented kid who didn't quite have what it takes to make it in this town.

There was no getting up from the bed, so I toured the familiar options for ending my life. *What would cause the least physical pain?* If I stole all the prescription pills from the cabinets, would they do the trick? If they failed, what would that do to the roommates who already hated me for taking up their space when Alex and I didn't move out together as planned? I couldn't deal with the blood from slitting any body part. I was way too squeamish, plus, again, a mess for the roommates. I was fixated on his roommates, even though their constant snubbing added to my own pile of self-hate.

Just the other day, after applying for the best apartment I thought I could get for the price, I hung around the hallway on my knees, hoping the phone — the one landline apartment phone — would ring with good news. The literary agent-roommate stood at the hallway entrance.

"I need the phone, and I need it NOW!" He screamed, adding for extra measure, "This is not your house!"

Shame lay over me like a wet blanket. I was once again a burden, a basket case that caused people to raise their voices. "I'm sorry," I moaned pathetically. "I am just trying to get out of here!"

I first fantasized about jumping from my New York City eighth-floor apartment window in high school, imagining myself going splat on the large square bluestone tiles of the courtyard where Marissa, Ricky, and I used to run around and ride our bikes. When I told Kate about wanting to jump, she looked at me with such compassion, I felt tender hands cupping my heart.

"I don't want to cry," I told her, breaking up inside.

"Why not?"

"It makes me feel weak," I said.

"Sweetie, you're in pain. It's not weakness to be where you are."

I cried and felt a million times lighter. Kate looked at me wryly and shook her head. "You're like the Queen of Perfection."

"What do you mean?"

"You think if you're not perfect, you won't be loved."

But I was alone now, and I couldn't cry. All I could do was roll over and return to stillness. Not moving made the ache more bearable. There was no one. Nothing. No point.

Another tour of the options: pills, slitting. If only I had a gun. Alex had a college friend, a genius, who jumped from a tall Chicago building. It was devastating. His way was quick, simple, painless. But too violent, too messy. I always circled back to pills as the winning method of choice. With the roommates gone, I could sneak into their bathrooms and see what their cabinets held.

I managed to get up and stare at my face in the chipped bathroom mirror. My eyes were dull. My face was bloated. A whole half-moon of extra chin hung under my jaw. I swapped out my image for the inside of the cabinet. Orange prescription bottles huddled between the mouthwash and deodorant. Because I didn't know what I was looking for, I wedged all the bottles between my fingers and shuffled back into Alex's bedroom, where I sat on the floor and arranged them on the grubby carpet. I tugged my oversized tee out from under my butt and tallied up the pills. Close to one hundred. I could almost taste the relief on the other side, not the pain of nothingness, just nothingness.

I needed alcohol, lots of alcohol to seal the deal if I didn't want to wake up in a hospital. I thought about getting the vodka in the freezer, but I just sat there staring at the cluster of bottles illuminated by a ray of early afternoon sun.

My whole life was ahead of me. Instead of that being a balm, a freeing thought, an understanding that my situation was temporary, it felt like a death sentence.

Go get the vodka.

Gabby entered my thoughts. My New York City born-and-raised comrade in spirit. I could call her. She'd understand, but she was impossible to reach now that she lived in an ashram. If I wanted to talk, I'd have to leave a message with the ashram switchboard, and eventually she'd call me "collect" — using an operator to ask me to accept the charges — from a payphone. If I picked up, she'd quickly give me her number, and I'd call her back. In our last conversation, she talked about her new job riding around on the back of an ashram garbage truck in an orange jumpsuit. It was an assignment from Gurumayi, Gabby's beautiful Indian guru, whom I'd seen in a video when I visited the Siddha Yoga Center of Chicago on a date.

"Spiritually, I have so much karmic garbage to clean up, Blair," Gabby told me on that call. I could hear her pretty nails tapping the payphone door and I wondered if she still polished them while at the ashram now that she was a garbage collector. Garbage duty as a spiritual practice? And yet, there was something compelling about what she said about picking up trash on the outside to clean up her trash on the inside. I had a landfill in my soul.

In that same phone call with Gab, I broke down and told her I'd had a dream with Gurumayi, though I'd been keeping it to myself. Her reaction was predictable and reassuring.

"You did?! Blair. People pray to have her in their dreams."

"Yeah. Well, you're not going to believe it," I went on, "but I was at my college waitressing job, and the food was ready to go to the tables, and — don't laugh — I couldn't find myself."

"Perfect!"

"The food was getting cold, and I was terrified I was going to be fired. I went back and forth through the double doors of the kitchen looking for myself, and ended up at a crowded theater party."

I remembered the dream in exquisite detail: scurrying between the restaurant and the party, frantically looking for myself, when all of a sudden, from way across the room — poof! — Gurumayi appeared, gliding towards me, red robes flowing behind her, like a bindi-wearing fairy godmother.

"So," Gurumayi said in her slight Indian accent, tilting her head to one side. "You are looking for yourself in these places?" She was perfectly still, moving only her eyes around the room. The accusation was so startling in its simple truth, it was as if a glass of water had been thrown in my face, but instead of feeling cold and wet, I felt tickled and refreshed. As the inanity of it dawned on me, I started to giggle. "Come," she said, with a huge smile. "Let's look for you." She took me by the hand and walked me through clouds of smoke and chatter, up the cold concrete stairs of the party. I laughed. She smiled mischievously as we continued in mock search for my Self.

The dream felt so real: the panic, the relief, and the ridiculousness of my plight. I *had* been searching for myself — outside myself. In places — at work, in the theater world, and who knows where else — where I'd never find it. Dream Gurumayi saw that and playfully brought it to my attention.

Gab was silent for a while. "It's all right there, isn't it?"

It was. But I was hesitant to assign too much meaning to the fact that dream Gurumayi, though she had saved me from false answers, was THE provider of true ones. The night I visited the Chicago center, I read a sign on the wall that said, *God dwells within you as you*. The promise of Siddha Yoga was that the guru lived in the awareness of this truth all the time, and through her gift of *Shaktipat* — that awakening of the Kundalini energy that happens in the transfer of spiritual energy from guru to disciple — you could, too.

But did I want a guru? Gabby sometimes sounded ridiculous in her praise. "Blair, she walked by me and smiled, and my whole mood literally shifted, like she'd taken my sadness with her as she passed."

Get the vodka, I thought. *You need relief.* I was midway to standing when an escape hatch presented itself.

Well, what if I just tried chanting that mantra I learned when I visited the Siddha Yoga Center? I didn't need a guru for that. The set designer who brought me there had dedicated a comforting corner of his apartment to meditation, with a special cushion, a picture of Gurumayi, a timer, and a brass elephant statue. He chanted and meditated regularly — I was sure his calm energy was what drew me to him because he wasn't my physical type. Gabby also described feeling blissful from doing the practices at the Siddha Yoga ashram. I had nothing to lose.

I took a deep breath and tried to remember the chant. What came to me was some cockamamie version I pieced together from that evening: *Om Manah Shinaya*. (It's actually *Om Namah Shivaya* — at least I got the "Om" part right.) I folded my legs, closed my eyes, and prayed for some relief: *Please take this weight from me.* After a few minutes or so, my prayers were answered when a sense of calm descended, a cool breeze blowing through me, clearing out some of the overheated cobwebs. And then the breeze became waves, the rhythm of the ocean was inside me, with an undertow pulling me in towards myself, and then a forward motion, expansion, energy gently moving out — contraction, swelling, and subsiding. It was lovely, quiet, blissful. I stopped chanting. And then I heard a voice, clear and distinct as the LA sun: *It will all be okay.*

The life-and-death grip of malaise loosened its hold on me. I smiled, looked around the room, suddenly a sweeter place to be, with a light breeze teasing the shades. The fog had lifted. I might have laughed.

People say that "gratitude can change your attitude," but gratitude can't be forced. The wave of thanks that permeated my being after chanting was instinctual and unbidden. But who was it for? *Thank you,* I said, to the guru of Gabby and the set designer, who was said to charge the mantra with her spiritual energy. *Thank you.*

I put the pills back in the bathroom cabinet and paced a bit before calling Phil, a friend I'd driven out west with, to get some coffee. Miraculously, he was available. I didn't tell him about the depression or the chant, about how low I'd fallen or how high I'd bounced, but he knew about Alex and our dashed living plans. I joked about how this town was kicking my ass. He had a rickety cackle that shook his whole body when he laughed.

Hearing it again soothed me. Things were going well for him: he'd gotten a job, found some friends. I felt, for the first time in weeks, like a "normal" twenty-two-year-old out in the world. There was space between me and the struggle, and I trusted that, yes, things were going to be okay.

When I got back to the apartment there was a message waiting for me. I had left a superintendent my number weeks ago, and now there was a unit available in his building, a small housing complex not ten blocks from Alex's West Hollywood apartment. I immediately ventured back out to take a look and fell in love. It was a perfect studio apartment for a young actress, complete with arched windows and cute little moldings, and a Murphy bed. The super was dubious because babysitting didn't count as a *job* job, and for a while, it looked like I wouldn't get the place. I made a vow to the powers that be: If I got this apartment, I would chant in it every single day.

4: Equipoise

In the You Can't Make This Shit Up Department, the next day, after I got up, waited for Alex to leave, and sat down to chant for three minutes, an old high school friend called.

"Hey! I know you just got to town. One of the receptionists in the spa at work is leaving. Do you need a job?"

I jumped into the stifling car and barely waited for the steering wheel to cool down before driving to Brentwood for the interview at a spa called, of all things, *A Sense of Self*.

I was literally going to work at a sense of Self. I got a part-time job as a receptionist.

The following morning after I chanted, Alex called. He had arranged a meet-and-greet for me with a reputable talent agent he knew. I danced around his room by myself. I was back in the game, a contender. That night, the landlord called. The apartment was mine.

It was all happening so quickly, and it felt like new love, like a montage in a rom-com. Scene by scene, my new life fell into place. The chant appeared to be the magic thread. It didn't take a lot. I sat there, sang until I felt vibration — maybe not the oceanic feeling from the first time, but certainly the blessing of breath running through me, more clarity, and a return to feeling hopeful. And things changed. I even stopped wanting cigarettes because the chanting left me feeling clean inside, and smoking made me feel dirty. Life in LA was beginning. I had to say, the chanting thing was going very well — but I only said it out loud to Gabby whenever we talked.

By the beginning of December, I'd landed a full-time job as a customer care service representative at a wildly successful new skin care company. I started scraping up every connection I could — my father's second cousin, old acquaintances from college, a big-deal casting agent from sleepaway camp — to try to jump-start my acting career.

"Hi, this message is for Blair Glaser," my answering machine announced one evening upon my return from work. "We were able to squeeze you in Tuesday at 11:00 for an audition for a Fox TV series, for the part of Parker. We're leaving audition sides — scripts that you'll need for the taping — on the front door of our office."

The best of messages! I skipped around my cozy apartment in celebration and then frantically searched for my date book to pencil in my first big LA audition, secured by the old camp acquaintance. But I couldn't believe it: the audition was on the same Tuesday of a beauty convention in Chicago, where everyone from my office needed to be.

Even though my boss said he could be flexible around auditions, this was a tricky situation. Our flights were booked. I immediately begged him to let me arrive in Chicago one-day later than everyone else so that I could attend the audition. He was pissed at having to find a replacement to man our booth for the time I'd be out, but I told him I'd pay for my own flight with a free voucher I had from my student American Express, and he caved. My first real LA audition. I could barely breathe.

Me on TV?! Oh, to have a high-paying, high-profile acting job and know my hard work after all these years of study paid off! Being able to tell my parents, calm their worries, give them something to brag about. Being one of the classmates — like Anna Gunn, who was already on a sitcom, or Jim True who was in movies — who "made it." I'd have to get an agent — a long-held dream of mine — and be able to say the self-important words, "*I need to talk to my agent about it.*"

But when I caught my breath, I knew my chances were slim. I was a theater person. When the agent I met through Alex saw my film acting reel, she said, to my heart's dismay, that I was "pretty green." She also said my talent really shined in the clips of shows when I was singing, but I had been trying to avoid singing lately. Thinking back to how joyful it once was and how unsteady it had become, singing brought up too much.

On the Tuesday of the audition, a virtual packet of Pop Rocks sizzling in my stomach, I called the casting agent's office to confirm my call time.

"What's the name?" the assistant said.

"Blair Glaser, 11:00."

"Um, hold on please." My armpits dampened as I waited, and I hoped I wouldn't have to change my blouse, because I'd spent hours picking out the right color and fit for the audition. When she returned, she let me know that the office had no record of my name or my booking. The slots were full. I had spent five days in deep prep. I had negotiated with work. The floor fell beneath me.

"There will be others," the assistant said, in response to my desperate attempts to negotiate. I hung up and cried, shrieking sobs as if someone had died, the entire way to the airport. I couldn't believe my one big chance had just slipped away, vanished into thin air. But I also couldn't believe how insistent the tears were. They trickled down through baggage drop-off, security, and boarding. I couldn't turn them off.

On the plane to the convention, I rested my head against the window shade and turned away from my seat mate, stifling my sobs, letting silent tears fall. When I finished the pack of Kleenex I'd brought, I started using the back of my sleeve. I was a puddle. *How could I be* so *upset*? The whole chapter of moving to LA, of losing the life I thought I wanted with Alex, of striving to put myself out there, and of the emptiness I now felt, seemed to be pouring out of my eyes.

Through the chanting I now knew a little more of what inner calm tasted like. Maybe if I devoted more time and energy to spiritual practice, I wouldn't freak out so much? Maybe I needed more than three minutes a day to become centered? I hinged my seat back and tried to shut my eyes.

Maybe I shouldn't judge Gabby, I thought. I was a little jealous of how focused she was on her *sadhana,* so steeped in healing and growing, and how much she loved Gurumayi. But she'd gotten in with Gurumayi's program so quickly. Chanting and meditation now made sense to me on an experiential level, but the guru thing remained mysterious. Scary even.

I kept replaying a night when I was around eleven and moseyed into my parents' room after dinner, where the nightly news flashed images of a white-robed man getting into a Rolls-Royce. My mother's jaw hung low. "This man stole all these people's jewelry and money." She pointed to the sex guru Osho/Rajneesh on the screen. "And they took over an entire town in Oregon."

"Who did?" I asked.

"His followers."

I looked up at the images. Rows and rows of people in red waiting for the white-robed man.

"Listen," she said, turning her gaze to me, her jaw now set tight. "Don't ever get involved with gurus. They're very dangerous."

From everything I'd heard, Gurumayi didn't seem dangerous. And yet, the first time I saw *darshan* in Chicago, the time to kneel before the guru and receive blessings, when people stood in line to bow down to the empty chair with the picture of Gurumayi on it, my reaction pulled me in two. I was moved by the tenderness the kneelers displayed when they bowed, and how humble and contemplative they looked as they did. At least they modeled a deep respect for someone, something. Respect seemed so foreign to me. But a mild repulsion curdled my stomach. The bowing of heads seemed so subservient. Bowing down to another person was debasing yourself enough, but bowing to a chair with a picture on it seemed deranged. And seeing people throw cash into baskets that flanked the chair made the back of my neck itch.

Gab believed that her guru was divine energy incarnate. "She's a *Siddha*. That means an enlightened master, or perfected being." I didn't know what that really meant, but I sensed Gurumayi did have some true spiritual power. And if she could be perfected, why not me? But if I went to meet Gurumayi, would I end up like Gabby, saying airy fairy things and living in an ashram? Could I end up broke and wearing red, my least favorite wardrobe color? It was unthinkable. And yet, with being turned away for my one big audition and no idea how or if the next opportunity would come, it's not as if a clearer direction for my life presented itself.

The flight attendant asked me if I wanted a drink. I shut off my CD Walkman and turned to her. She gasped — I guessed from my bloodshot eyes and red nose. I looked at her blankly and asked for a ginger ale with extra napkins.

At the hair and beauty convention, still emotionally raw, I got a break from manning our booth to roam the cavernous hall. Hip-hop blasted. Flashing lights and models and hair products were everywhere. In one corner of the convention, there was a serene Japanese flute playing and a pleasant banner advertising Aveda products, a little oasis from all the bombardment. The popular company was in its infancy and displayed a product line of chakra-aligned essential oil fragrances that not only protected hair and skin but transmitted certain vibes to the wearers. The fragrance I was most attracted to was called Equipoise.

"Ahhh, Equipoise. My favorite," said the woman behind the counter.

I didn't know exactly what the word meant, but I craved it.

"It means evenness of mind," she said, as if reading mine. Well, now it made perfect sense as to why I was drawn to its smell. With all my ups, downs, and dramatic freak-outs, I definitely needed some Equipoise.

She sold me on its calming properties, but on the plane ride home, I knew a bottle of essential oil wasn't going to fix my problems. I feared returning to the depression I'd just clawed my way out of — the way it became the master of my life, flattening me, holding the rest of my heart's wants, needs, and desires hostage, isolating me from friends and family. I didn't want to collapse when I got back to LA. I needed more than Equipoise, more than a magic chant. I needed a path.

Back in LA, I called the LA center and listened to the outgoing message on the machine. It sounded soft and inviting. "Welcome to the Siddha Yoga Meditation Center of Los Angeles. We are located on 19th and Broadway in Santa Monica. The following schedule is a list of our free events ..." I hung up. I called again the next night, and the night after, and finally listened to the whole message. I didn't understand the Sanskrit names for the chants they had on the schedule: *Guru Gita, Rudram, Shiva Mahimna*, but when the message said, "Our Saturday Evening *Satsang* Programs with live chanting and a video of Gurumayi start every Saturday at 7:00 p.m.," my ears perked up. That was the one.

The LA center was grander and more beautiful than the Chicago one, modern with cozy lighting and plush carpeting. It smelled like incense, chai spices, and, strangely, like the after-bath fragrance Jean Naté, which brought me back in a pleasant way to childhood. Later I discovered it was Jean Naté, because in the 70s people would bring it as gifts to Gurumayi's guru Baba, who used it to refresh the hall, and it stuck. I was nervous to enter, but when a blonde woman in a Chanel suit looking a little like a friend of my mother gave me the warmest, most welcoming smile and extended her hand in the direction of the shoe rack, I relaxed. In the hall, I was gently guided to the stockpile of yoga cushions, known as *asanas*, and then to a seat on the floor on the women's side. Gender division, like temple! I thought. Live musicians played beautiful, soothing music for the chant, and as I sang and swayed along, a sense of well-being bubbled up.

Despite my fears about gurus, I was excited to see Gurumayi on video again. In the Chicago video shown on a big box TV, she was beautiful and funny. She sat straight-backed as a toddler: so still, so elegant. And she laughed with her whole body. I couldn't forget a story she told that night of a disciple that approached her at *darshan*.

"Gurumayi," the devotee said. "I would like your blessing to get a nose job." That was not what I expected someone to be talking to their guru about. The meaning of life, the burden of suffering, yes; but *plastic surgery?*

"But why?" Gurumayi responded sweetly, the "why" drawn out in a singsong-y, Indian accent. "Your face is the work of God. You are beautiful as you are."

The woman said, "I know, but I don't like my nose." So Gurumayi shrugged, gave her blessings, and moved on. The next time the woman came to *darshan*, she said, "Gurumayi, I decided not to get a nose job after all."

And Gurumayi replied in the same singsong tone, "But why?"

The story — presumably meant to illustrate the fickle nature of our thoughts and feelings, that there are no real rules, that if what you are looking for is Gurumayi's approval, you won't really find it — got a big laugh. For me, a young woman who had gotten a nose job, the story hit a soft spot. I carried guilt about being desperate to fix my nose at a mere fifteen, chaperoned by my mother, never given a chance to grow into it and choose to change it as an adult. And yet, the new nose did make me feel better about my appearance. That night in Chicago, I felt Gurumayi was showing me self-forgiveness: *Don't judge yourself for your vanity — it's all a part of the dance.*

But in LA, she appeared on huge wall-mounted screens, one on each side of the hall. It was soothing to hear her laugh and tell a story, like she always did, about some fabled Indian character to illustrate a deeper point. The story she told was about a great king who one day found himself very thirsty, and none of his attendants were around. He took himself to the well, but he didn't know how to operate it. An attendant found him by the well, where the king expressed humility. *For all my power, I don't know how to quench my own thirst.* I heard the message loud and clear. I didn't know how to quench my endless thirst either. Time to step down from my lofty sense of self and all my privilege, and learn to access the well within.

But during the meditation, I couldn't. My mind was a beehive, my thoughts buzzing around, trying to figure out what it meant that I was here and sort of enjoying it. I looked out at the hall full of people, maybe 250 or so, sitting peacefully. There were a few people with wooden bead necklaces, rat-tail hairdos, dangly earrings, and flowing skirts — the kind of garb you would expect at a spiritual gathering. But the majority of people looked like they came from a cocktail party, with comfy but dressy outfits, and it blew my mind. What were *they* doing here?

There is a certain look on the face of someone in inner bliss: a slight smile, a sense that they are absorbed in whatever is happening behind their gently closed eyes, without self-consciousness. It tickled me to see it, while sensing a deep stillness all around me.

After the program I waited in line at the snack bar, watching what seemed like hundreds of relaxed, shiny faces chatting in clusters. Some grabbed their shoes and headed out into the bustle of a Saturday night, others hung around, recognizing each other and hugging. A pretty lady whose voice captivated me while she was chanting at the mic marched up to me while I munched on a scrumptious homemade cookie.

"Are you a singer?" she asked. Her radiant face beamed light at me. No "hello". No introduction. Just the startling question. I finished chewing.

"Why?" I asked, catching a crumb with my tongue.

"Because you look like a singer," she said sweetly, blue eyes twinkling. The chanter told me her name was Nada, which means heavenly sound.

"How can you tell?"

"I dunno. I just can."

I told her about studying classical voice at the "Fame" school in New York, how a jazz pianist and vocal coach had scooped me up at thirteen, made me his mentee, and put me in his Soho cabaret, and my love for musical theater.

"Come lead chant with me at the mic sometime," she said, before walking away, leaving me in a bemused stupor to contemplate: *Was I a singer?*

Gabby said that Nada's intuitive question was not just a coincidence but a nudge from the guru herself. For once, that reasoning actually felt plausible. My first time visiting the LA Center and — boom! — an old wound and unresolved issue marched right up to me and interrupted my snack as if my spiritual work had been teed up for my arrival. Was I supposed to start paying attention to my voice again?

5: Knots of the Heart

At a sidewalk cafe with a bright yellow awning in West Hollywood, I sat with my legs crossed, sipped a four-dollar coffee, and jiggled my foot. The cute scene partner in my new acting class was late, and I really hoped he wouldn't stand me up like the actress who'd left me waiting outside the movie theater, minutes creeping past the start time, or the classmate who said we'd "meet Friday morning" and then never called. When I saw these students in class, they simply said, "Oh, sorry, I totally forgot."

The cafe was filled with fit blondes leaning in towards each other across metallic tables that sparkled in the sun. In my mind, I cast them as various biz people: *that one's an agent, there's a screenwriter, that's a table of TV actors,* until my scene partner's chiseled face appeared in the entrance and I uncrossed my legs. He ordered a soy latte and launched into a tedious commercial for his new commercial agent.

"One national is all it takes," he said, referring to big-deal, non-local commercials while stirring Sweet and Low into his mug. "And you can like, live on the earnings for a year."

"That's great," I said, scanning once more for anyone noteworthy, wishing I had worn my sunglasses to make it less obvious. "So. What are your thoughts about *The Glass Menagerie*? Because I'm feeling very nervous about this scene. It's such a classic."

"We'll be fine. Did you see Kilmer in *The Doors*? Oh my god, he totally nailed it."

The conversation flipped between commercials and Kilmer's "totally rad" performance for the remainder of our chat.

In contrast to flaky actors, the people at the Siddha Yoga Center were attentive, warm, and I could plug into conversations that mattered. I used to cringe when Gabby spoke of herself as a "devotee," but as I got to know the devotees in LA — Nada and the few friends she introduced me to — I felt a kinship with them. It was a relief to be able to discuss transformation and some of the new books I was reading: a collection of talks by Gurumayi, spiritual autobiographies like *Play of Consciousness* by Gurumayi's guru Baba Muktananda, and *Autobiography of a Yogi* by Paramahansa Yogananda. I ate up any book that revealed how to win inner freedom by committing to spiritual practices that quieted your ego, and to a meditation master who showed you your true Self.

Akira was one of my new Center friends who taught me about the Siddha Yoga path, people, and practices. "Don't point your feet towards the chair," she whispered one Saturday night as I unfurled my legs from their criss-cross position towards the front of the hall. "In India, it signifies disrespect."

"Thank you," I whispered back, recoiling my legs, a twinge of embarrassment coursing through them. At the end of the program, I followed her out of the hall and discovered we were both actors from New York.

"How did you get involved?" I asked, waiting in our socks on the Amrit line for cups of chai. Hers were red and blue striped: fancy, like she'd picked them out to wear for the program. Akira's New York acting teacher had told her to repeat the mantra along with doing specific sensory exercises to "attune her instrument." She started having intense spiritual experiences: seeing blue light and rainbows of color flow inside of her. When she asked the teacher what was happening, he introduced her to Siddha Yoga.

After getting a decent role in a famous indie film, Akira was having trouble getting cast in New York — she thought in part due to her being Asian — so she asked Gurumayi what to do next. She landed in LA after Gurumayi told her to "move where the work is."

Interactions with Gurumayi had a sort of magic that led to better outcomes or deep contemplation. Siddha yogis, like the yogis in the books

I was reading, turned to their guru for guidance on major life choices. The guru was said to have a broader perspective on the blueprint of your soul, so her guidance was elevated. Sometimes the guidance was direct and accessible, other times it was cryptic. One actress I met told me about struggling to film a scene in a major motion picture: after six takes she still hadn't given the director what he wanted. She went to see Gurumayi, who was visiting LA, and knelt for *darshan* with the weight of this struggle on her mind. When she lifted her head, Gurumayi looked right at her and, as if reading her thoughts, asked, "Are you doing the mantra?" The next day during filming she repeated the mantra. It steadied her nerves, her work felt inspired, and the director was happy.

I loved this story. Gurumayi could even coach actors!

A visiting swami from the ashram in India told of a time when Gurumayi visited his room bearing a physical — and spiritual — gift. As she dropped off a saffron linen swami outfit, she asked, in her inimitable, punny way, "And how is the *habit* of sadness fitting you?" It led him to contemplate his relationship to his default emotion. Naturally, I related to this question. Was my malaise a habit? Does that mean I had some choice in the matter? Maybe I could respond to my inevitable bouts of depression as if they were storm clouds I could steer clear of.

These stories and the programs solidified my own "long-distance relationship" with Gurumayi. One Saturday night, I arrived at the Center struggling with tightness in my chest that had persisted for days. It was like wearing a costume that was too small, but couldn't be removed until the show was over, except the show was my life and I couldn't shake off the tension no matter how much stretching I did to relieve myself of its grip. I wished I knew why it was there and what I could do about it. Was it anger? Sadness? I left the Center and walked the dark streets of Santa Monica, literally shaking my arms, trying to cast off the constriction, and returned just in time to watch the video. In the middle of her talk, Gurumayi said something like, "Hatred weighs heavily on the heart. When you feel a restricted feeling, a weight upon your chest, understand: it is hatred — for oneself or others." The message seemed cherry-picked for me, and left me with understanding and a place to focus: *Who did I hate?*

The answer came quickly. Myself, of course. "The queen of perfection," Kate's label echoed in my head as I shuffled out of the hall with the other devotees.

Prema, the head of the hall, stopped me before I could dig deeper into that contemplation. "Are you ready for *seva*?" she asked, jolting me out of my serendipity haze. Seeing I was becoming a regular, she wanted to know if I'd vacuum the hall after the programs. She added, "Selfless service has a mystical way of whittling down our resistance to our own inner Self."

Hmmm. Prema appeared to be a very devoted, accomplished yogi. An intellectual Venezuelan activist in her 40s who worked in energy conservation, she had short dark hair and a serious face. Her eyes were always shining, even while she kept the hall tidy, seated large numbers of people, and directed volunteer ushers to do the same. When things got busy, she remained quiet and calm.

I hated vacuuming. But maybe *seva* could help relieve my tension. I was coming to these evenings for free, so I said yes.

Being in the hall by myself after everyone had gone was intimate: just me, Gurumayi's picture sitting on her throne, a votive candle dancing in blue glass on the table beside her, the lingering sweet smell of incense, and the chant-like drone of the vacuum. I began chatting with Gurumayi inside myself as I worked the vacuum in long strides up and down the hall, creating wide ribbons of clean blue carpet. *Gurumayi, help me understand my path. Gurumayi, help me let go of my irritation towards Gabby. Gurumayi, help me stop eating out of control.* I imagined sucking up all the *Shakti*, the spiritual energy left in the hall by the meditators, and often finished my task with a pleasant, buzzing sensation.

Prema thought my work was satisfactory and assigned me weekly vacuuming *seva*. I started looking forward to it. One night, when I took the vacuum out of the closet where it had been shoved by a rogue *sevite*, I discovered an impossibly tangled cord. Prema walked by as I sat on the floor working my way through it.

"Ah," she said. "Untangling the knot of the heart."

The metaphor made me smile, but I didn't yet know how accurate it was.

I tried to share the elation I was feeling about the Center with Alex. We were still seeing each other, having sleepovers a couple of times a week.

"The host of the West Hollywood Center is a TV writer," I said. Alex had brought over a pizza after work, and the box sat on my little kitchen table while we sat on the carpet in front of the TV, plates on our laps, folding slices into our mouths. I'd started attending a smaller *satsang* closer to my apartment, monthly on Tuesday nights, chanting and meditating with other devotees in the TV writer's living room.

"Uh huh."

He was absorbed in the pizza. I wanted him to see the benefits of what I was committing to. "He told this story about having a fight in the writer's room, and it was making him uncomfortable, so he started saying the mantra. Then he remembered Gurumayi talking about treating everyone with respect and love, and asked himself what he could respect about his angry co-worker and his mediocre ideas. Once he found something to respect, there was this shift. They wrote their best episode yet."

"So ... are you gonna give her all your money?" he teased. Alex couldn't help making fun of me, and I understood because I could see how I must have looked through his eyes — I'd once felt the same about Gabby. But sometimes it was a little mean, like when he glared at the new gift I'd received from a fellow devotee and sneered, "Why do you have a picture of *feet* on your table?"

There was no way to explain the significance of the guru's feet as a symbol of surrender — how placing your head at those sacred body parts was a powerful act of humility — without sounding ridiculous. "It's just a cultural difference. It's very accepted in India," I said.

Alex raised his eyebrows at me.

"But I don't bow down to them." I didn't say my next thought out loud. *Not yet, anyway.*

He turned on the TV, while I picked at my pizza and tried to focus on the episode of *Cheers.*

As my relationship to Siddha Yoga blossomed, my relationship with acting wilted. I'd been accepted at a fancy acting school with weird rules. You had to pay in advance for monthly classes as if they were rent and leave a security deposit for your last month. And there was this irritating ritual of clapping for your teacher at the start of class.

Our teacher would make an entrance looking like the washed-up soap opera star he was and bow, and we all stood and clapped like he'd performed Hamlet. He wasn't a star. He'd had a few bit parts in major motion pictures fifteen years back. But the ceremonial clapping, he'd explained, was a way we'd learn to be generous with applause, for ourselves as well. That never really made sense to me. I felt dirty standing there clapping. He didn't deserve applause. Also, every time a woman took off a piece of her clothing in a scene, he cooed, "It was so reeeal." His praise — otherwise rare and deeply coveted — inspired all the female students to bake nudity into their scenework.

After three months, I'd finally started receiving something in the ballpark of praise from him: "Blair, you're *actually* becoming interesting to watch!" Yes, I had taken off my shirt in a scene where I was changing clothes, but even so, based on how hard I was working and the students congratulating me after my scenes, I knew that my ability to slow down, listen, and embody a character's motivation in every line was *actually* improving. But on the two days a week I had class, dread soured my stomach. The thought of clapping, watching hours of the bad scene work it took for students to grow, the anxiety of rehearsing for my own ... I wanted to quit.

But was this kind of thinking sabotage?

"I mean, after all these years, am I throwing away my career?" I asked Gabby on a phone call. "Career" sounded ridiculous after I'd said it. I'd made under 200 dollars in twelve years of performing. "I didn't put in all those years of study and training just to sell skincare," I said, lying on my little red Ikea foldout loveseat, staring out the window at the patch of darkening sky between my building and the one next door. It was a late autumn Sunday afternoon, and the twilight intensified with my Sunday night blues.

"I know," Gabby said. "Things start to lose meaning when you search for the Truth."

Those kinds of statements from Gabby had annoyed me when she first got involved, but now I found them soothing. I wanted to stay on the phone with her forever.

"At least you're not working the dullest marketing job on the planet," she said. After her summer of *seva*, Gabby returned to the city to live with her mom and work for a devotee who owned a small pharmaceutical PR firm. She'd wanted to stay at the ashram and continue to focus on her *sadhana*, but the ashram rejected her application for a full-time position. If she wanted to stay, she'd have to start paying for lodging. Paying to do selfless service seemed like a rip-off; something that would sound my mother's guru alarm bells, so I was glad she declined. I felt for her, but I was thankful because she was so much easier to reach.

"I'm sorry, Gab."

"Well, it's clear that being in the world is what Gurumayi wants for me," she said. "But surrender can be so challenging."

"I guess that's it, *surrender*," I said. The word somersaulted through my brain, revealing new dimensions with each tumble: an image of a dog showing its belly, a feeling of leaves falling to the earth, a sensation of floating in a wavy ocean. "'Cause for me, the truth is? Acting no longer brings me to the Truth."

"I hear ya," she said. "You need a real guru for that."

6: A Real Guru

My LA Center friend, Akira, and I met before *satsang* at a healthy diner in LA, the kind that served carrot juice and burgers. I wanted to share my thoughts about leaving acting. She'd heard my complaints about class, and cattle call auditions with long lines, and feeling like I'd never get an agent. I didn't know if she'd congratulate me or talk me out of it.

"You eat meat?" she said with a blank stare when I ordered a regular burger to her vegetarian one.

"You don't?" I asked, rubbing my hands on my skirt to warm them. LA winter was shocking. The sun blazed during the day, but once it went down, a searing cold took its place. Vegetarianism was not required to be on the Siddha path, but in keeping with the official diet of the Hindu mystical tradition, dairy was the only animal product served at the centers and ashrams.

"Nope. I don't want to eat animals. Plus. Think about how an animal feels when it is brutally slaughtered. It's scared, right? You don't want to digest their fear and shock. We are what we eat. You can hardly get yourself to an audition. Do you really want more fear in your system?"

Instead of sharing about leaving acting, I sat quietly and sipped my Diet Coke, looking at her carrot juice and wondering if soda was a no-no, too. "The body is a temple," I'd heard Gurumayi say. And what Akira said made sense, even though I loved meat and couldn't imagine, with my binging and food preoccupation, having a food restriction to obsess over.

She thanked the waitress for bringing our burgers, their bright orange platters clanking as they hit the table. I picked up my burger immediately, but she bowed her head, placing her hands in *namaste* before taking a bite. We chewed in silence for a bit.

"Do you want to be enlightened?" I asked her.

"Sure, but I don't think about it that way," she said, resting her burger on her plate. "I think about practicing so I can enjoy my life more, not be thrown up against the rocks every time something upsetting happens, you know? I mean — you know — acting is a hard business."

I did know.

My answer to the question, that I hadn't yet said out loud, was that I seriously wanted to be enlightened. In fact, it was the only thing I'd clearly wanted in a long while. The more I watched Gurumayi on video and the more calm I felt watching her, the more I wanted to live in her state: unperturbed, unmarred by self-consciousness, and most of all, a state that inspired others to be their best selves. It was hard to wrap my head around Gurumayi's existence, but it was clear to me that by devoting herself to her teacher and the practices, she'd attained the point of being human, an unshakeable knowing that *God dwelled with her as her.* She lived in a state of meditation all the time. She was the river of life and the banks that hold it together. She had access to all the wisdom that life had to offer because it was in her, and through her teachings she was saying, "I got here. With focus, effort, and discipline, you can, too."

If vegetarianism was in fact a requirement for enlightenment, I'd figure it out.

I found myself on all fours, on my apartment floor. A powerful earthquake had tossed me out of bed at 5:15 a.m. I braced for another, breathing heavily in the dark. I turned the light on and surveyed my little apartment. Everything, save for the picture of Gurumayi which had fallen over, was in its rightful place. *Maybe she protected me*, I thought, which was a quintessential Siddha Yoga way of interpreting the events.

I turned on the radio and called my parents to let them know all was okay. As the sun rose, the city, it seemed, was still intact. I was up so early, pacing around my apartment, at a loss for what to do next. I decided to drive to the Center to see if it was damaged, and if others would still show up at 6:00 a.m. for the daily recitation of a core practice I hadn't yet tried, the *Guru Gita,* or song of the guru: a ninety-minute, 181-stanza chant that was sung too early and was very intimidating.

I was relieved to discover the Center was fine, and about twenty people were grateful to come together, practice, and calm down. The *Guru Gita* was rigorous. I struggled with the pronunciation and phrasing of the phonetically written text, but by the chant's end, I had a better buzz than I'd had from any cup of coffee, which fueled my mission to get comfortable with it. In addition to monthly meetings in West Hollywood, I started attending the Center five times a week: for Saturday night *satsang,* Thursday night *hatha yoga* (the physical kind), Monday and Wednesdays at 6:00 a.m. for the early morning *Guru Gita,* which was sparsely populated, and the Sunday *Guru Gita* at 8:30, followed by an Amrit brunch.

"See that guy?" Akira said one Sunday during brunch after the *Gita.* She pointed to a white-haired man in fancy slacks and a button-down shirt. "He wrote the screenwriting bible. He and his wife are board members of the Center." I watched him and his wife shuffle in their socks to get a bowl of something called sour cereal, which wasn't sour at all, but some of the best hot cereal — a blend of millet, Indian spices, and oats — I'd ever tasted. I loved learning about the intelligent industry people involved in Siddha Yoga, especially the theater luminaries like André Gregory of *My Dinner with André* and the British theater director who'd written a book I studied in college. It made me feel safe and quelled my doubts about having a guru. There was also a famous actress from one of TVs top 80s sitcoms, a renowned Indie director or three, and a few other highly accomplished but largely unknown actors who came around. They didn't mingle with me and the group of friends I was starting to develop. But one morning after the Sunday *Gita,* I went to a celebrity's house, an exquisite home on Mulholland Drive. Akira had invited me to tag along on some errands, which included watering plants for her friend, a famous devotee, an actress who was filming on location.

A cinematic view of LA sprawled beneath the huge floor-to-ceiling windows. While Akira waltzed around the house with her watering can, I gawked at the view of the vast city leading all the way to the shore and the enormous painting of Gurumayi sitting in meditation on top of a snow-covered mountain, which hung on a 20-foot wall. A perfect bowl of fruit sat in the center of the spacious kitchen, which was bigger than my entire apartment. I thought, *I'd like to have a perfect bowl of fruit and a large portrait of Gurumayi in my house one day.*

But when I returned home from that expansive afternoon, I couldn't hold onto the good feelings. As I closed the door to my apartment, the nameless ache started to bubble up — a basin of need in the pit of my stomach, and it wasn't long before I found myself leaning over the counter, shoving Wheat Thins into my mouth as fast as I could, crumbs flying sideways, flattening my *Shakti* buzz with carbs and shame. I prayed that over time, the practices would help shift my compulsion.

A few Sundays later, standing in front of my kitchen cabinets after the *Guru Gita* chant and brunch, there was a shift. The siren song of the Oreos was strong and insistent. I ached for the relief of the crunch and cream filling in my mouth. But there was a new sliver of internal space between the craving to binge and the need to fill it, and I wondered what would happen if I did one of the practices instead. I forced myself to sit on my second-hand throw pillow — I was still holding out on buying an official meditation cushion — and focused on my breath. The craving was a painful sensation in my jaw and stomach, which migrated to my chest where that knot sat like a boulder. Every time I breathed into it, it was as if laces were tightening around my ribs. I wanted to escape, but I willed myself to keep breathing in the mantra. Then I slipped into a vision, what may have been my earliest memory. I was in a crib, surrounded by white wooden ribs extending up towards the ceiling. I could hear the high-pitched whir of an electric juicer, my mother pressing orange halves down over its plastic mound. Through the slats I could see the back of her green housecoat. All of a sudden, I needed her. Maybe I was wet. Maybe I was hungry. Whatever it was, a wordless discomfort was mounting and mounting. My mother was annoyed. She was looking down over the bars at me, desperate for me to stop fussing. Maybe she picked me up and dropped me, but suddenly I couldn't feel her, and then she was gone. My heart was shattered, a searing pain ripping my chest in two. STOP. STOP. STOP. I wanted the horrible pain and my mother's irritation to go away. I wailed, but there was no stopping it. I squeezed my little chest muscles in a concerted effort, trying to stop the pain flooding my heart.

Then, the whole frantic episode faded, like I'd plunged deep into the ocean and made it back up for air. *What just happened? A nonverbal memory?* Whatever it was, I knew for sure the pain was real. I also felt a sense of accomplishment. I had accessed my first *samskara*, a psychological impression or old wound — in psych parlance, a *trauma* — that impeded enlightenment, or the flow of *Shakti* in one's life. I understood the root cause of tension in my chest. Untangling the knot of the heart and lightening the load of hate demanded that every stone be turned and looked under, and I was fully committed to this work of self-confrontation. Going so deep led me to believe I was a little closer to being free.

I decided December was the month for breakups. I kept harping back to a dream I'd had with Alex, that my college therapist had interpreted one way, but I now understood. In the dream, after having sex with Alex, a snake emerged from my genitals and I was freaking out. I needed him to do something, pull it out, call for help, kill it — but he turned away in disgust. My therapist thought it was about me not feeling protected by him emotionally, but now I saw the snake as the *kundalini* — often symbolized as a snake coiled at the base of the spine until it is awakened — and how my spirituality turned him away from me. I realized Alex wasn't and would never be the curious, open, and daring soul-searcher I needed.

I found the courage to finally call it off while waiting to see *The Doors* on the top floor of a large indoor mall. We leaned over the railing looking down at the people on the floors below moving around like ants.

"You're just not *spiritual* enough for me," I told him. I couldn't think of any better way to say it. I needed to make a clean, final break, even if it meant I had to spend New Year's Eve alone.

"But ... we love each other. Isn't that spiritual enough?"

Not for me. On lonely nights when I thought about trying to win him back, I knew I wasn't equipped to have a guru *and* a somewhat philandering boyfriend with ultra-cool friends and little interest in his own spiritual development.

But it wasn't until January, after spending a month of nights lying awake on my Murphy bed, perseverating about leaving my acting class, that I worked up the courage to leave acting. You had to break your contract in front of the class, and I thought I would die of humiliation from how the teacher would react. I talked about it ad nauseam with Gabby and Akira. *What did it mean? What would I do now?* I consulted with a jolly friend who'd lived in the ashram for ten years, editing videos of Gurumayi before moving to LA and winning an editing Emmy. Her reflection on how to deal with the teacher was extremely perceptive. "He can't control you, even though you're used to being controlled."

During the announcements section of acting class, when most people shared good news about auditions or callbacks or getting an agent, I announced I'd be leaving the following month. I used my deposit as last month's rent.

"So, you're a quitter!" the acting teacher yelled out. The house lights were still on, and the entire class turned its eyes on me, sitting in the last row of risers. No one stood up to the acting guru, not without being trampled. I felt my heartbeat in my temples and alternately repeated the mantra and the devotee's words, over and over inside. *Om Namah Shivaya. He can't control me.*

"Yes, I am quitting this class," I said.

"You." He stopped and shook his head, clearly looking for the right hook, the right takedown. I waited. "You're going to let fear run your life."

I hoped he wasn't right. *Om Namah Shivaya.*

When he got no response, he went further. "What are you going to do with your creativity?" he asked, his bushy eyebrows joining in the middle of his forehead.

"I am focusing on my singing right now." I had started lead chanting at the Center, which meant I sat at a mic at the head of the hall with Nada and a bunch of other musicians and "called out" the Sanskrit chant, which everyone else repeated.

"Yeah ... how?" He was not letting up. I couldn't tell the class about the chanting.

"I'm making a demo tape with a musician in Laurel Canyon."

This was also true. Nada and her husband Joe, a Center musician and jingles composer, were convinced I should be doing more with my voice. Joe volunteered to make a demo tape in his home recording studio of me singing three songs from my NYC jazz days. I spent two Sunday afternoons in their funky Laurel Canyon love shack, making music and learning about a new fad diet called, "Fit for Life."

It seemed to do the trick. The teacher backed off for the moment.

When the next student went up to do her monologue, he continued his attacks by shouting thinly veiled "critiques" of her work to the back of the theater where I was sitting. "You're not committed, and not being committed can lead to breakdowns everywhere in your life!"

He was furious, but I was free. Free to commit to a new teacher, one who had mastered the art of inner freedom.

That Saturday night at the program, before *darshan*, the emcee — that actress from a big '80s TV show — said that whereas in life we mostly lead with our heads, when *pranam*ing, or going into child's pose during the practice of *darshan*, we place our heads below our hearts, placing love above our thoughts. This perspective opened something in me. I could approach *darshan* as bowing down to a bigger part of myself.

That night, I stood in line to bow down to a chair with a picture on it. It felt like a natural expression of gratitude. On my knees, breathing in the Jean Naté-smelling carpet and releasing any tension into the earth, I sank into a moment of silence. Then I sat up, stared into the eyes in the photo, and floated towards the back of the hall.

The next Saturday night at the evening program, I paid attention when they announced an upcoming Valentine's Day Intensive in New York. The only thing left to establish me as a full-fledged devotee was meeting the guru in person.

7: Tested
Shree Muktananda Ashram, 1992

The dining hall at the Catskills Shree Muktananda Ashram had a silent section, although you could hear murmurs of conversations from other tables and the clatter of trays and silverware landing in the dirty-dish tubs. I told Gab that's where I'd be sitting for lunch. I didn't want to talk to her. I was still mad at her for getting the bus schedule wrong, leaving us to wait pointlessly in the cold, moist dawn for fifteen minutes before realizing it wasn't coming. We had to chant my first ashram *Guru Gita* at Sadhana Kutir in the moldy dorm-building hall, with audio from the main building piped in. And she scolded me for resting my water bottle on the chanting book while I was arranging my seat. She scowled, "That's disrespectful!"

After spending the night before the Intensive staring at the springs of the bunk bed on top of me and listening to them creak every time the devotee in it stirred, I was exhausted. I was also disappointed that I'd come to see Gurumayi teach in person, but only swamis and scholars had guided us through the morning segments. Maybe the prickly sensation under my skin was, as Gabby called it, *tapasya*, my bad karma burning. Even if this irritation was the price of freedom, I hated being at a Valentine's Day Intensive, feeling anything but love.

I ate a few bites of chickpea stew, staring out the window at the cold damp gray. *Focus on why you're here*, I coached myself. I wanted a deep experience of my higher self in meditation, to touch the God within me. And after all these months of connecting with her inside myself, I wanted to meet Gurumayi, which they said was guaranteed at *darshan* at the Intensive's end. I dumped the contents of my tray in the big garbage pail and waited for the bus to go back to the main building to attend the afternoon session.

"*Sadgurunath Maharaj Ki Jay*! Welcome back to the Live in Love Intensive!" Swami Keshavananda said enthusiastically after the lunch break. He was the Intensive emcee, a handsome, articulate swami.

The meditation hall was cavernous, with lovely, soft aqua carpeting and a lighted path on the floor so people could move around in the dark. Hundreds, if not thousands, of us were packed in. A huge picture of Baba lit from inside glowed at the back of the meditation hall, so Gurumayi could see her teacher whenever she was in her chair, which continued to be empty.

I noticed certain people, special people — including a famous movie star with soft blond ringlets and a plush leather tote — being escorted to seats way upfront next to the guru's chair, coveted seats, closest to the master and her powerful energy. Watching the important people stride past me triggered feelings of jealousy. I wanted to be waltzed to the front, important enough to be in the guru's inner circle, to be known. But as a newbie, I felt invisible. I wrestled with this feeling. *It's just ego*, I told myself.

At the ashram, I was now seeing, there was no end to wrestling with ego. Every moment, every thought, judgment, and emotion felt magnified. It was overwhelming. I had read enough books explaining that all the things that happen in the presence of the guru — good and bad — are designed to point you to God, to look within. This was the nature of spiritual growth. Whatever made you feel bad was in the way of your experiencing the truth and needed to be examined. I looked at the packed hall behind me. I looked at the many in front of me. *Settle down, Goldilocks.* I took a breath and wiggled my sitz bones into position for the long haul.

"You all look different than you did this morning," Swami Keshavananda said. There were thousands of us, and I didn't know how he could say that with any authority. I knew I looked worse: tired, sweaty, wan. But

Swami Keshavananda, like most of the Intensive speakers, was smart and charming. He wore round, rimless wire glasses, a shaved head, and looked fit underneath his draped red garb. The Siddha Yoga swamis had taken vows of celibacy and non-ownership, wore only shades of red, and devoted their lives to spiritual practice, teaching, and serving the master.

A young female swami with a cute haircut of short layered black hair, about ten years my senior, gave a lecture about St. Valentine and the history of the holiday. She reminded me of someone, like we could have been good friends. Later, I discovered that she also grew up in the city and went to Dalton, the same high school as my next-door neighbor, Marissa. As the swami went on about the saint who married people in secret and fought for the right to love, I wondered: *What would it be like to be a swami and get to live in such a beautiful place, teach all over the world, meditate, chant, and serve God every day?* If she, a Jewish girl from the city, could become a Siddha swami, couldn't I? It seemed like a humble way to live, moving towards a great goal of inner peace, being able to share that peace with others, and having the messiest questions of my life — who should I be and what should I do? — neatly answered.

She spoke about *bhakti*, the state and practice of devotional love, dissecting the mysterious bond between gurus and disciples. The apostles devoted their hearts and lives to Jesus. The Sufi poet Rumi idealized his teacher Shams. Baba Muktananda gave everything up for his beloved Guru "Bade Baba" Nityananda, who was the life-sized centerpiece statue in the temple just down the hall. All this talk about love and devotion between student and teacher confronted me with a mysterious question: Did I *love* Gurumayi, a person that I spoke with daily inside myself but had never met? It sounded bizarre to put it that way, especially because my feelings, however big, were entirely platonic. But as the talk continued, I realized that, yes, it had gone that far. My heart got that fluttery sensation when I thought about her, and she was all I wanted to talk about. I started to giggle, maybe because loving a guru I'd never met — odd in and of itself — was such an unexpected turn of events for who I thought I would be.

Like a kid in church, I tried to keep my laughter quiet, but it kept escaping in little bursts. What had started way back in Chicago as intrigue and morphed into a vague sense of connection after that classic 'let's-look-for-you' dream, had resulted in falling in love in Los Angeles. She was my teacher, and I loved her. What else could explain the desire to be near her, see her, get to know her for real? Trying to wrap my brain around this love and the fact that she probably had no idea who I was, had no effect on the heart-inspired intimacy I felt. But the laughter subsided when I considered: *if we are this in sync inside myself, would she recognize me when we met? Would she love me back?*

We were given meditation instructions for our final session of the day, and it was clear, after a good while of sitting in the dark, that I was merely meditating on frustration. I was stewing in a sense of futility, the minutes dragging on, when a gentle breeze stirred. People started coughing and rustling. I opened my eyes to find Gurumayi sitting in perfect stillness on her chair. She was as beautiful in person as in the photos, perhaps more so as she sat there, eyes closed, spine erect, in bright red silk.

The energy in the room crackled. Gurumayi brought us out of meditation and then guided us in again, but still, I didn't feel much. That is until strange animal sounds erupted from meditators in the room. Spontaneous imitations of pigs, cows, and other animals were so life-like it made me think there was some kind of training people had attended to create the perfect mimicry. They were *kriyas,* a cleansing eruption of the *Shakti* during meditation, clearing out the channel from the base of the spine to the top of the head so that the meditative energy could flow freely. Gabby had seen a young woman, an ashram acquaintance, leave a course over the summer while having a *kriya,* eyes fixed and open wide as if she was possessed. The woman ended up in the parking lot doing yoga poses and had to be calmed down by a couple of swamis. The *kriyas* I was now listening to were both hilarious and unsettling. The crowd kept laughing, so now a room of hundreds was filled with animal sounds and laughter, like a huge, spooky group improv.

I also wondered if people taking the Intensive had been drugged, even though I'd eaten the same food and drunk the same chai. Though I hadn't had the meditation experience I'd hoped for, I was relieved to not find myself uncontrollably shrieking like a monkey. At the end of day one, I followed a large mob out of the building heading for the shuttle to the dining hall. I wiggled my feet into my shoes. Pictures of enlightened beings were everywhere, and Hindu deity statues like Lakshmi and Ganesh sat in pockets in the walls. Half-bodied elephants, multiple arms, skulls, tigers: everything that had once been mysterious and beautiful seemed strange. I was back on the creeped-out side of the interminable see-saw of my spiritual path. If only I didn't want to meet Gurumayi so badly at the end of the course, I might have planned an escape.

Gabby was waiting for me at the end of the hallway, her eyes and teeth sparkling. She had been doing *seva* in the Amrit, cleaning the tables and walls. The sight of her, my familiar, smiling friend, comforted me. My anger towards her melted.

"How was it?"

"Gurumayi finally showed up. But it was very weird. Lots of *kriyas*. I want to crawl out of my skin."

"Aww. More *tapasya*! Well, let's meet Bade Baba. He can help. The temple is very calming."

She led me down the hall to the temple, a legendary part of the ashram that everyone in LA said was magic. While we strolled towards it, I tried and failed to find good reasons to skip it. We put our shoes in the temple cubby and stood in a line to perform the customary bow before entering.

Gabby darted away and then rushed back over to me carrying an ivory pashmina shawl. "Wrap this over your pants," she whispered. I had worn wide-legged, skirt-like pants that I thought would do, but women were only allowed to wear skirts or saris in the temple.

The power of the temple was evident upon entering. An octagonal addition with large, single-pane windows letting in the natural beauty on all sides, it was home to a huge, life-sized statue of "Bade (Bah-day) Baba" Nityananda, the enlightened grandfather of the Siddha tradition. The statue of Bade Baba was known as a *murti* — it had been infused with divine life force in a ceremony by Brahmin priests. Draped in real Indian silk robes, Bade Baba sat on a circular platform in the temple's center and was surrounded by oil candles, piles of fruit, and so many beautiful flowers; the intoxicating smell of gardenias filled my nostrils and went to my head. A slightly audible recording of the tamboura tinkled in the background.

Legend had it that Nityananda was born a realized being and walked all over India, eventually settling in the town of Ganeshpuri, where his successor, Baba Muktananda — Gurumayi's guru — meditated, became enlightened, and built an ashram that still operates today. Imitating what I saw the devotees in line before me doing, I bowed, or *pranamed* to a pedestal in front of the statue that held a silver tray with a pair of silver *padukas* — sandals — and fresh-cut blossoms. Then I followed Gabby in a customary walk around the statue, before sitting for meditation. Behind the statue, against the wall, was an enormous amethyst geode the size of a small car. I could feel its energy as I passed.

We sat. I gazed up at the life-like bronze figure. Compared to the zoo I'd just come from, communing with a spirit-infused statue didn't feel so strange. I became quiet and opened to a connection with Bade Baba, as if I had a loving spirit Grandpa who would listen to my heart. *Help me connect*, I pleaded. I did connect with something — my evening plans: *get dinner, skip the evening activities, and go to bed.* The simple directives were comforting. Gabby tapped me on the shoulder. "You'll miss dinner," she whispered, took my blanket back to the pile from where it came, and wished me luck before returning to her *seva*.

Sunday, the final afternoon of the Intensive arrived and I still hadn't fallen into meditation. I sat up straight in the dark. Gurumayi's words pierced me.

"Those of you who are trying to sit up very straight and force meditation with your will — it won't happen," she said from her chair. I was sure she was talking directly to me. I was *trying* to be good. I was *trying* to breathe, *trying* to focus, *trying* to have an experience — I was meditating on trying, and mostly I just felt hardened and stiff.

I didn't know how to stop running the show with my will, not in my life, not when we chanted with Gurumayi for the next part of the Intensive, and not when she brought us into the final meditation. So I let it go — everything. I just slumped. If I was going to fall asleep during the guru-led meditation, or sit there twiddling my thumbs, so be it. Since I couldn't force myself to have a deep inner experience, I just wanted to enjoy the remainder of my time in her presence. After a few moments, I found myself feeling stretched, as though a string was pulling my head up, and sitting became effortless. I was drawn to a river within, a palpable experience of being magnetically pulled into my body, somewhere deep within my consciousness. I was residing in the inside of my belly, but instead of guts, there was space. Lots of glorious space. An image arose from within this space: tree tops. I was walking, looking up at limbs of rustling leaves, glistening with light, and as they shimmied in a soft breeze, I recognized the leaves. They looked and felt ... like me. They were not just leaves, they were *Blair* leaves, made up of the same me that was witnessing them. And then, literally, like pulling up a curtain, a veil was lifted, the trees vanished, and all that existed behind everything was blue, pulsating sky blue, the most exquisite blue I'd ever been in everywhere, and there were no thoughts, just spasms of deep, blue recognition of true, true, truth. The Truth! Once that word formed in my mind, the spell was broken. The intensity of the ecstasy waned and the pulsating lessened and the room came back and my belly came back and I was a young woman again, a young woman who had touched the very fabric of the universe and understood something about it, something deeper than I could put into words.

"*Sadgurunath, Maharaj ki Jai!*" Swami Keshavananda shouted, the Siddha Yoga catchphrase — "Hail to the true guru!" at the Intensive's end. As was custom, everyone bowed their heads and placed their hands in prayer position in front of their hearts, and the most exquisite, otherworldly music began, a long poem-song called the *Pasayadan*. The tamboura was followed by a steady flute, which preceded pure women's voices, one of whom I later discovered was a mildly renowned folk singer. I was spent. I sat there in blissful exhaustion, watching people purposefully move about, until I realized it was time for *darshan*. People started forming a line, six across. I was finally going to meet Gurumayi, to bow down to a living being on the chair, not just a picture.

Those sitting towards the middle of the hall started moving their *asanas* to the sides, to make space for the wide line. I moved my meditation cushion gingerly, not just because I was learning to respect it (thank you,

Gabby) as a sacred tool, but because my *asana* was fresh off the bookstore shelves. During the break after the mega-meditation, I meandered into the bookstore where there were meticulously designed tables and cases of books written by Baba, Gurumayi, the Siddha swamis, and a few other ascended masters; CDs of chants and talks; delicate jewelry, bracelets, and necklaces you could remove and use like a rosary to say the mantra with, and then, there were the cushions. My eyes zeroed in on a bright purple wool beanbag *asana* with a silk-trimmed wool cover blanket and a chanting book cover to match. I wanted it. I knew it would be pricey, but I had the American Express with me. I spent a few minutes pretending to talk myself out of it, but that cushion set was mine. I invested $180 in my *sadhana* for a proper *asana* and my very own chanting book with a silk cover to take back to LA. It was time to own my own seat. I put the set on the card and hoped the money would come back to me.

Darshan was mesmerizing. People *pranamed* tenderly before Gurumayi, touching their foreheads to the floor. While they did, she would transmit blessings by bopping the top of their head with a wand made of peacock feathers. There were six people in various states of coming and going in front of her at any time, and all of them had different needs and experiences. Some simply knelt down, received the blessings, and walked away. Others stayed and talked with her, and some lucky ones were addressed by her.

Even a complete atheist would marvel at the composure and multi-tasking dance of the straight-sitting teacher, peacock wand moving effortlessly between her hands, bopping each person on the head all while engaging in conversations with devotees and negotiations with her staff. I wished my non-believing friends could see it. There was a seamless rhythm to it. As the devotees came and went, it was as if her arms were operating on their own. Gurumayi, within an aura of stillness, would move the feathers furiously atop one kneeler's head, as if rubbing in extra blessings or shooing a demon out, while ever so gently tap-tapping the head of another, while simultaneously engaging in lighthearted conversation. She looked at one devotee sternly and then turned to beam a wide-eyed smile at the next. She was a mirror. She was full and empty at the same time. People gave her gifts, fruit, money, and sometimes she gave gifts back. The first time

Gabby met Gurumayi in *darshan*, she received a bracelet. I wondered what present might be waiting for me but then slapped my inner wrist at the thought. More ego! I knew I had already received a gift — an experience of the truth — that would last a lifetime, and that should be enough, even though I still wanted a token of my spiritual teacher's love and a good story to share with Gab.

I joined the others in line waiting to greet Gurumayi, and my mind went blank. A kind lady named Sharon approached, noticing from the color of my name tag that I was a first-timer. She offered to introduce me to Gurumayi and plucked me off the line to bring me to the front. I felt special and giddy. I couldn't think of anything to say in person to Gurumayi except that I was so happy to finally meet her, and suddenly we were on our knees, shuffling up to her from the side of the line.

"Gurumayi, this is Blair Glaser from Los Angeles," Sharon started.

It was happening so fast. Grinning, I beamed up at her on her chair, stunned to be so close. She barely glanced at me. Bop. Bop. Bop. She blessed a few people on the line.

"She has been practicing at the Center in LA," Sharon continued. "She is an actress and a singer."

"... and a what?" Gurumayi snarled, her wand bobbing up and down.

"A singer," Sharon repeated, a little louder.

"Oh," Gurumayi said, disinterested.

"She wants you to know that she is so happy to meet you."

Gurumayi turned to me for one intense moment — boring into me with her unfettered gaze — bopped me with the feathers, and then, unimpressed, turned away. We were shooed away by a pretty *darshan* girl, like Santa's little helper, who nodded as if to say, this is complete.

I stumbled away as though I had been bopped on the head not by a peacock feather, but by a wooden bat. My jaw hung open. There had been no recognition of me, no welcoming, sweet smile. She couldn't have been less interested. Apparently, Sharon didn't know what had happened up there either.

"Are you okay?" She stood by my side and repeated helplessly, "I'm so, so sorry. That's never happened."

I just wanted Sharon to leave me alone. Gurumayi didn't recognize me, but at the very least, I thought she would show interest in me as the devoted student I'd become. My hopes for the beginning of an outer relationship with my teacher were crushed. As I gathered up my new purple seat, tears of humiliation leaked from my eyes. I ran out of the hall and found Gabby in the Amrit.

"It didn't go well!" I sobbed, placing my head in my hands.

"Oh my god!" She hugged me. We were making a scene. "We'll talk about it on the drive back."

I couldn't wait to get out of there and lick my wounds. Gabby was taking her time, wrapping up a deep conversation with one of the swamis. I grabbed my shoes and bag from the cubby area and motioned to her, mouthing, "I'll wait for you in the courtyard."

Under a darkening, cloudy sky, I replayed what had happened. A kind voice inside nudged: *Before the guru ignored you, you had the most amazing inner experience. Don't forget it. Don't let this ruin it.*

On the ride back to the city, where I'd sleep before heading back to LA early in the morning, I stared mindlessly out at the barren evening landscape, my heart heavy in my chest. I'd heard a few stories about the guru's wrath. She could be very harsh at times, although it was said that she wasn't really angry. The point was to wake you up, pierce through that part of you that was *jada* (fittingly pronounced JUDD), the part that was stubbornly asleep. When I was able to catch my breath, Gabby and I dissected the diss. We loved pouring through interactions with the guru, looking for the hidden meaning or teaching, knowing her words and actions were laden with layers of impact.

Maybe Gurumayi was testing me to see if I could hold on to my inner experience of the Self and of her, which was love, the whole theme of the weekend. Earlier in the day, I was directly connected to all that is! Well, I failed that test. But maybe it was more detailed, more literal. My lack of commitment to being an actress and especially a singer was why she appeared unimpressed and had to ask again ("a what?"), as if billing myself as an actress and a singer was a lie. Maybe she was rejecting me because I was rejecting my higher self. Maybe all of it was true. I didn't bother to consider that none of it was.

By the time we got to the city, I fashioned myself a spiritual warrior, in way too deep to reject the path just because Gurumayi rejected me. I didn't need a bracelet that carried her blessings. I had the practices, and they were helping me heal and grow.

On the flight home, a final wave of panic crashed through. Now that I had traveled across the country, met my teacher, and skyrocketed into the cosmos, there was no turning back. Siddha Yoga had become a major part of my life, not just an LA thing. How would I explain it to my parents? What if it was all bunk? What if it *was* a cult? How would I know? I kept having to remind myself of how I first got involved: by seeing the set designer walk down a theater aisle and feeling attracted to him. That was all. Everything unfolded from there.

When I got off the plane in LA, there was some noise and commotion. A group of Hare Krishnas were in a corner, dancing in robes and chanting *Hare Krishna, Hare Rama*, a chant I now knew. I paused for a moment. They looked silly and happy. One of them spotted me and approached carrying a huge book, *The Bhagavad Gita*, one of the Hindu texts that had been quoted over the weekend. When he offered it to me, I politely declined and walked away. I giggled, thinking it could be worse: *at least I wasn't dancing in the airport.*

Finally back home, I opened my mailbox to find a random check. Weeks before and without communicating it to me, my parents had closed my childhood savings account, where the cash gifts of friends and relatives had been stored until I was old enough to use them. The amount totaled a little over $900, covering the cost of the Intensive and the cushion. The note from my parents said, "Here ya go, we closed the account." But in my heart I pretended — or more accurately, I *believed* — it was from Gurumayi. I stopped doubting. I was in.

8: Longing

My hands shook as I held onto the steering wheel, waiting for the light to change. A few random people were running down La Cienega Boulevard, perhaps escaping the fires or coming from igniting one. A 7-Eleven was burning across the street, and pieces of the building were flying off the roof. If the wind changed before the light did, a piece of burning building could land on my car.

As the Rodney King riots exploded in late April throughout Los Angeles and angry Angelinos looted stores and set them alight, I felt the fire on many levels. I seethed at the injustice of the verdict that let the police officers — who had so clearly beaten up an innocent man — go free, although my anger was from an outsider perspective. My boss, distraught as I had never seen him, talked to family members on the phone. He called the owner and announced he would be leaving, told us to go home early. As I drove through the burning streets, I tried to comprehend what had happened and what I could do.

At the Center, sitting in multicultural circles, the famous Black TV actress led us through exercises in which we talked about spiritual practice as a way to change the world. By seeing God in others, we treat them with respect. By being a calm and luminous presence, we impact the world around us. By watching our thoughts, by contemplating what we say and how we say it, we uplift those around us. I wasn't sure if it was all we could do, but it felt like a start.

The riots marked a turning point when my day job as a customer service representative for a cutting-edge brand of skincare began to feel pointless and deadening. I wasn't making a contribution to bettering the world. Immediately upon entering the office, I felt sluggish, entranced by the soporific buzz of the computers.

And my spiritual practice could do nothing to shift it. Just two months after returning from the Intensive, my practice no longer gave me a big pick-me-up in the mornings. Was this normal? Was I still heading towards enlightenment?

"I'm just going through the motions of life, to work and back each day," I complained to Akira at *satsang*. "I feel disconnected, like I've lost my *sadhana*, my spiritual path."

"It happens," she said. "Stick with it. It comes back."

"But what else can I do?"

Akira let me know about an open, paid position at the Catskills ashram she'd heard of, for an initiative called the Prison Project, teaching meditation to prisoners. This sounded like a great way to give back, to be a more active participant in justice and live close to the guru. I wasn't sure I was trained for that kind of work, but I wanted to devote myself fully to the path and get back in the groove. I signed up for an interview.

"How long have you been practicing Siddha Yoga?" The Prison Project director asked me in our phone interview.

I was at work, and put my head down low in my cubicle, resting my forehead on my fist, trying to be discreet. "I guess since November."

"Less than a year?!"

I didn't expect her to be shocked, or her manner to be so brass tacks. This wasn't going well.

"What makes you think you are ready to devote yourself to a more monastic lifestyle?"

I shifted the receiver to the other ear, fighting the urge to hang up and pretend we got disconnected. "I just know I feel most inspired when I'm focused on my spiritual practice."

"What might you be running away from?"

She sure got me on that one. Was I running away? I knew skincare wasn't my life's work. I wasn't acting anymore. Was I doing a-void-dance?

Or, was I running towards the Self? I derived meaning from focusing on my growth, immersing myself in practice and striving to get back to that true blue faith. I felt in my bones that my *sadhana* was a big part of my *dharma*, my life purpose. I had to learn how to steady my mind in order to discover what my true purpose was.

"Hmmmm ..." I said, fantasizing about being back at the ashram, waking up in the electric darkness, chanting before dawn. "I feel like I'm running towards something."

The Prison Project's response to my application, in a phone message three days later, was: "We don't think you're ready. Maybe in a few more years."

I was a little relieved to be spared the fire of intense *sadhana*, but the rejection stung. And the idea of moving back east to be closer to the guru was now lodged in my being. I imagined myself living in New York City and taking weekend trips with Gabby to the ashram to do *seva*, sitting for meditation in the temple, burning my bad karma, and becoming pure. I didn't know if giving up on LA was the right thing to do, especially now that I was lead chanting at the Center, enjoying community, and focusing on singing again. I poured my heart out in my first-ever letter to Gurumayi, telling her I didn't want to run away from my life, but I didn't know how to make sense of my disinterest in the world and my desire to only immerse myself in spiritual practice. *Gurumayi, I know you teach us that God is in everything, but I wish to be in an environment where more people see it that way.* Word in the community was that it sometimes took up to a year for Gurumayi to respond to a letter, but the writing in and of itself was what mattered.

Gurumayi's reply arrived ten months later, on a grimy, overcast, winter day in New York — when I'd forgotten all about writing that letter. I'd crawled home after a lunch shift at one of my two Manhattan waitressing jobs to the vermin-infested apartment that I shared with Gabby. My insides felt like the city sidewalks, with the dirty slush lining the streets. I just wanted to sleep. I got into my pj's and closed the door to my room.

Leaving LA had been another churning drama. Despite the point of spiritual growth being to trust yourself and your inner voice, I could not. I went back and forth about the pros and cons of moving until I worked up the courage to call Kate for the first time in over a year.

"I'm driving myself nuts," I told her. "I want to move back to New York, but I've just gotten a life here."

Her response was classic Kate: a drag of the cigarette, a deep pause, and then a truth bomb.

"You've completed your task. You needed to move away from your parents to see if you could make a life of your own without them. Now that you have, you can live near them again."

It blew my mind. She probably knew the whole time that things with Alex would fall apart. But she wasn't judging me. She was rooting for me. And her explanation freed me to move back.

The day I decided to leave LA was, in classic Siddha Yoga fashion, the day I heard there would be a Labor Day *Dharma* Intensive at the ashram. I'd been intent on discovering my life's purpose, and an intensive on that very topic was on my birthday weekend! So I signed up for my second Intensive at the ashram with Gurumayi — paid for with my untaken vacation days from quitting my LA skincare job — and put the move to New York in motion.

I had prepared for my second visit to the ashram to be filled with agitation. But since I arrived early in the day, there was no registration line. Gurumayi walked by Atma Nidhi after I registered, which I felt was auspicious, as if her presence this time was welcoming me. And the *Dharma* Intensive was easy to follow and to slip into meditation. I received some surprising guidance. During a contemplation focused on what we're here to do, I heard the words "be a teacher." *Be a teacher.* I understood that teaching had always been a part of my big-sister nature: the way I interacted with friends, the way I guided younger campers as a team captain at camp, the way I gave feedback in my college acting classes. It was a role I relished. *But what would I actually teach?* There was no TikTok or YouTube to log onto and start building an audience for my spiritual insights.

Even if there had been, I was all too aware of how limited my true knowledge was. I was at the beginning. I was only twenty-three. The guidance to be a teacher was both an answer and a question.

At the *darshan* after the Intensive, Gabby and I asked Gurumayi for blessings to be roommates when I moved to New York. Gabby, with her personal relationship to Gurumayi, shuffled up on her knees, and I knelt beside her.

"Gurumayi, Blair and I would like your blessings to live together in New York."

She held us in suspense while she bopped other devotees on the heads. She looked us over, smiled woozily, and gazed up at the right corner of the hall, as though it held a movie screen, playing out our future. Her big eyes gradually drifted back to us.

"It's okay," she shrugged.

Not great, not bad, but okay. Gabby and I decided it was enough of a blessing to move forward, so we got a big, cheap apartment near 100th and West End Ave, just over ten blocks from the Manhattan ashram.

In the immediate aftermath, the move to New York was, as most major life changes, new and exciting. I loved the smells of my new, old city, the feeling of turning the key in the door of my own apartment, figuring out where everything should go. Gab and I had set up our space with a little meditation room in our tiny laundry area, with the altar on top of the stackable. I got a few waitressing jobs and went back to acting and studying voice, thinking that since it was what I knew best, if I didn't get work, I could teach acting one day. Hope crackled in the crisp autumn air that stung my cheeks. Living with Gabby made life less lonely. Plus, she'd started going to therapy with Kate, so we had a lot to talk about. We rented movies from the video store and listened to chanting and Indian music CDs from the ashram. I tried to see my parents as little as possible.

But as autumn wound down, my mood plummeted with the encroaching darkness. This moving and then crashing was a distressing pattern. *How was I submerged in this low-grade depression, yet again?*

On a slushy gray Friday, on the train uptown from my fancy restaurant job in Tribeca, I tried to piece it together while listening to Gurumayi chanting *Om Namah Shivaya* on my CD Walkman. Listening to chants had become my only spiritual practice. I liked the contrast of the clean, deep, peaceful tones in my ears while walking the noisy streets, or staring out at the subway riders and underground filth. Beyond that, meditation had become impossible. I hated the claustrophobic feel of the Manhattan ashram, a brownstone that had a railroad layout, so I no longer attended *satsang*. Dust bunnies crowded the altar on top of the dryer. The guru lived only two hours away, but I only went to the ashram twice. I had to prepare for the *tapasya*, the constant ego wrestle, and I didn't feel strong. Gurumayi, if she even registered who I was, didn't seem to like me. And staying at the ashram cost money and meant giving up valuable waitressing shifts.

As the train rocked back and forth, it dawned on me that I was living the stereotypical young artist's life, but there was no romance in it for me, literally or figuratively. After waitressing shifts, I'd have a late-night drink with the staff, having little to say. None of the cute bartenders were interested in me, and the two gorgeous actress-servers, slightly older, made my life feel so small in comparison. I felt chunky in my waiter costume of black pants and a white button-down shirt, the buttons straining at my chest, my bushy curls fanning out from the rubber band at the back of my head like a raccoon's tail. I'd spent the last three Saturdays in bed, thinking about bagels. I'd wake up and fantasize about getting one with cream cheese at the shop around the corner. Then I'd argue with myself that I'd better not — too fattening. Then I'd end up midday at the bagel store, and I'd get two, one presumably for the next day, and eat them both. I didn't want to face the emptiness of another bagel-y Saturday. I just wanted to hole up and stay in my room until spring.

I kicked off my snow boots, dragged myself into my room, and shut the door, curling around myself on my unmade bed.

Gabby knocked when she came home from her lame marketing job. "You have a letter from the ashram! It might be from Gurumayi!"

I flung the door open and tore at the letter in disbelief. It was typed on stationary with an ornate header, //OM GURU OM//, and written on the guru's behalf by Swami Kripananda, an elegant elder swami. Kripananda wrote that Gurumayi received my first letter — the one I'd written saying

I didn't want to run away but I did want to pursue my *sadhana* more seriously — when she was in the *Namaste* room, where she did official business. She was watching the dance of snow falling outside her window, which brought her great joy. The response didn't address anything I had written about head-on, but included a poem that Gurumayi wanted me to have, printed on a pastel yellow and green postcard, with two birds in flight in the upper corner.

There is so much love in waiting.
What you search for is within your search.
It is longing; not anguish, but longing.

It is this incredible longing
That makes our meeting possible.

Longing. That was it. That was the word for so much of my malaise, my anguish. To consider the nameless ache as "longing," and be able to know that it was a part of the wholeness I craved was a total relief. I briefly considered that the postcard was a canned response to everyone who wrote to her for the first time, but ultimately, I decided it didn't matter. It made me feel loved.

A few nights later, I had a dream in which I was at the ashram, walking down a brick path to a house that had belonged to Gurumayi's deceased Guru, Baba. In the dream, Baba's house had become a museum of sorts that had preserved his living quarters and was said to have incredible spiritual power. As I was heading to it, Gurumayi materialized, always in her flowing red robes, and stopped me on the path.

"So," she said tilting her head sideways, "You are walking on the ashram path?" the *th* in path pronounced *teh*, an idiosyncrasy of her Indian accent.

"No, Gurumayi," I replied rather hastily. "I'm headed towards Baba's house."

She straightened her head, slightly pursed her mouth, and nodded slowly, the kind of nod that says, *You just don't get it.*

That look — which she will eventually give me in real life and make me kick myself for not getting her intended meaning sooner — made me reconsider her words, and in the dream, I turn to yell after her, "Yes, yes I am! I am walking the ashram path! I want to be at the ashram!" But it's too late. Gurumayi has already walked down the path and is onto something else.

Chapter 9: Bridge

I saved up for a four-day ashram stay to allow myself to shed my winter skin and sink into the *Shakti*. When I stepped off the shuttle bus from the Manhattan ashram to the Catskills one, a gentle country breeze and the pop of new green on the trees lightened my mood immediately. The city trees were already in full bloom, but upstate everything was in that glorious phase of just coming alive. Even as I carried my bags, it was as if an invisible backpack of tension lifted off my shoulders.

I knew my way around now. The buildings. The ashram schedule. The bus schedule. The way people started walking when they heard Gurumayi was around, a little bit frantic like dogs sensing their owner is near, a movement that both excited me and made me feel silly when I got swept up.

"In India," I was scolded by a South Asian devotee as I started walking fast to catch the guru in the Atma Nidhi parking lot, "to follow the guru around like a hungry puppy is undignified." I heard him, but I still wanted to see her, to have a welcome *darshan*. When Gurumayi waltzed by with a cluster of attendants, her radiant smile was like a delicious breeze coming through a window on a scorching day. But trying to focus on the God within, I decided not to follow her and stand my ground after she passed. Just as I planted my feet, she turned around and smiled my way. She was wearing sunglasses and I couldn't see her eyes. But I felt the smile was for me.

My first morning, after the *Guru Gita*, as I went to dump my tray in the dining hall dishwashing tub after breakfast, a sweet *sevite* smiled at me.

"Would you like to do some chopping *seva* today?" I was on my way to the temple, but I couldn't resist her smile. *I'll just chop for a few minutes.*

I entered the kitchen to find ten sacks the size of small horses full of carrots that needed to be scrubbed, peeled, and chopped for Gurumayi's birthday celebration on the weekend. *This will take days, if not years,* I thought. I put the apron around my neck and the net on my hair and the gloves on my hands and got to work with a team of others, peeling, looking at the clock to see when I could exit. I stood in front of a growing mound of orange strips and quietly sang along with a lively chant from the boombox. Then I moved to the chopping area, standing around a large work table, tossing chunks of carrot into huge stainless steel bowls. The sweet, smiling *sevite* put her hand on my shoulder.

"Would you like to join us for the lunch *puja*?"

I looked around, and the rest of the choppers had taken off their aprons and were gathering around the kitchen altar for a brief chant to honor the guru. I walked in at 8:00. It was noon. The carrots were almost all gone.

I was so blown away by my level of absorption in what I thought would be an impossible task, I thought *this is how life should be.* Not outside myself, always resisting life, wondering when I could leave the boring task to get to the good part. The point was to be absorbed in where I was. To find pleasure in the simplicity of it. I was always rushing to be in a better place. In LA, I wanted to be famous. In New York, I wanted to fit in. At work I wanted to be at home, and at home I wanted to be in the ashram.

But the Miracle of the Carrots changed the course of my life.

I would be happy doing this, living this kind of life. I made an appointment at the *seva* office for a summer job interview, even though chances were slim since the summer was underway. Applications were still being accepted for a few remaining full-time seasonal positions in exchange for room and board. I wanted to try my luck at walking the "ashram path."

The next day, walking the wooded trail connecting the dining hall with the main building, en route to my first *seva* interview, I daydreamed about ashram life: waking up every day to the sweet smell of incense and the pre-dawn light, meditating, chanting the *Guru Gita,* wearing a *shmata* on my head and chopping vegetables, or doing dishes in the cavernous kitchen while quietly chanting the name of God. My reverie was interrupted by a small cluster of people gathered on a footbridge. I thought Gurumayi might be around but instead came upon a short-haired, red-robed swami on the ground, clutching her ankle. She was hurt. Help was on the way.

I stood there, wondering if I could be of service. The wind shook the tree leaves. The only thing I could think to do was close my eyes and offer a prayer that she would heal smoothly and quickly, and continue on my way.

The interview with the *seva* supervisors went well. It was nothing like the call I'd had with the Prison Project director. The two women, dressed as if for a corporate job in skirt suits, were welcoming. But they weren't sure where to place me.

A week later, they called me at home with urgency. "We have a great *seva* for you, a *maha seva*," the director told me. "How soon can you be here?"

"I can't believe you're forcing me to live with a *stranger*!" Gabby yelled, as we stood awkwardly in our living room. We had no air conditioning, and the heat was stifling.

"I know. I'm sorry!"

"That's easy for you to say! But this is not what I signed up for."

This was the biggest fight we'd ever had and I worried about the volume of our voices. I didn't want to upset our neighbors. But there was nothing I could do. She was pissed. Little beads of moisture formed above her pursed lips.

"Now I understand why Gurumayi wasn't so enthusiastic," she said, referring to the *darshan* where we asked for her blessings to live together after the Dharma Intensive.

Gabby blamed me for blowing up our lives. I blamed the carrots. Now that I had been accepted to live at the ashram as a summer *sevite*, I couldn't wait to get there, and fighting with her made me want to leave even faster. I understood why Gabby was upset, but I had been talking about living at the ashram for months since the dream. Now that it was actually happening, I didn't want to deal with her feelings about it, and I didn't know what was worse: that I was making her live with someone else, or the fact that I had gotten in and she hadn't. I didn't want to face the possibility that my literal dream-come-true could permanently damage our friendship.

My parents took the news even worse.

After I dropped the bomb on my mother, she took a beat before laying into me.

"I don't understand. After all that time and money invested in college, this is what you're doing with your life?" She called for my father to pick up the phone. He was calmer.

"So, why do you want to move into an ashram?"

"It's just for the summer, Dad. Focusing on my spiritual growth is helping me deal with depression and anxiety."

"But I don't understand. Why do you need to live in an ashram to do that?"

"It's an immersion, Dad."

It was so hard to articulate! But I knew in every cell of my body that this was the right place, the right move. They demanded we go see a therapist, and I acquiesced because I thought maybe it could help them understand. It didn't. While I appreciated that the therapist confirmed I didn't appear to be psychotic and I was old enough to make my own decisions, it increased the rift between my parents and me.

After two interminable weeks of hunting for a suitable subletter, a young male devotee that Gabby knew from the Siddha community rented my room for two months. As soon as I got the check, I shoved a bunch of comfy clothes for yoga and meditation, plain clothes for hands-on *seva*s like cooking and cleaning, and dressier clothes for ashram events, into a dusty old duffle I still had from camp and stowed all my personal stuff in a bin under the bed.

Swami Sajjananda looked familiar. Her spacious sunlit room was filled with flowers, including a bustling *Get Well Soon!* bouquet/balloon combo from Swami Chidvilasananda, otherwise known as Gurumayi. Gurumayi had also given Sajjananda a blanket, which she draped across her lap, as gifts from the guru were believed to hold the power and vibrations of the guru's blessings. In our initial meeting, a few days after I arrived for the rest of the summer, the swami was seated in a cushy recliner, her huge, boot-like cast propped up on an ottoman. Her ankle had suffered a bad and complex break, and I was tasked with being her caretaker until it healed.

As the sunlight illuminated her salt and pepper hair, I realized the same swami I passed on the bridge, the one I'd said a prayer for, was the one sitting in front of me. I didn't need more proof that in this place, my prayers were *literally* answered — but there it was.

Sajjananda eyed me up and down, as if looking for something to dismiss me right off the bat. I tried to ease the tension and find a connection. "You know, I walked by you after you fell on the bridge and said a get well prayer."

"Oh," she nodded with a slight smile, but she might as well have rolled her flinty eyes, as if she'd heard it all before. I took a deep breath as she instructed me on all the things I'd be doing for her, starting with bringing her breakfast and ending with running her a bath at night.

I was intensely curious about Sajjananda, this new person I was charged with caring for, affectionately known as Swamiji (all swamis had this moniker) or Saj for short. A prior assistant had to leave due to a family emergency and had left her in the lurch. Saj was not one of the eight or so swamis who regularly spoke at programs and Intensives, so I didn't know exactly what she did — other than meditate a lot. Baba had initiated her into monkhood, and she'd taken a vow of celibacy, vegetarianism, and non-ownership, which meant that even though she had possessions, they were not really hers.

My room was right down the hall from hers, in Anugraha, the main building where all the action was: the temple, the hall, the fancy Amrit, and Gurumayi's residence. I was thrilled to be so close to all the action and not way out in Sadhana Kutir, the camp-like dorm building with the 50s decor. But my swell of pride receded immediately that first night when I opened the door and saw four bunk beds with only one top bed unmade and seven women in various stages of undress. I put my sheets and blanket on the remaining top bunk, shoved my duffle on a small area of a shelf in the back of the jammed closet, and immediately shut down any thoughts of how claustrophobic it was going to be living in a room with seven other people and one small bathroom. I was where I'd wanted to be since I'd fantasized about it after the riots in LA. Crowded or not, I would wake up in spiritual paradise day after day — even if it was now going to be extra early to beat the other women to the bathroom — and breathe in the summer pre-dawn blueness. I'd won the spiritual lottery. I just had to share it with seven strangers.

That very first morning, breathless with excitement, I thought I'd play it big and get to as many practices as I could. I woke up at 4:00 a.m., quickly showered, and rushed in the pitch black to the temple to chant the *Arati*, the first chant of the day. It was a Saturday, and people visiting from the city and surrounding areas poured into the temple. I couldn't believe how many showed up at such an early hour: the *Arati*, a thirty-minute chant done standing every morning and afternoon at 4:30, was not popular like the *Gita*. The one other time I had chanted it, I had trouble following along with the sudden changes in the melody and tempo.

In the temple, the statue of Bade Baba Nityananda, dressed regally each day, was wearing a stunning royal blue robe with a gold trim and a matching grand silk turban. The small oil lamps, continually lit to keep the energy of the statue vital, illuminated the bronze body with an unearthly glow. The tamboura tinkled and the air smelled of the potent spicy morning incense blend of frankincense, dhoop, and champa. Live loud drums and horns blared at the top of the chant, aiming to stir the gods — and presumably the humans — awake.

In the middle of the chant, struggling with the tune and the text, I felt my insides start to rumble. At first, I thought it might be hunger. I hadn't eaten since early the night before. But then my guts were in chaos. I was going to have to make my way out of the crowded temple, fast. It was not easy to move with all the people packed in. I waited in distress. I held it together the entire chant, sweating. But the minute the *Arati* ended and people were moving to sit for a few minutes of meditation, I zig-zagged out of the temple, ran down the stairs and made it to the bathroom in the nick of time. It felt like the stress of all the days and months of waiting to arrive at the ashram for an extended stay poured out of me. *Purification*.

After the *Arati*, big vats of steaming chai tea were brought out from the kitchen and offered in little cups. People sat, sipping the spicy sweetness in deep silence, watching the daylight consume the darkness. It was my favorite ashram time of day, this reflective space between darkness and daylight and the two morning chants. When the chime pierced the air, everyone shuffled in a sleepy, trance-like mass into the main hall for the long *Guru Gita*, followed by a few minutes of meditation, allowing for all the efforts of the morning practices and vibrations from the chanting to be absorbed.

When I entered the hall for the *Gita* that morning, a hall monitor stopped me.

"Do you sing?" she asked.

I blinked at her. This singing thing was surely a strange pattern. I barely nodded before she led me all the way down to the front, to a spot right by the guru's chair, in front of a floor mic near a cluster of lead chanters.

"Gurumayi wants young people lead-chanting," she whispered, and left me there.

I plopped my *asana* down in front of a mic, next to two other women at mics, one young, the other middle-aged. Was I actually about to lead chant the *Guru Gita* at the head of the main hall in the ashram? The enormity of it was surpassed by Gurumayi appearing seemingly out of nowhere and taking a seat in her chair. I was not only going to be lead chanting at the ashram on my first day as a staffer, but next to the guru herself! She was *right there*! *Would I do it right? Would she criticize me?* I was able to watch her radiate in person and blend my voice with hers. She noticed me, and I somehow made it through the entire chant without one harsh look from her.

By the end of the chant, I was practically bursting with excitement and gratitude. I had spent many mornings at the LA Center singing along with a videotape of Gurumayi chanting the *Gita* in India, and now a dream of chanting it with her live and in person had come true. As if the morning weren't bountiful enough, people started moving things out of the way, clearing a path for a *darshan* line. My first morning living at the ashram, and a spontaneous *darshan*! These, I was told, hardly ever happened in America, where *darshan* usually only took place at the end of big holiday programs and Intensives. I couldn't grasp my good fortune.

The following week, Gurumayi came to the *Gita* and offered *darshan* again, and then began coming even more regularly. Everyone kept saying, "You're so lucky to be here when she is so accessible. She's usually more reclusive! This is more like how it is when she is in Ganeshpuri!"

Ganeshpuri, India, was the home of the "real" ashram. The place that Gurumayi's guru, Baba, built, the place where a huge organization grew up around a cluster of practices. The lineage of the sacred energy of the Siddhas purportedly went back in time through many ascended masters, but the Ganeshpuri ashram was where the organization and practice of Siddha Yoga began and where serious seekers went to evolve.

One weekday afternoon, everyone standing on the lunch line fell silent as Gurumayi passed by on her way to the kitchen, to give the hardworking food prep *sevites* some love. "She's giving it all to us while she can," the devotee standing next to me said, shaking his head. "Once she goes to India, who knows when she'll be back?"

My mind raced. So the reason why Gurumayi was so accessible was because she was soon leaving for Ganeshpuri? I'd heard it could be as soon as January. I didn't want to think about India, or her leaving. I didn't want to think about my leaving either. I was the happiest I'd been in a long time: meditating, lead chanting, practicing *seva*, and getting closer to my guru and my goals of self-realization. But Gurumayi had started highlighting the temporary function of the ashram by referring to it as a school, or *gurukula*. In ancient India, she explained in a series of talks on the subject, a student would come to the *gurukula* and spend time with the guru, studying spiritual discipline. Then, the student would complete the learning and go home, back out into the world, where they would live an exemplary life and be an inspiration to others. The ashram was not, as she once put it, "a place to hang out, eat vegetarian food, and fart." She assigned all devotees the task of writing a thesis on the topic, "What is an ashram?" I took copious notes on my reflections on her questions, but I never went to the ashram library or wrote the thesis. On top of all the discipline I was engaging in, I couldn't find my way to the rigor of arranging my thoughts in any coherent manner.

Every morning at the *Guru Gita*, at about stanza 90 out of 181, I started strategizing about how to bring Swami Sajjananda her oatmeal, orange juice, and piece of fruit on time at 7:00. While chanting with a stern focused face, I plotted in my head: Forget the bus, it takes too long with everyone getting on and off. Run the path through the woods to the dining hall, wait in line (*maybe it will be shorter today*), get the tray, find the saran wrap, make it to the bus stop, and then take the 6:45 bus (*please, let it be on time!*) back to Anugraha. I could probably get breakfast to her by 7:05. After the whole ordeal, I'd arrive, sweaty and breathless, with a saran wrap-covered mess at 7:15. After the third such morning, the swami snarled at me.

"You're late *again*?"

Fiery and on the cusp of fifty, it was clear Saj was not used to being infirm or dependent. But what the swami lacked in tenderness, she made up for in realness. With Saj, there was no spiritual "love and light" persona.

She finagled it so instead of rushing to the dining hall, I could get breakfast in the main building Amrit with swamis and other important *sevites* who also didn't have to make the trek to the dining hall for breakfast. I thought the move would resolve the breakfast timing issues with the swami, but one morning I stood in an unusually long line of summer weekend devotees who didn't mind paying for breakfast at Amrit, and someone bumped into me from behind, spilling orange juice all over the swami's food tray. I cleaned up and had to wait in line again. Tearing out of there at a quarter past, I knew she'd be pissed.

As I rushed to her room, there were men moving large furniture into the main building, and I couldn't get in. I was frustrated and scared that Swamiji was going to explode. *I'm going to be fired for this,* I thought. I'd recently discovered, when the swami let it slip, that her prior assistant had no "family emergency." She left because things "just didn't work out." Saj was tough.

As I waited for the men to figure out how to get a big couch in the door and for my good fortune to go up in smoke, I had a game-changing thought: *Why did I feel like a little kid about to get in big trouble when I was an adult doing my best?* My raging mother wasn't here. *What really was the worst that could happen?* I took a deep breath. After the *Gita,* I felt centered and calm. Now my shoulders were up to my ears and stomach in knots, all because of a breakfast delay. I could go into the swami's room tense and frazzled, explaining all the things that happened that weren't my fault, or I could approach her in a relaxed, matter-of-fact manner. In those few moments of waiting, I knew I didn't need to race, make a million excuses, or feed her anger with my panic.

I entered the room and said, "I know. I'm twenty minutes late. I'm so sorry. It was rough out there this morning. It won't happen again."

She didn't yell or even grimace. "Yeah, I heard them moving furniture and directing traffic all morning. It's chaos in that hall." Compassion from her was the last thing I expected. Her atypical response felt connected to me changing my energy before the confrontation. Although preparing for conflict with calm acceptance is a lesson I would relearn over and over for decades after, it was a startling realization. It also helped me relax when chanting in front of Gurumayi. She wasn't my mother either. If it was true that she embodied love, then she loved me.

Ashram life felt like a marathon, a race I was delighted to run in which big life insights and lessons emerged. Being a summer staffer was often the opposite of peaceful, but I knew how to navigate this world. There were rules that I could follow. Do the practices, show up on time, don't wallow, keep confidences, as in: don't share private details from the swami's life. I could strive to be pure. I felt I was putting a big deposit in the life bank, setting myself up for a better shot at a happier future. I wanted to go all the way with my spiritual development, to rest eternally in a state of equipoise.

I didn't know how long it would take to reach enlightenment, but I knew it was going to take a lot longer than the duration of my subletter lease.

PART 2:
THE ORANGE FLAG

"To the mind that is still, the whole universe surrenders."
—Lao Tzu

Blair at the Ashram parking lot, wearing "the guru's hat" (Chapter 17), 1994

10: Recognition

A few weeks after I arrived for the summer, thank *Shiva* (pronounced Shee-vah — one of the major Hindu gods), the seven roommates whittled down to four, and in a rare moment in the room by myself, I laid down on my new bed, a bottom bunk. I got out my journal and began my daily practice of reflecting on the day's highlights and lessons. The faint murmurs of the evening chant across the courtyard wafted in through the window, along with a cool breeze and the smell of fresh cut grass.

Listening to the subdued, lyrical verses of the evening chant — which after the first week of trying to do it all, I never went to again — I put down my journal and opened my copy of Gurumayi's book of poetry, *Ashes at My Guru's Feet*. I sank into her words of devotion to her teacher Baba, in which she described being known at her core and loved at the deepest levels. Oh, to be seen like that! The intimacy of it! Tears of longing streamed down my cheeks as they always did when I read about Gurumayi's relationship with Baba. The bond they had was enviable. They recognized each other. She was his star student and he was her everything. Every time Gurumayi told a story about Baba, like when he told her she would be his translator but she barely knew English, forcing her to dig deep and realize how much she did know, I craved the sensation of having a teacher who could push me into a deeper state of surrender. I mean, the guru had already given me so much — deep experiences of the Self, many teachings, a set of practices, and an ashram life — but I was aware that she didn't know my name. Sometimes, when lead chanting the *Gita* at her feet, or bowing before her during the recent morning *darshans*, I looked up at her and we exchanged timeless gazes, as though she was pouring love into me through her eyes. At least the days of outright snubbing appeared to be over. But I wanted more. The inner relationship with the guru was what everyone said mattered, and for me — in the insights I was having and the experiences of inner calm after the practices — that was going pretty well. But it felt lonely. I pulled the elegant, olive-green hardcover with its protective plastic cover to my chest and wondered if I, one devotee among thousands and thousands all over the world, had good enough karma to be known and taught by Gurumayi directly.

The next morning, after dropping off Swamiji's breakfast, I ran to the hall for the third *darshan* with Gurumayi that week. On my knees, I pleaded with her inside myself. *Gurumayi, I don't know how to speak to you, and I would very much like to. I am giving this desire up to you.* Handing painful desires and emotional strife over to the guru was a declaration of non-attachment and surrender. If you handed your troubles to the guru, it was said the guru offered grace and protection in return. As I got up from the floor, I heard her rich, resonant voice: "Blair."

Or so I thought. She started talking with another devotee, so I turned to leave, wondering whether I actually heard her say my name out loud or just made it up in my head. A step later I felt a tug on my sleeve. One of the *darshan* girls, Sukhala, a beautiful Brazilian teenager, pulled me back.

"Gurumayi would like to meet you," Sukhala said and asked where I was from, what I did, and what my *seva* was. When there was a break in the *darshan* flow, Sukhala stepped in and introduced me to Gurumayi as "an actress, here for the summer, working with Swami Sajjananda." Gurumayi, radiant, turned her massive eyes on me. She kept bopping others on the head as we spoke.

"How long are you here for?"

"Through the summer," I replied, my mouth a mealy desert.

She smiled big and nodded. "What do you do for Sajjananda?"

Time slowed, and, as if a drug had just kicked in, we were encased in our own heightened reality. I stammered, trying to collect myself. "I ... I'm assisting her ... you know, her ankle."

At first she looked confused. "Oh!" she exclaimed, throwing her head back when it clicked. "You're taking care of her! You're her nurse!"

"Yes," I nodded, an adverse reaction to her choice of words — *taking care of her, nurse* — simmering inside me. Taking care of others was a noble thing to do, but somehow in that timeless moment, it registered as familiar and small — a codependent habit, something I didn't really want to do anymore.

"OK," she said, and bobbed her head Indian-style from side to side, signaling *that was nice and we are done.*

"Nice to meet you," I said, as though we hadn't met before.

Satisfied and elated by the idea that an outer relationship with my guru had finally begun, I practically floated to Sajjananda's room to pick up her dirty breakfast dishes.

"Gurumayi is giving *darshan* this morning," I said. "Do you want to go?"

Sajjananda lived to see Gurumayi, but she hadn't felt up to attending public *darshan* yet. She thought about it while I hummed through my daily chores of tidying, dusting, and picking up the previous night's candy and ice cream wrappers from the floor. Swamiji was a fellow food user. At first, when picking up her wrappers in the morning, I didn't know where she'd gotten the Snickers or ice cream sandwiches, items not sold on ashram grounds, but then I noticed the little fridge under her desk.

"Yes, let's do it. Hand me the crutches."

I passed the crutches to her so she could get from her recliner to her wheelchair, but not carefully enough, and as she went to grab them, they crisscrossed to the floor. She looked at me like I had two heads.

"Sorry."

"Just hold the chair in place for me," she said, puffs of exasperation escaping the sides of her mouth. It was a jab, a thinly veiled reference to a few days ago when I forgot to put the lock on her wheelchair as she stood, causing her to wobble and chew me out for putting her in peril. I carefully helped her make her way from the recliner to the wheelchair, smarting from being caught once again in my discombobulation.

We wheeled out into the sunny courtyard, stopping every few minutes to say hello to someone she knew, mostly old-timer devotees who had been around since Baba. I got used to the small talk, the exclamations of *What happened?!* and the responses Saj gave. She was not super-friendly, but she often introduced me. Contrary to the chopping and cleaning *seva* I thought I'd be doing, I felt visible and important when wheeling Saj around. People noticed me, learned my name, and I secretly hoped they held me in high esteem, equating the exalted position of assisting a swami with my level of spiritual advancement: there were all these beliefs that the closer to the guru and to the swamis, the better karma you had. I vacillated between knowing that line of thinking was very stupid and very real, and the joke was on me. The position was entirely mundane. Saj would normally dismiss me after the morning chores, and if she didn't need me to drop off or pick up her undergarments and PJs at Swami Laundry, I'd have stretches of the afternoons to myself. There were no philosophical debates, no pouring over ancient texts like the *Upanishads*, no meditating together. Each night at around 7:30, I'd do some more straightening, run her a bath, and make sure the shower chair was in place in the tub and the crutches were where they needed to be so she could get to and from her bed. Occasionally I would deliver a message to someone else. That was the extent of the glamorous job.

When I wheeled Saj in front of Gurumayi later that morning, Gurumayi looked at me and raised her eyebrows.

"You came back?"

She said it exuberantly, but the message was clear: *Only come once.* There was no double-dipping with *darshan* — I would have to share *darshan* with Swamiji when she wanted to go. But I was elated that Gurumayi addressed me! And I appreciated her gentleness in getting the message across. With each interaction, my fears that she would rage at or reject me faded away.

"Did you get your driver's license checked out?" Swamiji asked one morning while I wiped down her chest of drawers.

"Yes, I got the pass." It was my job to take Saj to the drugstore, dry cleaners, and doctors' appointments. In order to use ashram vehicles, the organization had to vet you as a driver.

"Good, I need you to take me to the doctor's later today."

The thought of leaving filled me with dread. Out in the world, she would be my sole responsibility. Out in the world, there were bad drivers and depressed rural towns. I was not excited or ready to leave the sacred cradle of the ashram.

When I arrived that afternoon, she was dressed in maroon jeans and an orange sweatshirt, with a red pocketbook on her lap: a civilian swami. It was jarring. I was used to seeing her in her fancy handmade linen outfits that had to be sent to the dry cleaners. I managed to pass Swamiji the crutches with a steady hand, locking the chair down as she made her way into the car's front seat. After folding up the chair and heaving it into the back of the car, I came back around to shut her door. She stared at me expectantly.

"My bag?" She asked, holding out her hand.

I'd left her bag on the back of the wheelchair as I folded it up to put it in the car, creating a mess to untangle. I heaved the handlebars up and struggled to get the bag free. As I handed it to her, she looked straight ahead with a smirk.

After a long silent stretch driving on a tree-lined county road, we emerged into the surrounding Catskill town. Hasidim in heavy black coats lollygagged in front of decrepit storefronts. Children with long curls framing their faces ran around a convenience store parking lot. A bunch of downtrodden, ashen-looking older men and women, many wearing jackets even though it was summer, congregated around a church entrance, I assumed for an AA meeting. The poverty of the surrounding towns lived in stark contrast to the bountiful ashram grounds.

The swami didn't get great news at the doctor's. The complex fracture wasn't healing as quickly as projected, and the appointment to get her cast off was extended by three weeks. She was despondent. "Let's go get some Chinese food."

Our trips outside the ashram began to ritually include visits to the diner or the Chinese food restaurant. In the once fancy but now shabby Monticello joint from the Catskills heyday era, Swamiji ordered an egg roll and a vegetable dish with wrinkled brown snap peas. I sipped the free tea.

"You're not gonna get anything?"

I had no disposable income. "I'm on a budget."

"Oh. Well. I'll get you an egg roll," she said in a sullen bid of generosity.

I picked at the greasy crust and tried to manage my intense curiosity about Saj. Did she get paid? She bought things with a credit card. Who did the bill go to? And on a more intimate level: Was she lonely? Did she have regrets about choosing to become a monk? Was she satisfied and fulfilled by her meditation practice? I felt I could be happy living this life, but Saj didn't seem happy. She didn't seem enlightened like the guru. I thought that someone who had taken such vows would have risen above their crankiness and self-pity, and their dependence on junk food. But clearly, this was not the case. I began to wonder: *Was she hiding from life? What does her family think? Do the practices work for some people and not others?*

Of course, I couldn't ask her any of these questions. So, mostly, we sat in silence.

On the way home, we stopped at the supermarket. She picked out a few things: trail mix, moisturizer, and frozen candy bars and ice cream sandwiches for her room. Her addiction to sweets bothered me. I wanted her, as an elder and a swami, to be beyond food issues. The enlightenment I sought didn't include using food as a crutch. I wanted proof that a monastic life was an answer to emptiness, and I wanted the swami to have figured it out.

I was careful to make sure she had her bag on her lap when we were back in the car. She barely looked at me. I braced against her grumpy mood. I was anxious to return to the ashram, get her settled, and head to the temple to meditate and burn off the stress of the afternoon. When we returned, there was a sticky note with hand-drawn hearts around it on her door: *Hellooo! Sending you lots of healing and love - GC*

The swami pulled the note off the door and shook her head.

"I can't believe I missed a visit from Gurumayi! All because we were at the stupid supermarket," she nearly cried. Even with a huge ashram to run, the guru had remembered that the swami was going to the doctor and stopped by to see how it went.

"Don't worry. You'll probably see her at *darshan* tomorrow!" I knew visits from Gurumayi were special, but Saj seemed so young, like Gurumayi was her mommy and not her teacher. I tried to console her. "You must be upset because of the delay in removing your cast."

She glared at me. We were in a spiritual growth environment, but my Kate-learned psychobabble did not fly with the swami. At a later doctor's appointment scheduled on an ashram holiday, she complained, "I just hate that I'm missing the morning program."

"But you never go to the programs. I thought you didn't care for them." I mistakenly hoped reminding her would help. She shook her head. I added: "It would make sense that you're afraid of going to the doctors after what happened last time."

She tightened her jaw and swallowed. I knew I was rubbing her the wrong way.

About three weeks into my stay, it all came to a head. I'd pleasantly gotten a little lost in the final meditation of the *Gita*, and arrived, once again, just a few minutes late with her breakfast. Her chilly countenance sliced through me.

"I'm sorry, I know. Are you okay?"

She glared at me from her chair.

"Are you still feeling depressed?" I asked.

"No," she snapped. "But I'll feel a lot better once you get out of my head and focus on your job. Stop being my therapist!"

It was shocking and slightly embarrassing, but strangely, I was relieved that she felt comfortable enough to be direct with me. We were having a real exchange, and I appreciated her deeply in that moment. I now knew where I stood with her, and an unspoken tension between us had been released. The truth was, I had no idea how to be with her. But now I was more comfortable with having to figure it out.

"And another thing. I understand you want to do the practices, that's why you're here. But I need you when I need you. I come first."

"Okay," I said, taking it in. "Okay."

The blowout cleared the air for a time. And I realized I was learning how to pay attention to detail. I was hyper-vigilant when we were out and about, forcing myself to be present. I bit my tongue with the analyzing and always left the *Gita* on time. And I did get better at paying attention to detail and pre-empting her requests.

One day, I overslept and missed the *Guru Gita* but was still right on time delivering breakfast. After my breakfast and picking up the swami's dishes, I heard that Gurumayi was giving *darshan* in the huge hall known as the Mandap, which I would have known had I made it to the *Gita*. Thinking *darshan* would be ending soon, I ran back to Swamiji's room and transferred her to her wheelchair so we could go. Swamiji was annoyed that we had to rush. As we entered the large hall, the line had evaporated, which meant we might have missed it. I rushed the chair into the hall, and as we approached the guru, I lost control, and the footrests of the chair bumped smack into the base of the guru's elevated platform.

I panicked. Did I hurt the swami? Would Gurumayi blast me for rushing and being so clumsy?

I looked down. Swamiji was unhurt. I looked up. Gurumayi was laughing. And laughing. There was a small pool of people at her feet, and everyone sitting around giggled with her, and I felt so relieved and silly that I backed the chair away while doing a little jig, mocking myself as if I had planned the whole thing. This got more laughs from Gurumayi and the crowd.

I had made Gurumayi laugh. It was the best feeling in the world, even though Swami Sajjananda was not so happy with me.

11: The Orange Flag

"When do you get a break?" asked Pete, the guy who ladled out my cereal every morning when I picked up the Swami's breakfast.

I froze. Was this an ashram date? I didn't want to get involved. I was at the ashram to study, to go deep, to clear out. Plus, I was a good girl. Someone who was focused, who followed the rules.

And the rules were clear: in addition to no entertainment like TV or radio, there was also no sex on ashram grounds. The *Gurukula* was designed to help you go inside yourself, not look for or cavort with a mate. Sexual energy, according to the classic mystic Indian scriptures, can be transmuted into spiritual energy via meditation and other yogic practices. Orgasm and sexual release were said to diffuse the spiritual energy that a seeker aims to cultivate, but through meditation, one could raise sexual energy from the base of the spine up a central channel called the *sushumna nadi* to the head, to cultivate enlightenment, that highly coveted, permanent state of nirvana and awareness. All the Siddha gurus and swamis had taken vows of renunciation and were purportedly celibate in service of enlightenment. Only married couples visiting at the ashram could stay in the same room but were advised to visit the ashram for short spurts in order to stay chaste, build up spiritual energy, and remain pure.

As a devoted disciple, I took all the spiritual guidelines and ashram rules seriously. Being known by Gurumayi and establishing a rapport with Saj grounded me in a sense of spiritual progression on my path. But after so many months of feeling invisible in the city, overlooked by most men, and uninspired by the few who showed interest, I was enjoying connecting with so many cute, interesting, and open-minded guys. There was the strapping, sandy-haired Englishman who lit up my entire being when we went toe-to-toe in sloppily masked, flirtatious banter about spiritual dogma. There was the former New York graphic designer who consistently set down his tray at my meal table, who was wise and funny and felt like family, probably because he was old enough to be my father. There was the seductive charm of the practically ten-foot-tall, ex-model-turned-massage therapist named Bo. My knees went weak when Gabby Prita introduced us and he flashed me his dashing blue-eyed grin.

Pete the Cereal Guy was there to greet me every morning. He was on kitchen staff and brought the breakfast food over from Atma Nidhi for the "special" *sevites* who couldn't make it to the dining hall. He started making little flirtatious bids.

"I can tell you're just coming from the *Gita* this morning." He looked me in the eyes as he ladled out the oatmeal.

"Oh? How can you tell?"

"You always radiate when you come from chanting."

Pete was short and fit and had a joyful face, bearing coffee-colored, almond shaped eyes that sparkled behind his glasses. But he was not my type. He had long curly locks, a mustache, and a big nose. His hippie-rocker look reminded me of the '70s magician, Doug Henning.

When he asked about my break, I thought: *I don't want to get entangled with boys. I'm here to focus on my spiritual growth*. As if my alter ego — or at the ashram, we would simply call it *ego* — took the reins, I replied, "After I pick up the swami's dishes, I usually have a half-hour."

"Great, that's when I'm done!"

Why did I say that? We started hanging out in the mornings.

Pete grew up in Seattle. His older sister had introduced him to Baba, and the two of them devoted their lives to spiritual service. They had lived for a time in another SYDA (Siddha Yoga Dham Association) ashram in Oakland, California. He let me in on the fact that most "old-timers," people who had been around since Baba's time, did not strive for such a rigid, monastic existence as I did. Full-time staff would often leave the ashram and go out to dinner and the movies. Some read the news. Others went to the gym. Sometimes, swamis were even spotted at a devotee's nearby home, watching TV, or — back when Baba was the guru — smoking a little pot. I found all of these things shocking.

I liked that Pete was so steeped in Siddha Yoga and seemed so relaxed with who he was. He had an embarrassingly silly sense of humor, like the way he always said to the bald swamis, "Hey, what happened to your hair?" But he was kind and warm to everyone. I especially liked watching his face light up as I approached. He listened to my circular inner struggles — about Gabby, about what I was going to do with my life, about wanting to stay at the ashram and sublet my apartment for longer than the summer, about whether or not I was avoiding my acting career. He always offered rational input. He teased me for being so serious, invited me on walks and even to explore the world outside the ashram. But if leaving the sacred environment wasn't linked to my *seva* with the swami, I wasn't interested.

On the celebrated Hindu holiday *Rhaki* Day, it was customary to exchange thread bracelets with loved ones, symbolizing devotion.

"Here," said Pete, as he grabbed my wrist to tie on a purple and red twist.

"Thanks," I said, suddenly very uncomfortable.

"Don't worry," he caught on. "It's not a ring. Everyone will give you one of these today. No one will think we're going out."

Phew. I wasn't ready for that and didn't know if I'd ever be. The ashram was a small village, a fishbowl existence. We all moved, meditated, and ate in the same spaces. I was utterly aware of everyone seeing us together and making assumptions. The joke was that if you were seen eating together in the dining hall more than three times, you were engaged to be married. Already, the head of the music department looked at me askance after I walked by with Pete for the third time that week. My discomfort only thickened when he did things like swap out the lyrics of a Michael Jackson song, singing loudly — *I'm gonna Rhaki you, Rhaki you, all night* — leaving a cloud in the air that smelled of trying too hard.

Despite Pete's odd looks, and others looking, I started to look forward to seeing him, and this made me very nervous.

That evening at *darshan* after the Rhaki Day program, I wheeled the swami up to the guru's chair. Gurumayi watched us approach, and threw her head back and laughed. I felt very in sync with her playfulness and laughed with her, but afterwards, Swamiji told me she thought Gurumayi was laughing at, not with, us. My hair, which was wild and wide with humidity that night, was what Saj perceived to be the source of the guru's laughter.

"Gurumayi likes things neat and tidy, not so big and all over the place," she began. "That's why all the *darshan* girls wear their hair pulled back in a tight ponytail or bun. The *Shakti* is better contained when things are neat and smooth. Male swamis have no hair, and we wear ours short. You should do the same."

Ouch. I had suffered my mother's judgmental eye, always feeling too messy, too heavy, and not put together enough for her rigid aesthetic taste. "Brush your hair," my mother often said, when I thought it looked good.

All you had to do was look at the posse of well-kempt girls surrounding Gurumayi to know what Saj was saying about the guru's regard for neatness was true. But I didn't want to accept that she was laughing at my hair. When I chanted at her feet, I could feel waves of love radiating from her to me — actually, to all of us. If she was one with all-that-is, why would my hair be an issue?

I also had had a recent brush with the guru's disapproval, and by contrast knew what that looked like. Huge piles of sesame bagels from a nearby bakery decorated the breakfast line each morning, and I got in the habit of toasting one and slathering it with lots of butter. They were always so good going down, but left me feeling like a tugboat afterwards, and the mornings dragged on as a result. One morning, at the bagel table waiting for the toaster, Gurumayi walked by and gave me a very stern look. That message seemed clear: *Don't*.

Still, I was beside myself with curiosity: could Swamiji be right? Would my guru laugh in my face at my appearance? After my evening chores, I went back to *darshan*, as it was winding down. I knew I had been instructed not to, but I got in line and approached Gurumayi again. A stream of nervous energy made my hands tingle. Maybe this time I would piss her off, and I would be out of favor. But God dwelled in me, too. And I had to find out.

"You came back?" she asked, never missing a beat, even after hundreds had passed through the line that night. She had her signature wide-eyed twinkle, as if to say, "how bold!"

"Yes ... Swamiji thought you were laughing at my hair!" I tried to remain playful, though there was a waver in my voice. I wanted to see how far I could go with being myself and bringing a true hurt to the master. I wanted to see if she would ask me to pull my hair back herself.

Instead, she shook her head and made a grimace, as if she'd tasted something horribly sour and was appalled at the accusation. Then she said softly, "Swami and you looked so funny," and somehow in that moment, without her being explicit, I understood that what she was seeing went way beyond my hair, as if she could see the whole drama of my relationship with the swami playing out, and it tickled her. Relieved, I turned to go, but not before a *darshan* girl handed me a little tissue-paper package. It was my first gift: a *rhaki*, a delicate gold bracelet with five hearts. A reward for speaking my truth? I wore it every day.

One bright morning after breakfast, Pete and I hiked up a grassy knoll on ashram grounds, far from the Anugraha entrance. We looked back at the building in silence, a light breeze tousling our wild, Jewish curls.

"There's the orange flag ..."

I hadn't noticed it before, but there it was, outstretched like a windsock at a small airport, waving hello from a pole on the multi-tiered roof.

"It means the guru is in residence."

He leaned closer and looked at my lips, as someone who wants to kiss you does, and I hedged.

"Pete," I said, feeling trapped in awkward goo. I didn't want to lead him on, but I didn't want to reject him either. "I enjoy hanging out with you. I just really want to focus on the practices while I'm here. Are you open to being my friend?"

"Yeah, sure," he leaned back. "For a while, anyway."

One sultry summer evening, I was bragging to some city folk dining on the Anugraha porch about how Gurumayi had been giving *darshan* almost every morning. I used to be jealous of people who told stories of sharing time with the guru, and now I had a whole stack of my own. Pete emerged from the kitchen and silently waved me towards him. I excused myself and walked his way. Gurumayi was standing behind the corner of the building, amidst a small cluster of devotees. She was addressing a mother and child.

"What did she say?" Gurumayi asked the mother, of her little girl.

"She wanted to know if Gurumayi was a boy or a girl," the mother said shyly.

"Well. *That* is a very mysterious question!"

I guffawed out loud, prompting Gurumayi to turn and place herself a mere foot in front of me. I'd never been so close, not even in a formal *darshan* setting.

"Hi!" I said, riveted.

"Are you going to the dancing *sapta*?" she asked liltingly, wide eyes suggesting, *you're going to the* sapta, *right?* The *sapta* was a dance that reminded me of the Jewish dance the Hora, except it was done to a *kirtan*, a call-and-response Sanskrit chant. A big one was taking place in the two labyrinth-like circles in the garden that evening.

I nodded yes. Then, with her eyes only, she looked at Pete standing next to me, then back at me, with a cat-who-ate-the-canary smirk — *I know what you two are up to* — and moved on.

Being seen with Pete by the guru intensified my inner conflict about him. Gurumayi didn't seem to care, but I wondered. You're not supposed to come to an ashram to date. Instead of spending time going within, I was spending it with Pete. He walked me to the entrance outside the swami's room after the *sapta*, and sweetly brushed my cheek with his hand as he said goodbye.

"What's with you? You look all smiley," Swamiji said when I entered her room.

"I just said goodnight to a guy who likes me."

"Wow, you're all … gushy. It's so funny to see you like this."

Instead of feeling lovingly teased, I felt caught and belittled. My need to hang out with Pete defied my own desire to be pure, to be perfect, and the swami could see it. I shut down, as if the swami was a Catholic school nun.

"Don't make fun of me," I replied.

"What? I'm not making fun of you!" Saj hollered in defense.

"I thought you were judging." I moved silently around the room, preparing her bath, straightening things, my lips in a tight line.

"Wow," she said. "I wasn't making fun. Or judging. Just marveling. I guess it makes sense that you would hear it that way though."

I looked up at her. She was truly sorry. I saw a woman in a red costume in a wheelchair, stifled by the knowledge that who she really was at that moment would not register because of what she represented.

"It's okay." I said, feeling at a loss.

The next morning, while chanting the *Gita*, I replayed the scene in my mind and felt sorry I'd pushed Saj away. Shame was like an electric current running through me, and I tried to bring my attention back to the repetitive drone of the chant, but instead of the oneness I'd started accessing more easily, I felt dirty.

The ashram accepted Pete's application to come on board as a full-time *sevite*, which meant he could live and eat for free and even receive a small stipend — something I hoped and prayed I would be invited to do as well. He went back to the West Coast to pack up his life. Phew. I was able to put all that drama on hold, for a few weeks at least. Later that week, Gurumayi spoke at an evening program about the ego's hold over us, and told some funny anecdotes about how at the ashram we try to hide our shadow side, our baser instincts, from ourselves. While listening to her soothing, resonant voice, I got in touch with how much energy I had been putting towards being the perfect disciple. Trying to hide my demons of lust, jealousy, ambition, and judgment did not make them invisible, and I realized I was no better than anyone else struggling to figure things out. I felt the grip of my perfectionism start to loosen, as though a corset was being untied from my midriff. A rare breeze of self-acceptance blew through me.

After the program, I went to retrieve the swami to bring her to *darshan*. Sajjananda had put on one of her fancier swami outfits and a little make-up. I wheeled the swami before the Guru and bowed my head.

"The swami has joined the club!" Gurumayi said, bopping and smiling at Sajjananda. Then she bopped me on the head and repeated, "The swami has joined the club!"

Somehow, I knew the second time was for me.

12: A New Nurse

"What's that?" My mother asked when she spotted the delicate gold string of hearts on my wrist. We were in the inside dining area of the Amrit. People were whooshing by with their dosas and cookies. The screeches of forks scraping plates and chairs scraping the floor added to the din.

"A bracelet."

"It's nice," my sister said, trying to be kind. Somehow, my mother had snared my sister, four years younger and still in college, into coming with her to visit — no, *spy on* — me at the ashram.

Families and friends were welcome, and I was hoping that would soften her conviction that I was in a cult, because cults usually isolate people from friends and family. It didn't. Though my mother meditated, believed in reincarnation, and once spent a weekend in her early twenties with a levitating guru, she wasn't really a *seeker*. She possessed no urgent need to discover the truth about the mysteries of life or human behavior. She was not obsessed with the questions of existence and life's meaning as I was. She was certain that by living in an ashram I had gone too far, and the bracelet didn't do a thing to disabuse her of that notion.

She reached for my wrist for a better view. "I still can't believe you told me to wear *my* jewelry."

The clove/cardamom smell of chai spices wafted through the Amrit, and I tried to focus on its sweetness instead of the bitterness in my mother's voice. In a phone call before her arrival, I'd attempted to prepare her to feel welcome at the ashram.

"People dress up here for holidays and programs, like at church or temple," I told her. "It's a way to embody self-respect. You can even wear your jewelry," I added, trying to show her it was a dressy place and thinking it would help her to fit in with the clique of ashram devotees who looked like they materialized from Manhattan's Upper East Side.

"Are you serious?" she said. Through the phone I could hear how tightly clenched her jaw was.

Sitting in the Amrit, watching her watch the devotees, swamis, and *sevites* bustling around, I realized it had been a terrible thing to say. It fit right into her suspicions of me being in a cult, and she'd heard it as a request, not a suggestion. The chances of my family getting involved in Siddha Yoga and joining me on the spiritual path were slim, and now the odds were even worse. Despite that deep down knowing, I still hoped that the *Shakti* would find a way to help my mom and sis experience their true selves, and the visit would bring us closer.

They came on a holiday, Bade Baba's *punyatithi,* or death anniversary, so they would experience a program and get to meet Gurumayi if she gave *darshan,* which was likely. The Shakti Mandap, the big hall with the high glass wall doors and heated marble floors, was packed with thousands of people as usual. The doors opened on a slant, pointing to the vast rural Catskill landscape with the golf course just over the ashram fence, and the summer scent of fresh-cut grass blended in with the incense. A slideshow of black-and-white photos on the Mandap screens revealed the powerful Indian renunciate Bade Baba, the grandfather guru of Siddha Yoga, walking around India in a diaper-looking thingy, a big distended belly, long arms, and a very serene gaze. Swami Keshavananda, the one who emceed my first Intensive, talked about celebrating the *punyatithi.* "To most people, death is a sad or scary thing. But to the *sannyasin,* the true teacher — the one who has achieved permanent oneness — death is liberation."

My mother and sister gawked at the environment, while I thought about death as the ultimate goal of a spiritual life. I wanted to embrace death, but the whole concept was like the little fish that slipped through my fingers when I'd try to catch them in the camp lake. It was impossible to wrap my head around. I would die. I would cease to exist. I felt so removed from the notion — just as I did when Gurumayi told us one morning after the *Gita* about a recent devastating earthquake in India. I knew thousands died, but they were so far away, I couldn't feel it. Being at the ashram where TV and news consumption was forbidden, I hadn't seen images to cement the reality in my head.

But maybe, I thought, as Kesh's words landed, the point was that we continue to exist beyond the body, in that realm of "I am" awareness that I was getting better at accessing through the *Guru Gita* and sitting in the temple and meditation cave. Maybe this promise could calm me in moments like this, in which I felt, as my mother and sister tried to make sense of this zany world that had become my life, that so much was at stake. I so badly wanted them to like, or at least approve of, the experience.

And on the subject of death, whereas I felt my mother, in her fear of having lost me for good, may have wanted to kill me, I was glad my father didn't come. He would have died. *Sadgurnath Maharaj ki jay* for sparing all of us from having to deal with the look on his face. He would have left. I'm sure of it.

Gurumayi entered the hall and glided into her seat. The energy in the room buzzed. I was too fixated on the upcoming introductions to listen to her talk. *Would they get her? Would she charm them? Open their eyes?* The chant began, and I tried to get into it, but I kept peeking to see if they joined in. My sister closed her eyes as she struggled to sing the right Sanskrit words. For a moment, she looked peaceful.

I closed my eyes, realizing that I hardly knew her now. With four years between us, we never had enough common ground. As young girls, our fighting could be so brutal, it once caused our grandmother to shout, "I can't take it with you girls anymore!" before bursting into tears. When I started sneaking into our apartment building stairwell to try smoking at age twelve, she was still holed up in her room playing pretend. But now I was grateful she was here. We both shared the brunt of our mother's temper, and here at the ashram, she was a buffer between me and my mother's simmering angst.

Afterwards, we joined the long *darshan* line, where we had a close-up view of the guru in her element. *Look. Look at what she is capable of!* I wanted to say to them, watching Gurumayi in her glorious dexterity, talking to some while bopping others, placing the wand gently on top of one kneeler's head while talking animatedly with another. *Can't you see how perfect her concentration is? How effortless it appears? Don't you want to live with such ease and mastery?* A *darshan* girl welcomed me to approach the chair. Because I had first-time visitors, I was allowed to cut to the front. As we got close, Gurumayi was still speaking to a small group of women huddled at her feet.

"Angie is trying to be independent with all these mothers!" the group she was addressing laughed and nodded.

"And sisters!" one of the posse piped in.

"And sisters!" Gurumayi agreed.

The synchronicity was reliable, and the message was not lost on me. I, like Angie, was trying to be independent. But with mothers and sisters present, I wasn't free. I was bound up in a ball about what they thought of me and my life choice.

I wiggled closer to the guru on my knees. Gurumayi turned to witness the three of us, my mother and sister standing in a cluster behind me. Now more at ease and familiar with her, I jumped in:

"Gurumayi, this is my mother and sister. They are visiting from New York."

"Oh!" Gurumayi bellowed out. "You came to see the nurse!"

She was making a joke, but they looked up at her blankly.

"She is a nurse!" Gurumayi pointed at me, amused.

I froze. My mother and sister — not familiar with my *seva* nursing the swami — didn't get it and were mute.

That word again: *Nurse*. It hit me funny. A nurse isn't a bad thing. But every time she said it, it was as if she was pointing out my default, as if I was simply stuck in caretaking mode. It made me wonder if I would ever be free. The guru's force field of energy created a suspended moment in which I clearly saw, as in a video, how I nursed my mother and sister, how my shoulders were knotted with concern over whether or not my mother was upset, that if she was, it was my fault, and I was responsible to fix it. I was trying to protect my mother from me, and my sister from my mother.

Nursing was exhausting.

Bop, bop, bop. Gurumayi continued to bless others that knelt and walked away while we remained there, waiting. She often had someone, like a swami or a devotee of high esteem, sitting next to her at *darshan*. That day, the mildly renowned folk singer who recorded the beautiful *Pasaydan* was sitting beside her, so Gurumayi explained it to her.

"She takes care of Sajjananda."

"She's a good nurse," the folk singer said, recognizing me from wheeling the swami around.

Gurumayi corrected her. "She's a NEW nurse!"

The addition of the word "new" took the edge off of my reaction. If I was a *new* nurse, maybe I wasn't stuck in being an emotional caretaker?

Gurumayi smiled with a soft, soulful gaze as she bopped my mother and sister with blessings, giving us each different but matching homespun silk scarves. My mother, as if it were a worthless rag, thrust hers at me, and my chest went concave. I knew my mother was determined to hate the experience, but it was still a blow. I was at least hoping my sister would taste that sparkling feeling of peace within and be curious enough to come back. She reported loving Gurumayi and feeling calmer after chanting, but I quickly understood that opening to anything more would have put her in too precarious a position between my mother and me. My mother needed my sister on her side. There was no way she could lose control over the two of us.

After an uncomfortable and mostly silent lunch, I walked them to the parking lot and said goodbye.

"I hope you come to your senses soon," my mother said.

"Bye, Blair," my sister said with a look that communicated, *I'm sorry that Mom's being like this*. We hugged awkwardly before they piled into the car. I watched them pull onto the country road, red taillights vanishing into the mist.

I thought I would be so relieved when they were gone, but the space they left was filled with a horrible sadness, as if we had said goodbye forever. In a way, we had. I was changing, and as I continued to do so, things permanently drifted from the way they once were. I sat down on the Anugraha porch and looked at the gloomy sky. Way in the distance, the sun's rays poked through little holes in the clouds like slanted ribbons of light.

My mother, such a talented artist, taught me to see the sky. "Hon, pull over," she said to my father one Sunday on our way to a sculpture garden in the country. It wasn't even a designated lookout point, just the side of an uphill road. We all got out, took deep breaths, and looked at the hazy, vast expanse of New York's Orange County leading all the way to the Hudson River in the distance.

"Look at the way the clouds create shadows on the land," she said in awe. "And the colors in the distance where the river meets the sky."

It was gorgeous.

Staring at those Catskill sunbeams and thinking back on it, I wanted to cry, but the tears were locked in the pit of my stomach. I shared my woes with Swami Kripananda, the one who had written to me on Gurumayi's behalf, while she sipped her tea. Kripananda was one of the eighteen Siddha swamis, and the first to be ordained by Baba.

"Yes, it's very painful," she said in her mature, crackly voice. "You know, in certain traditions, *sannyasins* perform a ceremony in which they bury their parents — not literally, of course — but in order to fully step into monkhood, they have to abolish the parts of themselves that remain a daughter, son, or child, or have social standing. They have to abandon the construct of their familial role in order to realize the Self, and serve the world."

Thanks to Kripananda, I understood a little more about the spirituality of death.

The summer season was ending in a few weeks and I wanted to stay, but I was probably going to have to start paying to do so, and there was no way I could make that work. The thought of going back to that apartment and waitressing filled me with dread. I was in a spiritual incubator, and if removed before ready, I was sure I would perish. I wanted to go deeper, continue building my confidence and my focus, and negotiate staying as long as possible, even though it meant I would have to find yet another suitable roommate to finish out my lease with Gabby Prita.

A late-summer chill started to pervade the early mornings, and I left my room wearing layers of clothes. One August morning as the sun regained its strength, I returned to drop off my extra sweaters and found a note under my door — the preferred way for the administration to communicate with *sevites*. It requested my presence at the *seva* office. I was sure they were plotting my exit, and my lower lip started to quiver. When I got there, the two women, dressed in skirt suits, smiled and welcomed me to sit. I now understood. Everybody at the ashram was encouraged to dress their part. Swamis wore shades of red. The *sevites* who were responsible for the business of the ashram — registration officers, managers, etc. — wore business clothes. The *sevites* in food service all wore hair nets and yoga wear, looking much more ashram-y.

"Are you having a good summer here?"

"Oh, yes." I conveyed my gratitude, my sense of personal flourishing, and the hope that I could stay on past the end of my two-month stint in mid-September.

"Well, we have another temporary job for you, if you can stay longer."

I stifled a gasp of relief. "Yes?"

"Gurumayi thought you would be the perfect person to care for Bhama's sister, Jody, while she recovers from back surgery."

Bhama, around my age, was one of Gurumayi's top aides. Born to an Indian mother and sharing an American father with Jody, Bhama exuded a calm detachment, and I envied her for her demeanor and closeness to the guru. I couldn't believe I would be caring for her half-sister. Jody lived in California but was invited by Gurumayi to recover at the ashram from her back surgery at a New York hospital. I was tasked with bringing Jody food from the dining hall, helping her get around, and generally assisting with her recovery.

I was on Gurumayi's mind. She thought of *me* for this honor. I couldn't believe my good fortune. I was a new nurse, indeed. And this job meant I would have a *seva* for the entire month of September without having to pay to stay. Miraculously, my subletter back in New York wanted to stay in the apartment an extra two weeks before leaving town for good.

When I first met Jody in her lovely single room close to the Guru's private dwellings, with a little cot for her three-and-a-half-year-old daughter, Thea, she was a day out of surgery, spaced out on painkillers. She smiled groggily when I appeared with soup or extra pillows or to make sure she took her meds. At first, I was nervous, with her sister, Bhama, being so calm, cool, and collected, that — metaphorically speaking — my hair would be too wide for the job. But Jody was very different from Bhama, and I quickly got the sense that more than the disks on her spine was out of alignment in her life.

Once she was more coherent, Jody and I became fast friends.

"Do you actually ride?" I asked one morning when I helped her put on her leather motorcycle jacket over her PJs for a walk down the chilly hall.

"Oh, yeah!"

Jody was in her mid-thirties and had lots of ink — a butterfly tramp stamp, a big flower on her shoulder, and the name of her baby daddy on the other arm — before multiple tattoos were so in vogue.

"Well, I'm glad you've got your pearls on," I said, and we laughed at the fact that despite the PJs and the jacket, she wore her pearls and her hair pulled back whenever she left the room so as to fit in as best she could with the Siddha Yoga dress code.

She shared with me about the challenging history of her teenage years and her resulting struggles with substance abuse, as well as her strained relationship with Thea's father. I was happy Jody trusted me with her story and was secretly jazzed to be let in on the inner lives of people close to the Guru. I wasn't happy that Jody was hurting, but the fact that her life was messed up released the pressure of having to be perfect around her. If she were Bhama, I would want her to think I was more evolved, but Jody's grit and tattoos helped me to relax. As we walked arm in arm, very slowly down the former hotel hallways, I shared with her my ambivalence about Pete, who was staying in touch with me while he was out West packing up his life.

Eventually, I walked Jody to *darshan*. She couldn't bow down, but she stood and lowered her eyes, and Gurumayi bopped her tenderly with the feathers, looked at her sweetly and asked how she was doing, followed by a little chat with me.

"Is she taking care of herself? Are you making sure she drinks fluids?"

"Yes, Gurumayi."

My little conferences with the guru were my favorite part of the *seva*.

When Jody was walking more easily, I accompanied her slowly down the hill to a *darshan* in the Mandap, where I encouraged her to remove her socks so she wouldn't slip on the marble floor. Gurumayi greeted her and, as if it were planned, immediately told me to make sure she wears thick socks next time, to provide cushion on the hard marble floors.

Jody asked me to sit with her in her room one morning after *darshan*. I was due to check in on Saj, who now walked with a boot and cane instead of a cast and crutches, but I acquiesced.

"I don't know what to do about Thea," she confessed. "Two other moms told me that she's acting kinda hyper, raising her voice and even tugging on Gurumayi to get her attention. I like that Thea feels entitled to be herself and asks for what she wants. But I don't want her bothering others or behaving badly. I'm not sure what to do."

It seemed she was asking for my advice, which, with my propensity to analyze, I usually gave in a heartbeat. But I didn't have a clue what to tell her, especially since Thea was right there, listening. Before I could come up with a reply, Thea made it clear she didn't want us to be having this conversation.

"I want my daddy."

"He's in California, sweetie. We can try to call him later."

"Where's my daddy? I miss my daddy!"

"I know, sweetie. He's sleeping now."

"I want my daddy!!!" Thea slipped into a wild demonstration, repeating the words over and over, "I want my daddy!" while crying and kicking her little legs up the wall.

My heart broke for her. And I related to her. An ache, an old ache emerged from a patched crack in my heart where my own feelings of wanting my daddy bubbled up. My dad was a great playmate and provider, but with all us females around him, he was absent in his own ways. He worked long hours, and at dinners and family gatherings, he often seemed checked out.

The day I got my period I really lost him. Trailing behind my mother, we found my father reading the paper in the kitchen. "Blair is a woman. She got her period!" she announced. I felt embarrassed. I didn't know if I was supposed to embrace my father for the occasion, so I just stood in front of him, waiting for his lead.

"Well, that's great. Congrats," he said and went back to his paper. The awkwardness of that moment followed me around for the rest of the day. Something had died. I was no longer my daddy's little girl, and I never would be again. I felt rejected, being too young to understand that maybe he was sad I was growing up, too.

Thea's cries finally subsided, and she let Jody hold her while she sniffled. It was an intense, churning episode that left the three of us quiet and spent. I moved through the rest of the day feeling sore, like there was a cavity in my soul that kept getting pummeled by air. But alongside that rawness was that same sense of progression: real healing was happening. Another *samskara* faced and felt.

Gurumayi held *darshan* the morning of my birthday. I wrote her a devotional poem and put it, with a little money from the fifty bucks I'd brought with me, in a basket at her feet. After *pranam*ing, I looked up at her.

"You came by yourself?" she nearly sang. Jody was at a post-surgery check-up, and the swami had let me have the morning off.

"Yes, I came by myself. It's my birthday, Gurumayi."

"It's your birthday?!" she said in classic mock-surprise.

"Yes. I wrote you a poem, and I wanted to know if I could have a name?"

"A name?"

Now that I would be staying a bit longer, and she and I had an outer relationship, I wanted to belong. Really belong. I wanted her to initiate me into the community. Gurumayi nodded to a *darshan* girl, who went behind her chair and returned to hand me a pretty bag with a present inside. Then the guru motioned with one long finger for me to sit over on the side and wait beside her. The gift of her company was huge, and I relished sitting by her feet and watching the dance of *darshan* — people kneeling with their most tender hearts — and absorbing all the spiritual energy. I was woozy by the time the line ended, and I looked up at her expectantly, thinking for sure that by now the right name had come to her. But instead, she stood, turned, and walked away.

Huh. I looked in my bag. It held a stunning teal-green sari with a gold trim. A silk sari wasn't a name, but it was a precious, generous gift. It was also a message: I was to wear it during ashram celebrations and holidays instead of nice civilian clothes. I was to represent her and the ashram in traditional Indian garb. Owning a sari also meant I could perform sacred *sevas* like offering *arati puja*, a special type of worship in which you wave candles on a tray towards the master. Lastly, the gift seemed like it could be an investment in me, validation that I'd be staying a while. I certainly wasn't going to wear it as a waitress. I hoped and prayed it was.

"Do you think she just forgot to give me a name?" I asked friends and acquaintances at meals and on walks. I asked Jody, who had healed enough to be transferred to a family living unit with a kitchenette in Atma Nidhi, where she rested while she figured out her next life move. We spent less and less time together, but I was always thankful for it.

"No, honey, I don't," she said. "But, maybe? What do I know?"

Every scenario in my life in which I was an outsider suddenly surfaced: in my family, when I was ostracized in middle school, in LA and New York. I had to belong here. I became obsessed with the idea that Gurumayi simply forgot she told me to sit beside her in response to my request. Everyone I told looked at me askance, as if to say, "the guru doesn't forget." To me, she had so many people approaching her, so many requests. It seemed natural that she could drop a small detail like my desire for a spiritual name. In subsequent *darshan*s, I hoped for an interaction that would jog her memory.

She ignored me or smiled occasionally but didn't say anything about a name.

Finally, I got up the courage to approach Gurumayi's main *darshan* girl, Sukhala, as she cut through the Anugraha courtyard, probably on her way to the guru's house.

"I asked Gurumayi for a name a few weeks ago, and she nodded and told me to sit by the side and wait, but then she never gave me one."

"Well, then. I'm sure that was her answer." She turned to go, her black bun quickly replacing her face.

"I know, I know. But would you just ask her, just in case?"

She turned to stare at me blankly. I had added another frivolous task to her hefty to-do list. "Okay," she said, before dashing off to serve the master.

I fantasized about what the inside of Gurumayi's house looked like and what it must be like to watch her in daily life. Did she ever kick off her shoes and watch TV? Did she ever toss off the robes, wear pjs, and talk to her friends on the phone in India? Was she always the guru, the teacher, the God we'd cast her as?

Three days later, Sukhala approached me while I was writing in my journal and sipping a Siddha Coffee — a luxurious combination of coffee, sugar, milk, and chai spices — in the Anugraha courtyard.

"About your name," she said. "Gurumayi says, 'Blair is fine.'"

I nodded, and she walked away. Rejection flared, and then a familiar hangover of not fully belonging anywhere bubbled up. I walked around in a funk, and sometimes it seemed that everyone in the ashram whom I passed looked at me with disdain. What she said wasn't even exclusionary, but it was as if I'd put myself in exile.

After a few mopey days, I went to the temple. The smell of gardenias on the pedestal jolted me back into pleasure. As I sat there, gazing up at Bade Baba, I realized: I always liked my name. I was freed from the constraints of adopting a new one and of the awkwardness of training others to adopt it, too. Relief poured out of my eyes, and what emerged was a feeling of acceptance: *Blair is fine*. That was Gurumayi's true message. I opened my journal to write about it, and it fell onto the page in which she said, "The swami has joined the club!" A warmth spread over my heart. My name was fine, and my hair was, too. The subject of belonging now felt layered — I could belong and be a little different. In fact, my difference was fine. I felt satisfied, but as the summer light faded, a different anxiety mounted.

13: Absolute Faith

The autumn leaves began to emulate the brilliant hues of the guru's robes, blanketing the wooded path with shades of red, saffron, and orange. I'd been living at the ashram for ten glorious weeks, and the golden maple leaves set against a clear blue sky — so much statelier and more vivid than they appeared in the city — filled me with hope and wonder. I was receiving so much, the gratitude pressed up against the edges of my being, and every so often when I couldn't tolerate it, it soured into guilt. Life was too good, and I was living rent-free.

The days were rich and long, but the chill in the air reminded me they were numbered: one more week. Just imagining the dry, rudderless city existence waiting for me along with its endless concrete, gave me anxiety, which replaced wonder as the soundtrack underscoring daily ashram life. One early morning in meditation, in a dark room called the meditation cave, I prayed to be invited to stay on as a staff member, going round and round about what would happen if I wasn't (surely sinking into depression) or what would happen if I was (immediately having to find a new roommate for Gab in the city). The word "*kubja*" presented itself in my mind. I didn't know what it meant, so even though our relationship was strained, I called Gabby Prita because I thought she would know. I missed her and hoped we would survive my leaving and my need to submerge myself in my *sadhana*.

"I heard the word *kubja* in meditation this morning. Do you know what it means?" I asked.

"It means divine, or absolute faith,"[1] she began, "but the only reason I know that is because Kubja is the name of a wonderful woman who lives at the ashram and I once asked her what her name meant. She was an award-winning journalist and is now a philosopher who does research for the ashram. She and her brother Mahadev both have Muscular Dystrophy and live at the ashram. He is such a wise old soul. And she's fierce. You would love her."

I got the message. I had to have faith.

Later that very same day, I passed a young woman wheeling a man in a wheelchair on the colorful wooded path from the dining hall. I asked the man, "Are you Mahadev?"

He nodded.

"Prita said I should meet you."

"I'm a big fan of Prita," Mahadev said, cheerily. "Any friend of hers is a friend of mine. This is Amy."

"You're Blair, right?" his wheeler, Amy, asked. Prita had mentioned me, and Amy recognized me from wheeling the swami around. She had short hair with beautiful blue eyes and an inviting smile. I liked her immediately.

I told them about hearing the word 'Kubja' in meditation.

"Wow. The *Shakti* never fails to amaze," Amy marveled. "I just heard that Kubja's assistant is probably leaving at the end of the month, and you're good with a wheelchair, right?"

This meant I might have a job. I might have found a way to stay.

Amy and Mahadev told me all about Kubja, thinking I would make a perfect match for her.

"Truth be told," Amy confessed at dinner the next night when we bumped into each other in the dining hall. "Kubja doesn't get along that well with Connie. Or the assistant she had before that. But you seem smart, and she'll love that."

I liked the way she said "smart." It made me feel a little intellectual, but I was nervous about the track record of failed assistants. *Caretaking someone more intense than Swamiji?*

---

1   Not quite an accurate translation. Kubja was a hunchback in Hindu mythology who made an offering to Krishna and he turned her into a beautiful woman.

We chatted over dinner, and it felt nice to connect with a woman my age. Gab and her friend Deb, a.k.a Menake, sometimes came on the weekends, and I tried to eat with them if my schedule allowed. But mostly, I ate with guys or older people.

"Well, good luck. I'm going to go meet my boyfriend," she said.

What? She had a boyfriend! I couldn't hold back my questions. *Does Gurumayi know? How do you get around the rules?*

I was stunned to learn that Gurumayi accepted their relationship and, in order to respect ashram policy, they took an overnight once a week at a nearby motel. People who lived and worked at the ashram were figuring out how to live normal lives in a spiritual setting. Not everyone was trying so hard to be enlightened. Some were content to simply practice and evolve. Gurumayi wanted people to have relationships if that's what they wanted. It felt inclusive and made me relax a bit. It made me think about Pete. Should I just go out with him? I wished I felt more attracted. It was nice to have a break from all the drama his presence caused, even though I missed him.

One peaceful evening, the chorus of crickets chanting and the endless sky striped with various shades of gray, I strolled down to Kubja's living quarters, a two-room suite in a small cabin, a few yards from the main building courtyard. Connie opened the door to a dark, crowded room with a huge desk. Kubja sat in her wheelchair as if it were a throne. She appeared confident and beautiful, radiating authority. A stunning parrot sat on her shoulder, which fascinated me as much as it creeped me out. I'd never been that close to a bird in my life. Within minutes, the bird tried to sit on my shoulder.

"His feet may pinch a little. Can you take it?" Kubja said, testing me right off the bat.

I nodded, but once I felt the talons dig into my shoulder, I motioned to Connie to take the bird back.

"It's something you have to get used to," Kubja said. "But he doesn't always want to be close to new people. So I'll take that as a good sign."

Kubja interrogated me on my *sadhana*, my upbringing, and if I could tolerate wheeling her places and moving a wheelchair in and out of a variety of spaces, cars, etc. She went over her daily schedule. It seemed way too intense a care-taking job for me, and I was sick of being a nurse — having to focus so intensely on someone else's needs and details — but if it meant I could live at the ashram, and continue to have close contact with Gurumayi, I would do it as happily as possible.

"Relax," she instructed me, probably seeing my shoulders by my ears. "It will all work out."

The meeting went well enough that Kubja said she would ask Gurumayi about the matter. Back out under the now dark, chilly evening sky, I imagined life as Kubja's assistant. I saw myself opting to be a nurse yet again. I hated the thought of it. Then I thought about the emptiness of the city and hated it more.

Gurumayi, I give this up to you. I will do this job if it is the best thing for my spiritual growth. It was all I could do to have faith it would all work out.

On Sajjananda's forty-ninth birthday, I pulled the wheelchair close to Gurumayi's chair at *darshan* so Sajj could present her with a gift, as is custom. The cranky swami, who still needed to be wheeled in for darshan so she didn't have to stand on line in her boot and cane, regressed into a beaming little girl.

"It's my birthday, Gurumayi," she said, handing over the carefully decorated bag.

"Oh?" Gurumayi asked playfully, a *darshan* girl swiftly taking the gift. "How old are you now?"

"I'm forty-nine!"

"You look so young!" Gurumayi exclaimed. "You look twenty-four!"

Swamiji laughed and pointed to me.

"That's my age," I piped in.

"You?" Gurumayi inquired, studying my face while bopping another's bowed head. "No," she corrected me. "You look much older."

"Like, forty-nine?" I asked, pointing at the swami.

"No," she contemplated. "More like sixty."

We all laughed. I wanted to pretend to hobble away like an elder, but our moment was over and the guru had turned her attention elsewhere. It was all in good fun, but I also understood: my guru had just called me an old soul.

"You know," Swamiji confessed to me later that day, "each time I've unleashed my fire on you, I thought I was going to have to find another assistant. But you didn't crumble. Even though you're a pain, you can handle the fire."

The last thing I expected was a sort of compliment from her, but I guessed that our *darshan* had opened the space for it. We were learning from each other. I had assumed, with me being so much younger and less steeped in practice, I would be the one doing all the learning.

When word got around with the other swamis that Gurumayi had called me sixty, Keshavananda, Gurumayi's Number One and most popular swami, approached me. I was intimidated by his height, humor, and rimless eyewear. If someone told me how much time he and I would soon be spending together, I wouldn't have believed them.

"I hear that you're older in age than me."

I kibitzed back with him. "Yeah. At least I still have my teeth."

I wrote Gurumayi to let her know I was willing to work for Kubja if she thought it best and asked for her blessing to find a subletter for my apartment so that I could stay. Letters from ashram *sevites* were often read quickly.

The next morning, as I raised my head from her feet in *darshan*, she said, "After Sajjananda, Parvati."

It was my first command: an invitation to stay, and a new *seva* boss — a woman named Parvati — all in one.

A command from the Guru was a big deal. When she told you to do something directly, there were often blessings and growth opportunities packed within. Mystical dogma suggested that the guru, able to see your soul blueprint, knows what is best for your soul growth. Commands, in addition to helping you hone innate gifts and important skills such as thinking ahead, organizing, and communication, could help you burn negative karma instead of having to act it out. As a story I once heard illustrated, if you had done something awful in a past life, the guru might assign a very difficult or boring task, like raking leaves on a two-acre lot on a windy day. The task might feel pointless and like you're dying, but it might save you from a more tragic payback for past karma.

Not only did Gurumayi command me to stay, but I graduated from nurse karma! I discovered that Parvati, the next person I was to assist, was the fully intact head of the newly formed *Dakshina* Committee. *Dakshina* is the Sanskrit word meaning gifts to the master and was the spiritual practice akin to tithing. Our department would be in charge of increasing opportunities for people to offer monetary contributions to the ashram, in other words, *fundraising*.

Parvati, my boss-to-be, was a sweet, single, middle-aged psychotherapist from Arkansas. She had frosted blond hair and a soft, Southern way of speaking — a manner so diametrically opposed to my Manhattan upbringing that it was comical. Sometimes I was soothed by her soft, purring tones and flittery smile; other times I wanted to stop her eyes from their excessive blinking and wipe the smile off her face. The other Dakshina co-worker was Triveni, a grandmother from Connecticut. Triveni was more than twice, maybe three times my age, but her full-on seeker mentality, open and gullible, made her seem like a 1950s teeny-bopper in old hippie garb.

Before I had a chance to tell Kubja the news that I had gotten a different "job," the *Seva* office called me in for a meeting with Parvati. After the expectations of the job were laid out — mostly administrative work, six days a week, 8:00 - 4:00, with room, board, and a small monthly stipend to cover cost-of-living expenses like toothpaste and tampons — I let them know that Kubja requested I be her assistant and that I wasn't sure how to handle it now that I had been assigned an official *seva*.

Parvati knew all about it. "Gurumayi told Kubja that you are not right for the position."

"Oh." Uh oh. *Did Sajjananda give me a bad review?*

"Well." Parvati paused, and then looked at the *seva* director as if they shared a secret. "Gurumayi told Kubja that you are enormously talented."

"Me?" What talent was Gurumayi referring to? She knew I sang from my lead-chanting the *Gita* at her feet, but the only other thing she had seen me do was push the swami around in a wheelchair. Maybe she meant, *overqualified*. Parvati must have been lying. Buttering me up.

"Oh yes," Parvati nodded and blinked repeatedly. "When I asked for a helper to grow this department, Gurumayi said, 'Blair has great energy.'"

I wanted to get out of there. I wanted to hyperventilate, to explode, to reckon with what she was saying. Gurumayi had thousands of devotees around the world, probably over 500 in residence in the ashram right then. Just months ago, I was on my back, staring at the ceiling, feeling powerless, unknown, and longing to feel alive, connected to my teacher, and of concrete value to her mission. Those longings had been fulfilled. It was a prayer met, a healing. I could hear a crackling noise in the background, where a glacier of belief that I was broken began folding in on itself.

14: Quarantine

The first time I wore a sari was at the *punyatithi* celebration for Baba, Gurumayi's guru. Baba, aka Swami Muktananda, was the teacher who brought Siddha Yoga to the West in 1971 and died in 1982. His name translates as "the bliss of freedom." I felt, through seeing archived video, hearing Gurumayi talk about him, looking at his pictures, and reading his autobiography, that I knew Baba — warm, playful, ironic Baba. The photos of bearded Baba lining the ashram walls, showcasing his eccentric posture with his sunglasses and red ski hat, comforted me, even the one picture of him looking stern. His was the Papa presence to the maternal force of Gurumayi.

The anniversary of his death took place on what appeared to be a beautiful Indian summer day. The ashram was so full, they had to put extra dining tables at the main building under tents in its courtyard. A 24-hour chant praising his name was happening live in the main hall and played over the loudspeakers.

After purchasing a *choli*, a t-shirt-like silk undergarment, at a nearby shop with my new stipend, I spent hours in my room with my Indian roommate, learning how to iron and fold the sari. I never got it right. Even though I felt like a goddess in the garment, I was a messy one. The folds over the shoulder were not crisp, but loosely bunched. The bottom half barely stayed tucked into my underskirt.

At dinner, I got my tray and shuffled outside to the tents, my legs restricted by the bottom half of the garment. The sky turned a muddy gray. It was going to rain — in a major way. My first day in the sari was about to get even messier.

Sure enough, as I sat down next to a group of dining devotees, the skies cracked open. We didn't stand a chance under those tents, with the rain slanting down hard, and we all got soaked. In the Hindu tradition, rain is auspicious, carrying God's blessings. I forgot about the sari and accepted the blessings, chanting and clapping along with the loudspeaker streaming from the hall, letting our dinner trays flood and laughing while the rain pelted us, the presence of Baba in surround sound via the chant, thunder, and lightning.

That night, everyone at those tables felt as though we were in a conversation with Baba through nature. The chant peaked in speed just as the thunder roared so vehemently, everything shook. It was as if it came from the earth and not the sky. Baba's thunder had cracked us even more open, and we looked at each other in recognition as the lightning electrified the space without and within.

I hadn't been to the city since I'd arrived in July. But one October morning, I *pranam*ed before the guru and asked for her blessings to go to the city for a few days for errands and the Jewish holiday of *Yom Kippur*.

"Family duty!" Gurumayi said cheerfully, followed by a scrunched-up face that reflected exactly how I felt about it, and we laughed. She nodded to her *darshan* girl who materialized a box of chocolates out of thin air.

"For your family," the *darshan* girl said, presenting it to me. I felt such a swell of love for Gurumayi at that moment. As a monk, she didn't go home for family visits, and yet she totally got what it meant for me, while sending chocolate blessings for them. In addition to family duty, I had to get my teeth cleaned, collect the rest of my clothes and belongings from my apartment, and do what I could to rectify the subletter situation. Even though I had secured a new full-time *seva*, every day that passed without my finding a roommate replacement was a day I was in jeopardy of losing it: I couldn't afford to stay. As I turned to leave, Gurumayi leaned over to talk about me with a Spanish swami sitting beside her.

"Blair is so happy," she said to him. He nodded with a half-smile. I was glad she sensed my satisfaction with my ashram life. Gurumayi looked back at me — standing there bewitched — and gave a decisive, *you-can-go-we're-done-now* nod. But she must have known that I was still in earshot when she turned back to the swami and added, "Tsk. She is alone so much during that *seva*."

Her words, compassionately uttered, caught me off guard. Was she referring to my *seva* with Sajjananda? I still visited her with breakfast in the morning, and occasionally left my new post at the *Dakshina* office to take her to town or to the doctor. Or was she referring to my new *seva?* How did she know that, despite being thrilled to get away from caretaking and to be working with more people, I didn't feel like I belonged with those elder ladies either?

Dakshina *seva* was more like an office job. It was the same routine every day. After the morning practices and breakfast, our trio crammed into our makeshift office — a trailer outside the dining hall — for lengthy morning chants to Laxmi, the goddess of abundance. I attended the morning meetings about our goals, took instructions, and made documents at the computer. When they were in the trailer, I listened to Triveni boast about her son and his corporate lifestyle and new baby, while Parvati had her head down, studying papers over and over, scouring them for mistakes before turning them in to Gurumayi.

I *was* alone. I thought the entire point of ashram life was to be alone, to convene with your own Self, so I had ignored the fact of it, even though deep down I sensed that too much alone time didn't suit me. I wanted to be the type of person who thrived in endless solitude, but after hearing the guru's words, the truth of my loneliness started to congeal.

Was I supposed to make more friends? At the ashram, that was hard. There was always some upcoming celebration or deadline that kept everyone at the ashram prepping, decorating, furiously overworked. I started to see that serious *sevites* hardly did any practices but *seva*. The sense of urgency around getting things done and getting them right made people unavailable for the kind of connection that fed my soul — relaxed, lengthy exchanges filled with intensity, deep sharing, and revelation. Occasionally, if my day-off matched someone else's, then we could do something that lasted more than a hurried dining hall meal. But that was rare. Creating a welcoming, peaceful environment for others was a full-time, high-stakes, anxiety-provoking job.

In reflecting on all the people I'd met, I did have a real friend in Vera, a lovely, soft person with wide, innocent blue eyes. She worked in the video department and also ate her breakfast at the main building, so I saw her most mornings at the Amrit. The routine contact allowed something organic to develop. Coming from New York, where everyone was so tough and jaded, I was startled by Vera's incredible Midwestern earnestness. Her open face often expressed genuine wonder, and there were no hard edges with her. Little by little, we tested the waters to see if it was safe to share our struggles and the gossip about some of the crazier people or ashram dramas that we heard were happening in other departments. I was so grateful to have a friend for twenty minutes in the mornings, and yet, due to the extreme differences of our upbringing — with me recovering from growing up too fast and her doe-eyed innocence — a spacious gap loomed between us.

Visiting New York exacerbated any feelings of isolation.

In a cheap Thai food restaurant around the corner from our apartment, Gabby and I tried to rekindle our friendship. Paper lanterns swooshed over our heads as waitresses moved quickly around the narrow dining room. The attempt to reconnect was forced.

"Ugh, stop. You're in your defenses," she complained after I gave her advice on a work problem she shared. "You don't have to know everything. I'm not asking for advice."

We'd done a type of do-si-do: she'd been going to therapy with Kate and started using therapy lingo, with words like "defenses," "boundaries," and "safe space," and I'd started peppering my language with Siddha speak, injecting Sanskrit words like "what *prasad*!" (sacred gift) and "that was a *maha* (great) talk!" She'd moved on from being angry that I left to being angry with who I was. Plus, the apartment was a total mess, and I couldn't see how a subletter would be attracted to it. I thought it might be better if we were both freed from the tyranny of the apartment.

I took a gulp of green tea and offered what I thought could be a good solution. "Since the whole apartment situation with finding a new subletter has been so hard, would you consider breaking the lease?"

"Are you serious?!" she exploded. "How dare you? I didn't ask for this. And now you want me to move — for you?"

The ferocity of her response startled me, but I felt I deserved it. I apologized, took it back, and said we should keep looking for the right person.

Things with my parents were better only in that we managed to avoid talking about my leaving the ashram. I accompanied them to a Yom Kippur break-the-fast gathering at the home of a family friend, and they were happy that I made an appearance and that their friends could see I wasn't lost for good. I knew they wanted to know what I was going to do with my life now that fall had begun, but I managed to avoid telling them that I planned to stay through the winter.

I returned to the ashram and discovered Pete had returned from packing up his life. We caught up with each other one night at dinner.

"What's going on?" he asked in a sing-songy manner, feeling my reticence as we walked the path from the dining hall after dinner — where we had gotten a few stares — to the main building. The path was lit but now near dark at 6:30. Leaves crunched under our feet, and the earth smelled like decomposing summer.

"I just want to stay celibate while I'm here."

"Well, I can't wait forever. But I'm not in a rush."

His desire elicited claustrophobia in me. In an attempt at honesty and perhaps to kill off his hope, I added, "I'm just not feeling attracted."

The hurt formed in folds on his face. I tried to backtrack, but he said he couldn't be my friend anymore; it had gotten past that point for him. With the busy summer season over, his *seva* moved back to the Atma Nidhi kitchen anyway, and we hardly saw each other. I was free from the conflict, but not my aloneness.

It drove me deeper into dogma. The answer was within. I would use the alone time to befriend my inner self.

Three days before having to tell the *seva* department, "Sorry, I need to move back to the city to get a job to pay for my rent," I sat in the temple and pleaded with the forces-that-be for a miracle to let me stay. *Trust*, I heard a voice say. I really had to work on that. My anxious thoughts always won! But by the day's end, the miracle of a sufficient subletter presented herself to take over the rest of my lease under one condition: I lower the rent. I was willing to give over my entire monthly stipend if I had to, but I only had to give a little more than a third, around $75, to make the deal. I was free from the apartment share with Gabby, free to live at the ashram forevermore.

I didn't have much time to celebrate. I got a message that my father called, so I closed the doors of the rickety wooden phone booth and told him I'd gotten a new job and would be staying at the ashram for the foreseeable future.

"I don't understand why, with all the education you have, you are choosing this as a career?"

Here we go again, I thought. I felt like I was in a Cat Stevens song as I tried to tell him I was in the middle of something that I couldn't quite explain, and when I try to explain, it doesn't work. Whatever it is, it wasn't over yet, and I didn't know when or if it would be.

"But Dad, you always said you just wanted me to be happy. I'm happy here."

To his credit, my father said that although he didn't really understand it, he was glad I was happy. I felt free to pursue my spiritual life and keep our connection.

My mother became rabid.

"You're wasting your life at that place!"

I hated when my mother got like this. When she wasn't angry, her voice was upbeat, expressing her zest for life. But when she was, her voice was so menacing. I didn't know that was how she expressed fear, but even if I did, it was brutal. She tried to warn me that I was in a cult, and when I refuted with all the evidence to the contrary — I still came home, I had no secrets, no one was forcing me to do anything — she called me an idiot for not seeing what I had gotten into.

"Mom," I said, finally getting up the gumption to retaliate. "Did you ever stop to think that maybe my need for such concentrated practice, healing, and time away has something to do with *you*?"

I held the phone in stunned silence. I had said it. My mother knew that her temper could be out of control, but she could never grasp its impact. That last question had caught her off guard. She hung up, and I was finally free — free from my parents, free to be one hundred percent committed to my *sadhana*, free to live with like-minded people — but instead of feeling light and elated, I was all twisted up inside. The alone-ness mounted. I thought about going to the temple to burn through the pain, but the pull to Amrit was stronger. The situation called for cookies.

At the Amrit entrance, I saw the big white food truck pull up to the courtyard and was shocked when Pete stepped out of it. His long, bushy locks were gone. He looked a lot cuter, though I wished he'd lost the mustache, too.

"Wow!" I said, realizing how much I'd missed his company. I wanted to sit down and hear what made him do it and tell him everything that was going on.

He smiled with his whole face. "I know! And the funniest thing? Gurumayi told me that now that I've cut my hair, I'll get a girlfriend."

I could only afford two cookies. I ate them quickly.

As the temperatures got colder, I got a cold. Resting alone in the room with my books, chanting CDs, and tissues, and depending on roommates to bring a tray from the dining hall with cold, crusty dahl, got old fast. I was missing chanting the *Guru Gita* with Gurumayi, and seeing her — the one person I wanted to be near and never felt lonely around — at *darshan* afterwards. One morning, feeling mostly better, I went to the hall to lead-chant the *Gita*. I couldn't smell the incense or the Jean Naté, and I had to bring a bundle of cough lozenges and tissues with me to my seat. Even so, I knew I could sing. A burst of joy warmed my heart when Gurumayi took her seat in the hall. I closed my eyes. A few stanzas in, getting myself into the zone, I stifled a little leftover dry throat cough. I felt a *tap tap* on my shoulder. It was Sukhala, Gurumayi's assistant, motioning for me to leave, with my stuff. I followed her through a private door on the side of the hall (so that's how the Guru gets in!), where she shuffled me out into the hallway.

"You are sick," Sukhala said. "This is where you should chant." She turned and left me in the hallway outside of the hall.

Of course, Gurumayi didn't want sick people infecting others or disturbing the *Gita* with throat clearing and muffled coughs. I was ashamed I hadn't excused myself in the first place, but I just hated to pass up the opportunity to be with her, especially since I knew she was leaving soon and this time of physical proximity was winding down. I giggled to myself as I sat outside the hall, chanting in quarantine.

This isolation was well-deserved.

15: Blazing

Nine Brahmin priests arrived from India for the Hindu *Navaratri* celebrations of the goddess. Their sturdy forms, silk orange jumpers, and shaved heads with little ponytails on top graced the halls of the ashram, adding a vibe of gravitas and severity. The highlight of their visit from India was a weeklong *yagna* (yad-nya), a Vedic fire ceremony, intended to purify the ashram. They sat around a square fire pit in the courtyard, splashing ghee, spices, and other offerings into the flames, chanting in a drone-like manner, starting each prayer with *Om* and ending with the phrase *Swaha*, which means 'and so it is.' I sat down to witness the *yagna* and went blank, my mind empty of thoughts, only registering the sound of the chant, the splashes hitting the flames, and the deep pauses in between the prayers that were full of emptiness, with a few coughs and throat-clearing noises mixed in. The air crackled with clean, vibrant energy — the kind you'd find on a clear day on a cold mountaintop, and I awoke each day feeling refreshed. Everyone at the ashram, including Gurumayi, commented on how powerful the *yagna* was. The last day of the ceremony, I sat in the temple, which was bursting with fresh flowers, watching intently as Gurumayi entered, took off her hat, and dove into prostration at the feet of Bade Baba's statue. I buried my head in my hands. Watching her make herself that humble made me weep.

The final night of the Brahmins' stay coincided with the *Diwali* celebrations, the festival of lights. The Anugraha courtyard was filled with stringed lights, and a fire danced in the Shiva statue's fire pit. Many visitors, especially South Asian ones, milled about in the warm glow of a cool autumn evening, cradling small plastic glasses of cider *prasad*. I wore a pink sari, a new one given to me by a friend of Gabby's, a devotee who was leaving for India to prepare for Gurumayi's arrival and was planning to get new ones there.

My *seva* boss, Parvati, had encouraged me to talk to visitors, get to know them as an ambassador of the Dakshina department. I looked around the courtyard and reflected on my first-month performance review, in which Parvati sat me down and blinked at me with an apologetic smile. "It seems you don't like to talk to people," she said.

"It does?" As an actress, this seemed like strange feedback for me. She just didn't know me.

"Well, I don't think it's true," she said, pulling the front pieces of her frosted bob behind her ears. "I think you're shy." Blink, blink, blink.

"Me, *shy*?" Admitting shyness seemed at odds with my actor self.

"You need to mingle. To chat. To get to know visitors. I think you'll get the hang of it," Parvati said.

I couldn't deny that talking with strangers and forging new connections had always made me uncomfortable. I hated small talk and wasn't good at starting interesting conversations on demand. But what was the point of forcing chit-chat with devotees? *Dakshina* was actually a spiritual practice. You couldn't make people do it. Didn't people naturally want to give back to the guru because of how much they received?

Soliciting funds for a spiritual cause felt slimy. The chit chat seemed part of a calculated departmental show of friendliness. But as I listened to Parvati purr on about the significance of our newly formed department, I began to understand that this paradise consisted of three large buildings that needed the kind of heat and light that the *Shakti* didn't provide. In those buildings, there were lodgings and offices which all required furnishings, computers, supplies, and funds to carry out initiatives, and in those rooms, there were hundreds of people that needed to be fed. And some of those people, like me, needed money for toiletries, underwear, and gas, or an occasional ticket home. The practice of *Dakshina* made the whole thing work.

Money, which in my mind had seemed so antithetical to spiritual life, was now becoming central to it. Questions that had whispered in the background became louder: *How much money does this organization have? What do they do with it? How do they keep it all going?* Siddha Yoga was no longer free, as it had been in my mind since I first set foot in the Siddha Yoga Center of Chicago, and it would never be free again. The matter of money crashed through my naïveté. I not only needed to overcome my shyness, I had to reckon with the business of spirituality. The slimy feeling gave way to something else, a sense that I was becoming seasoned, real, more grown up.

On that last night of *Diwali*, in an effort to do my *seva* well, I circled the courtyard, nodding at a few devotees I knew and looking around for someone new to talk to. I stood beside a cluster of people chatting but couldn't gain traction after saying hello. Feeling awkward and at a loss for words, I finally spotted a figure on the other side of the courtyard, alone in a sari, and moved towards her. As I got closer, I saw a glow emanating from her sun-kissed face. I recognized her long, soft, wide curls. She was me, reflected in the closed glass doors of the main building lobby: a slimmer, sari-clad version of the girl who arrived. I gazed into the doors, realizing just how much I had changed inside and out.

Way back in Los Angeles, when I longed to know Gurumayi in person, I never dreamed in a million years I'd attend a private *darshan*, sitting in her "living room," also known as the Namaste room. Private *darshan*s were the stuff of legends. Everyone wanted private time with the Guru, so these were highly sought after and very hard to get. A request for a private *darshan* in no way meant it would be granted. Mostly, people didn't even think of asking for them unless they had either donated huge amounts of money and felt entitled, traveled to see her from another country, or were in a life-and-death situation.

One night, I returned from dinner to find a note under my door requesting my presence to welcome a couple named Leon and Beth, who would be arriving at the ashram the next day at 11:00 for their private *darshan*. Nothing else. I arrived at the appointed time, as instructed, in front of the

Namaste room in the lobby when Mahadev wheeled up. He was invited to partake in the private *darshan*, he told me, because the guest also had a degenerative muscular disease. I was being recruited in my trusty nurse role to help the guests get around the ashram.

Gurumayi, as if she had beamed herself into the space between us, appeared. "Are your friends here?"

Our eyes widened at her sudden presence. We shook our heads. "Not yet," I replied. She referred to a couple I'd never met as my "friends," so I made a mental note to treat Leon and his wife as such.

"When did they say they were arriving? What part of the ashram are they arriving at?"

I shrugged, and my belly tightened. I was simply following the directions I'd received in the note and didn't bother to follow up on them. She turned to Mahadev with the expectation that after all these years he should know better and should have made the effort to follow up on the details.

"Gurumayi," he sputtered, "I just got the note yesterday. I had some appointments I had to move ..." Gurumayi cut him off. She gave us clear instructions on what to do when they came: first, take them to the temple, then to their room, and then back to the lobby. We nodded aye-aye, and she vanished into her house through a door in the Namaste room. Nothing seemed strange to me about her brusque manner. It was part of efficiency: it was part of my upbringing.

An old, beat-up van eventually pulled up to the Anugraha courtyard, and Leon's wife, Beth, and a security guard helped lower Leon out of it. Leon was a Vietnam vet, Southern, with long, straggly hair — a physical cross between Sam Shepard and Ron Kovic. He didn't look at me as I introduced myself before getting behind the wheelchair. Mahadev and Beth trailed behind as I wheeled Leon to the temple, then to their fancy, softly lit room with a welcome fruit basket, and back down the hall and into the Namaste room in front of the guru's chair.

Sukhala shut the accordion doors and signaled Mahadev to sit on one side of the room, while Leon, Beth, and I sat in the middle across from the guru's chair, with Beth and I flanking Leon's wheelchair on the floor. I was nervous and giddy. *How on earth did I get to be part of a private* darshan?

I focused on taking deep, long breaths.

Gurumayi entered with Maya, an old-timer who'd forever been in a vague administrative role. As someone personally close to the guru, Maya was very respected. Sukhala stood waiting a few feet behind Gurumayi on the raised, stage-like platform. Leon's entire face burst into a grin. We sat in silence for a little while, and the world slowed.

Gurumayi sat in her chair and broke the silence. "Welcome. I got your letters. So, what propelled you to request Gurumayi's time?" she said, addressing herself in third person.

Leon had MS, PTSD, and was nearly blind, which explained why he had hardly looked at me. He was one of Baba's earliest American devotees and had lost touch with the ashram around the time Gurumayi took over. Unsure of how much time he had left on Earth, something in the Correspondence Course — a spiritual program sent out monthly by mail to students around the world — had made him think long and hard about his spiritual development. He wanted one last visit with his guru and had sent several letters requesting this meeting.

Gurumayi immediately invited the down-to-earth writer of the Correspondence Course, the popular and humorous Ram Butler, to join us in the Namaste room. Minutes later, Ram appeared and was directed to sit on the sidelines with Mahadev. Now I was sitting with the guru and the Siddha Yoga celebrity, Ram.

Gurumayi asked Leon many questions about his life since Baba. He revealed that he had been a writer and literary professor, but he hated academia and didn't last long.

"I couldn't stand it, all those parties, all those self-important academics in one room, their egos blazing. I mean just blazing."

Leon didn't look directly at Gurumayi when he talked because he couldn't see her, and it appeared as if he were talking to someone imaginary. But he was so natural, so unabashed of who he was when he interacted with her. He was not overly deferential or meek. The only sign he was nervous was that he continually played with his long, scraggly hair, by moving a few key strands away from his face with his fingers acting as a comb.

"Are you itchy? Blair will scratch," Gurumayi offered.

Another command. But this one was harder to swallow. Leon smelled like someone who maybe didn't shower daily — at the very least he had sat in a car for hours waiting in anticipation. I didn't want to scratch his scalp.

"Nah," he said. "My hair just falls in my face."

Gurumayi suggested he would look good with his hair in a braid, and Beth agreed. "I often try to get him to braid it."

I took the cue and stood behind his chair, picked up his oily, stringy locks, and began to braid, hoping it would look halfway decent.

"What did Leon say about those egos, Blair?" Gurumayi asked, nudging my own ego a bit, testing to see if I was paying attention.

"I believe he said, 'they were blazing.'"

She nodded. Phew. I had gotten it right.

"Maya's ego is blazing today," she added, giggling and throwing a little Guru-fire Maya's way. Maya did not seem hurt or embarrassed by this. She stood planted with her hands behind her back and her head bent slightly, wearing a teeny smile, as though she'd been caught with her hand in the cookie jar.

As Leon reflected on his time years ago with Baba in Santa Monica, he recalled a woman named Rhada, whom he befriended when they had done *seva* together. As it turned out, the same Rhada was currently on staff in the sewing department, and Gurumayi sent an assistant on a search to locate her. The sewing department was on lunch break, and no one answered the phone. Calls to the dining hall were made, but no one could locate Rhada. Gurumayi was surrounding Leon with a web of people to whom he had been connected, honoring threads I couldn't see, modeling a rare brand of inclusivity.

Gurumayi's name, Chidvilasananda, translates to the "bliss of the play of consciousness." My experience of this *darshan* was definitely theatrical. The whole thing, with the slightly raised platform, had the quality of an abstract play, with heightened lines and layers of meaning woven throughout. Everyone had their role. I was playing the part of the good nurse devotee. In my role, I couldn't see that the guru's play was a little sadistic. Nurses deal with all kinds of body messes, so the strangeness of her bid for me to scratch his head and braid his hair went over my head. I was too good of an actress, too focused on pleasing her, to allow for anything but devotion.

I didn't know if it was twenty minutes or two hours, but a prolonged silence and dip in energy signaled the meeting's end. Gurumayi tilted her head and looked at me expectantly. I took her cue and announced it was time to get a move on.

"Okay! We're going to lunch now?"

"I hope you saved some for them!" Gurumayi said, laughing.

Just that morning I had prayed to her about helping me eat smaller portions, so her words struck me as a personal attack on my piggishness. But also, it was the end of the lunch hour, and we hadn't called the kitchen to reserve food for them. The guru asked if we had let the kitchen know or asked about any food restrictions Leon might have. Mahadev and I shook our heads no, and she gave us a "Tsk," before rising from her chair. She approached Leon to say goodbye. I was sitting on the floor beside him as she looked into his eyes and placed one hand on his arm, while gently stroking the side of his face with the other. That was her parting gift to him. Her robes brushed back and forth on my face as she did. I inhaled her presence, and my head swam.

When I opened my eyes, she was gone. The play was over.

The morning after the enormous private *darshan*, I bowed before Gurumayi in public *darshan*. I was overflowing with *darshan*. So many blessings, it was as if my life and spiritual development were playing on fast forward. I *pranam*ed before her, and when I looked up, she was staring into me.

"Did you contact Radha?" she asked.

I had to think fast. I had no idea who Radha was, or why I was supposed to contact her. I searched my brain, and as I began to wonder if she had made a mistake, she reminded me.

"Leon's friend, who we were trying to reach from the sewing department yesterday."

"Oh. No," I replied.

"You should contact her and let her know she was missed."

She illuminated that one small detail from yesterday, that one missed thread I couldn't have cared less about. I was only focused on what I had received by being there, my good fortune. Another person in the room may have meant less interaction for me. Her reminder humbled me. I wasn't operating within an attitude of service but rather self-centeredness and scarcity. I wanted to learn to include people and follow the guru's example of casting a wide and generous net. I wanted to learn how to be proactive in making plans, not just follow them. I wanted to check my blazing ego. I wanted to mine the rest of the time we'd share for all the lessons I could.

16: Wannabe-ananda

I hit the alarm and peeled one eye open to check the time: 3:30 a.m. My roommate, Janet from the Lighting Department, responsible for lighting all events, talks, and programs, who usually didn't even get in until 11, turned over but, from the sound of her breath, appeared to still be sleeping. I raised my body against the weight of the early hour and tiptoed to the bathroom to brush my teeth and then turned my attention to the most daunting task of the morning, the sari hanging on the bathroom door. The night before, I'd practiced folding the shoulder folds and tucking the seam into my underskirt and then gave the silk sheet a good iron. In the dark of the morning, as quietly as I could, I folded, tucked, and wrapped, and then unfolded, untucked, and unwrapped only to try again, finally finishing with a pin at the left breast to keep it all in place. I twisted my hair into a bun. According to the barely-lit full-length mirror on the outside of the bathroom door, I looked frumpy, but it was time to go.

Despite the hideous hour, my special *seva* of opening the main hall once a week — inherited from one of my roommates who moved to Atma Nidhi, which was too far — resulted in a little precious blast of *Shakti* each week. I arrived at the hall at 4:00 and let myself into the sweet-smelling back room with all the supplies. I cleaned out the sacred bowl, lit a piece of charcoal in it, and topped it with a cone of *dhoop*, an intense sandalwood incense, adding some rocks of sticky frankincense and shredded myrrh on top. I stepped into the hall with the steaming bowl and stood before each of the lighted pictures of Baba and the other saints lining the hall and walls of Anugraha, moving the bowl in a circular fashion before them. I looked into their eyes as I waved *puja* in front of their images, feeling a connection, as if I knew them.

The silence at that hour was fertile. The ritual felt ancient. Knowing that I was opening the space for people to pray and go within and heal was an honor. Knowing that as I drifted down the halls trailing a banner of smoke, I had the gods and saints to myself while everyone slept, freed me temporarily from my circular thoughts and the gravitational pull of unworthiness.

There was one other person who had also been up for a while: the temple *dwallah*, who was responsible for maintaining the energized statue of Bhagawan Nityananda. One morning as I shuffled down the silent, smoke-scented hallway, she waved me inside the empty temple, past the larger-than-life bronze figure, ushering me and my bowl into a hidden, narrow room in the back. The tall room was stacked to the ceiling with shelves bearing colorful silk scarves, hats, and shawls, next to thin drawers of candles, wicks, special incense, and oils, next to an open closet of ornate robes protected by clear plastic covers.

"Fix your sari," the *dwallah* instructed me in a fierce whisper, even though no one was around. "It's too wrinkled. Plus, I'd like to invite you to do some temple *seva*, if you're interested. If you get approved, you need to look neat. You can do it before you open the hall."

I fended off the embarrassment and calculated a new wake-up time of 2:30 a.m., while she showed me how to change the bowls of water next to the statue of Bade Baba and refill the oil in the lamps and switch out their wicks. The oil candles were said to be a main element in keeping the energy of the statue vital, so it was essential to keep the flame lit as the wicks were changed and to do so without spilling oil or setting the platform on fire.

I imagined the possibility of being approved for temple *seva* as a gift from Bade Baba and a reflection of a new spiritual status. Not everyone was selected to go behind the scenes, where a *dwallah* ironed silk robes and puffed out fanciful silk hats and dressed the statue for the new day. Maybe through the rigor and intensity of almost three years of practice, some of my bad karma really had been burned.

And something new was taking its place. The silent awareness of the sacred mornings connected me to feelings of purity, like being a child all over again. After shame had taken up so much of my inner world, it was a marvel to experience myself, for longer stretches of time, as soft, open, and confident, feelings which for some reason reminded me of the Little Prince, a character in a children's book that I had long ago admired.

One morning at breakfast, after the hall-opening *seva* and chanting the *Gita*, I felt a new level of calm, as if my insides were a lake on a breezeless day. A handsome Italian elder named Guiliana sat down at my table and tilted her head back, observing me. "I like you like this," she said. After getting over the fact that she didn't like me when I was my regular self, I realized: I wanted to devote myself to this level of sanctity and peace forever. I wanted to be a monk.

Except for the weekly early morning *sevas*, every day I woke between 4:30 and 5:00 for the 5:20 *Guru Gita*. Though I started my day with chanting and meditation, my nights weren't for practice. They were for contemplation, writing in my journal, and reckoning with feelings.

I often found myself alone in my room, ruminating about Pete, which confused me. I was relieved to be done with him, so why did I still miss him so much? Why was I longing for anything when I was finally in the place that was the object of my longing? The thoughts circled round: *I pushed him away. I hurt someone who wanted to love me, and now I miss him. But I'm not here to be in a relationship*! Repeat.

I assumed, because I was generally happy, this yearning sprang from a very deep wound, a *samskara* in need of healing. With so few distractions, the ashram allowed me to tend to this longing with kindness. I lay on my bed and mothered myself, wiping my brow tenderly with one hand, just at the hairline, as I wished a nurturing mother would do. I never sobbed, but sometimes that tender motion would evoke tears. As far as Pete went, I decided I would try to rekindle our friendship.

Lying in the room one night, I heard a note slip under the door. It was authorization to perform temple *seva*. My heart swelled.

Changing the wicks for Bade Baba, which, while producing anxiety because I needed to get it right, also filled me with a rush of peace that almost had a sound, like an airplane far in the distance, a peaceful hum that would last throughout the morning. Each time I did it, I had to lie down at lunch because I was exhausted. After the first time, on my way back to the Dakshina office, my monk fantasies were fortified with a different reflection of my growth.

Mahadev rolled up to me on the breakfast line. "Blair, Blair! Wasn't that *darshan* amazing? You were amazing. I learned so much from you in there."

"Really?" I asked doubtfully. Mahadev, sweet soul, was flattering me. He had lived at the ashram for years. I hadn't thought to make arrangements with the kitchen. I forgot who Rhada was and was selfishly glad she didn't come. I was relieved when Leon and Beth left. Nothing *amazing*.

"Oh yeah. You seemed so comfortable, so at home with yourself with Gurumayi. Most people get all gobbledygook. They get tongue-tied, or they become young. But you held your own. Ram and I talked about it afterwards."

He talked about it with *Ram?* He was serious. Nervous, shy, compulsive, worrying, selfish — it didn't seem to matter. I was transmitting something positive without knowing it.

I was at risk for getting a big head. I didn't want my ego to blaze, to get any more puffed up from praise. But after sitting with it, I decided that even if Mahadev's reflection was yet another ego boost, it was useful to my spiritual growth. It signaled to me that, without formal training, without a job, without excessive years of life wisdom, I was already fulfilling the command "be a teacher."

If I could get better at being calm and share myself with people from that energetic place, I could be an inspiration. I started to contemplate monkhood more seriously, imagining all my bad feelings eventually evaporating, allowing me to remain in what is known in Vedic philosophy as a *Sattvic* — Little Prince — state of mind.

When I mentioned my monastic vision to Gabby Prita, she teasingly nicknamed me by adding the swami suffix *ananda*, which translates as *the bliss of*, to my fantasy: Swami Wanna-beananda.

After my second time performing temple *seva*, my lofty sense that I had reached a new level of even-mindedness deflated like a pin-pricked balloon.

Pete was in the Anugraha main building courtyard in the early morning dark before the *Gita*, unloading food trays from the big white truck. My heart lifted at the sight of him. He did look cuter with that haircut.

"Hey, you!" I waved.

"Hey," he said and kept unloading. I approached him. "Looks busy. How's it going?"

"Good," he said. His almond eyes did not sparkle. He nervously kept checking to see if his co-*sevites* were moving the trays quickly enough into the kitchen entrance.

And then a voice yelled out, "Any left?"

The head of the kitchen, a strong, hiking boot-wearing woman, emerged from Amrit, laid eyes on me and threw her arm around Pete. "Let's go get the last of it," she said. He nuzzled his face in her hair and turned back towards the truck and raised a hand towards me, without actually saying goodbye.

I had rejected him. I didn't want to be with him. But the rejection smarted all the same.

Barbara, the old-timer program director, knocked on the Dakshina Committee's door.

"You guys busy?"

She was joking. The holidays were fast approaching, and the entire ashram buzzed with busyness. Despite its link to mystical Hinduism, Siddha Yoga always looked for ways to honor different cultural and religious traditions, even celebrating the Jewish and Chinese New Years. Christmas was no exception. Gurumayi once referred to Jesus Christ as a great guru, which I imagined must have helped the large swaths of Christian devotees feel integrated.

"Your new office looks great, guys. Welcome to Anugraha!" Barbara said.

What started as the Dakshina Committee had evolved from a cobbled-together operation in a parking lot trailer to an official fundraising department in full swing. We were developing a campaign for a planned monthly giving practice. We were working in the main building where all the cool *sevas* like video and programming were, from 8:00 a.m. to sometimes 9:00 at night. Six days a week we tracked visitor numbers and set up meetings in our new office that had a lightly used computer. Barbara from the programming office was stopping by to spread the holiday cheer.

"I'm leaving some English Toffee with you," Barbara said before taking off. "Mukti makes it every year for Gurumayi for Christmas. It's to die for." The little tin of chocolate-covered chunks made my mouth water.

Each morning after chanting to Laxmi, the Goddess of Abundance, we buckled down on our used furniture with our paper scraps and lean office supplies to do the Goddess' bidding. The meeting topic of that particular morning was the upcoming Christmas Retreat, which started on the Friday night before Christmas Eve, and continued all the way through New Year's Day the following Sunday — a nine-day mix of free and paid programming. The ashram was expecting thousands of visitors because of how Christmas fell on the weekend that year and because Gurumayi's departure for India was impending and Western followers from many continents wanted to wish her farewell. We brainstormed ways to entice people to practice *dakshina*, and decided to print up a donation card as a way to remind people.

Two weeks before Christmas it snowed, and the ashram felt like a movie set. The spirit of Christmas infused the serene landscape and stole my Jewish heart. Decorating was fun. I was invited to sing in the holiday choir, which had a hefty rehearsal schedule leading up to the Christmas Eve program. Parvati let me attend all the rehearsals, and I was grateful for the time out of the office. I learned the words and harmonies to carols I'd loved and wanted to learn for as long as I could remember. The rehearsals brought me back to the best part of performing arts high school, where choir was a requirement. I *was* a singer, after all. And sweets were everywhere, delivered to our office from "donors" and colleagues in ribbon-tied, cellophane bags. Red and green foil-covered hearts, Hershey's kisses, Lindt balls, and Almond Roca filled the air with sweetness and amplified my sugar cravings. Munching on Christmas cookies one day in the early afternoon darkness, we reflected on the beauty and sacred feeling in the air, and I joked with my officemates that I was becoming a very devout Christian.

But something else was stirring, and it wasn't a mouse. As the intensity of fall colors faded and the darkness closed in on that magical summer, my mood followed suit. The holiday season marked the end of everything being new. Now that I was staff and not just a summer volunteer newbie, it was as if I had switched sides. I was STAFF, and the other devotees were GUESTS.

It was expected that ashram staffers work in behind-the-scenes *sevas* when the big programs and celebrations were occurring. As a summer volunteer, I resisted this and took every opportunity to go to the programs, soak up the wisdom, and be near the guru. But once I was officially on staff, I washed dishes, chopped veggies, or cleaned tables while listening to the programs over the loudspeaker. Gurumayi's talks were still reliably rich with poignant stories and useful teachings, but the programs themselves started to feel redundant and predictable: an emcee welcomed attendees, a swami introduced the practices for newcomers, a brief chant preceded meditation, and then a board member, famous author, or actor — someone *important* — hopefully, finally, introduced the guru herself.

During one of the Christmas Retreat programs, while prepping the main building Amrit for the stampede of peckish, post-program devotees, I listened to Gurumayi's voice over the loudspeaker. I realized the opportunity to see her speak live would be over in a matter of days or weeks, when she would leave for India. An overpowering desire to see her seized me. I hastily finished sponging crumbs off the Amrit tables and took off for the huge hall with the heated floors to watch the end of her talk and get in line for *darshan* early so I could go to bed and wake up for temple *seva*.

Rushing down the path to the Mandap, I saw from behind a familiar tall body walking in a slow, contemplative fashion. It couldn't be. I circled him just to make sure.

"James?"

It was the set designer who introduced me to Siddha Yoga. In a way, he was the whole reason I was here, and I'd practically forgotten about him.

"What are *you* doing here?" he said. We hugged. I hadn't seen him since Chicago.

"I'm living here now."

There was a long pause while we drank each other in. "Wow."

"Because of you."

"Well. I'll be here for a few days, let's catch up," he said.

"Yes!" I said, though I knew, with the hectic schedule, we wouldn't. I never saw him again.

When I arrived at the hall, the coat racks were stuffed, and there wasn't an empty hanger in sight. Once I figured out how to leave my coat sprawled over a rack, the hall monitors prevented me from entering, saying the hall was too packed and I had to stand in the entranceway. A stick of incense smoldered in a corner. I paced around, hugging myself to stay warm, peeking through the glass doors at Gurumayi, a red figure at the helm of a sea of heads. I just wanted to relax and fall into that sacred space arising from my connection with her and her words, but frustration coursed through me. Finally, a hall monitor who knew me pointed to a small opening on the floor in the back row and let me in.

I sat down, and, other than relief to be on a heated floor, I was totally surprised by what I felt: nothing. The experience of sitting there was completely two-dimensional, and Gurumayi was a flat, red triangle in the distance. Her words did not penetrate. Maybe this was my karma for leaving the Amrit *seva*. A baby cried and people shifted in their seats, looking around to locate the baby and who was responsible for bringing it into the hall. I rested my elbows on my knees and my head in my hands.

Feeling an absence of excitement or elation in Gurumayi's presence was jarring. Maybe I had reached a new level, and now, as the teachings constantly reminded me, I had to find it within. *Meditate on your own Self. Worship your own Self. Love your own Self. God dwells within You, as You.* Those oft-spoken words of Baba's had been on my mind as I contemplated what the ashram would be like when Gurumayi was in India.

Perhaps this experience was preparation.

17: The Guru's Hat

The retreat was a whirlwind of checklists, places to be, events to prepare for, friends to visit with. Akira, my friend from LA, arrived, and we had a rushed catch-up at the dining hall. She was both confused that I was living at the ashram because we had bonded as city girls, and seemingly impressed by how much I'd grown and how deeply involved I'd gotten. Gabby came with her ashram friend, a young woman we called Menake-Deb, who grew up in the ashram, lived in Manhattan, and had started seeing Kate. Friend meetings melded into Dakshina meetings melded into interdepartmental meetings about the retreat. Underneath the rush, that sore spot was pulsing. Occasionally — during a program that moved me, or when I walked away from lunch with Gabby and felt so far away from our friendship — it would get pricked, and I would cry. But I didn't have time to unpack what was really going on.

During the Christmas Eve program, I stood with sixteen choir members on risers in the back of the tastefully decorated Mandap. Thousands of devotees who had come for the holiday swiveled in their seats to face us as we sang out to Gurumayi, a ruby Christmas tree topped by the star of her pillbox hat sitting on the other side of the hall. We bellowed out carols, our voices piercing the black night on the other side of the glass walls. It was joyous and somber at once. I felt completely honored to be where I was on that stage, singing holy music for my teacher — which is why I was caught off guard later that evening after the program, when the choir director approached me.

"Were you okay up there tonight?"

"Yes, I loved it! I had a great time! It went well, right?"

"Interesting," she said. "I thought so, but Gurumayi said to me, 'Blair didn't look like herself.'"

In a hall packed with people, in which I couldn't have appeared bigger than a thumbnail from her vantage point, the guru detected my undercurrent of dismay. She sure hadn't left yet. And if she could see me that clearly from a mile away, maybe I wouldn't feel as bereft as I thought I might when she was eight thousand miles away in India. I had, I realized, been bracing for her departure.

I was sitting down to enjoy the special Christmas Day banquet when someone I didn't know approached me.

"Are you Blair? You're wanted in the main building."

"Okay," I said, alarmed. "What do I do?"

"I don't know. Just go to Anugraha. Get there as quickly as you can." I slid the contents of my tray into the huge garbage pail and made my way towards the shuttle stop, where two or three more people getting off the bus let me know someone had been asking for me over at the main building. I arrived in a swarm of people rushing to the Mandap to make the Christmas Day program on time. Sukhala, Gurumayi's main *darshan* girl, approached as if she had been waiting.

"Come this way." She escorted me into the main lobby and pointed to two chairs parked in front of the Namaste room. In one sat a beautiful woman whose face was damp with distress. "She is very upset," she said in a quiet voice, "and we don't know what to do. We think you can help her."

Sukhala turned and left me and the distraught devotee to figure it out. Huh.

I took a breath. "Hi," I said, sitting beside her and flushing my tone with warmth. "I'm Blair. I was told I should talk to you."

Her gorgeous strawberry ringlets fell into her face as she cupped it with her hands. "Oh, God," she uttered between gasps. "I'm just a mess."

"I can see." She laughed a little, then cried some more.

She wiped her nose on the back of her sleeve. I thought to get her a tissue but navigating the sea of people to get one would be impossible. People rushed by to get to the program, one of the last live talks of the year for who knew how many years. I imagined a little protective bubble around the woman and wondered, *who thought of* me *for this* seva?

"This director introduced me to Gurumayi," she said, her face wincing in pain. She shook her head. "I'm having an affair with him. And he's here with his wife."

"Oh, God. Sorry."

"I met him in this summer stock production, and it really should have been over at the end of the summer. I'm married! But now he's not talking to me. I shouldn't be this broken up about it. But I just am. I'm,"— sob, sob —"in love with him."

I breathed and focused on saying the mantra inside myself. The actress reminded me so much of the whole theater world I used to be in, and I wondered if the summer stock production was of Chekhov's *The Seagull*, a classic play we studied in school that had an irresistible, fragile ingénue who fell in love with a married director.

Gurumayi suddenly materialized, briskly charging by in a beautiful red wool coat, pulling on her gloves en route to the program. She flashed us a full-on, beaming smile.

The actress and I looked at one another. "Wow, that was special."

"Yeah," she agreed. "I want to go to the program, but I feel like I just can't."

I wanted to go to the program, too. But I also felt like this was the program. Like I was put on Earth to be with this stunning, vulnerable person. Gurumayi's smile said she knew it, too.

"I can sit here with you if you like."

She nodded.

"I studied theater in school," I offered after a spell of silence. We had been rather intimate for strangers, and it was time to back up. She told me her name and a little about her life as an actress in New York.

"How did you end up here?" she asked.

"Oh, it's a long story. I met a guy, too. And my best friend. She lived here before I did."

Before we parted, I told her I had a great therapist back in New York and gave her Kate's number.

"I feel so much better. Thank you." We hugged and said our farewells. She went to the Mandap for the program, and I went back to my room, where I knew I'd be alone, to reflect on what had happened. Unlike the weight and clumsiness of pushing a wheelchair around, holding emotional space for someone else felt light and seamless — sacred. It was amazing I could serve in this way. But again, I wondered, why did they pick me? I reflected on the summer and fall and ran scenes over in my mind: the analytical way I was with Sajjananda, the fact that I often cried when moved during programs, Gurumayi always calling me a nurse — perhaps news had traveled. But then I stopped. *Why was I trying to figure this out? Couldn't I accept by now that the* Shakti *was mysteriously serendipitous?*

How it all worked would always be a mystery.

New Year's Day, another bright, crisp winter day, seemed to bring every devotee in the Tristate area and their curious friends to the Catskills to hear Gurumayi's New Year's Message, an annual talk that included a saying to contemplate and live by for the year. After delivering the message for the year: "Have faith; everything is all right!" (Yes, I'd been working on that!) Gurumayi gave farewell *darshan* blessings for seven straight hours.

"Did you come with the Dakshina group?" she asked as I lifted my head from the floor.

Gurumayi liked it when departments came to *darshan* together, and the question was her way of signaling I had made a tactical error by showing up with Gabby.

"Come here," she motioned, inviting us to sit on the platform with her, with a smattering of other young people. Gabby and I looked at each other, smiling, glowing together in the most prized place on Earth. We'd been through so much since college, living together in New York, fighting through this transition, and now sitting together at Gurumayi's feet, probably for the last time in a long, long while.

"Blair," Gurumayi asked. "Do you want a hat?"

A pile of red hats flanked her chair, gifted to her by devotees. I never wore hats, but I scooped up an expensive-looking, tall red pillbox and turned to her for her opinion.

"Meh," she shrugged.

I put on a big red floppy one, enjoying her attention.

"No," she rolled her eyes, quickly shook her head, and returned to blessing her devotees.

Then, I spotted a red plaid wool bucket hat with a little rim. Plaid was not really my thing, and the hat's shape reminded me of Gilligan's from the 70s TV show *Gilligan's Island*, but there was something about it that was special, original, creative, and hip. It was woodsy and sophisticated all at once. I tried it on and looked up. She smiled and nodded.

I sat wearing the hat, staring out at the hall. The bright sun reflected off the snow and streamed in through the glass walls. I felt full and genuinely happy. Later that winter, when the guru was gone, a stranger stopped me in the dining hall.

"You're wearing the guru's hat!"

"What?" I exclaimed.

"The hat! I gave Gurumayi that hat for Christmas! I am so happy to know she got it, and that someone is wearing it!"

We marveled at the coincidence. She was a literature professor in Michigan, visiting the ashram for a long weekend, and had written a poem, *The Guru's Hat*, to go along with it. Together we relived the hat exchange that New Year's Day on the platform, those rich, final moments I spent in Gurumayi's presence. The professor sent me a copy of the poem, and I cried reading about her vision of what the guru would do in the hat, knowing I had received the blessing of that vision.

As the New Year's *darshan* line thinned out, a bunch of devotees gathered around as Siddha Yogis from Mexico hoisted a huge pink donkey piñata to the ceiling. Different people took turns putting on a blindfold, picking up a bat, and swiping at the air, while the rest of us cheered them on. Gurumayi turned to those of us sitting with her.

"No one wants to give it a try?"

I shook my head. Not one of us wanted to move from that spot. And I didn't want to be caught whacking away at nothing, teetering off balance and missing the target.

"Those batters are brave," she reminded us.

I felt ashamed that I didn't have the balls to play, to engage in the fun. As I searched for my courage, a young woman drove her bat into the donkey's belly, giving birth to an explosion of colorful candies which skittered their way across the marble floor to all corners of the hall.

The visitors returned to their lives in the real world, and the buzz about Gurumayi's departure took their place. It would be tomorrow. It would be next week. It would be early in the morning on Sunday, when everyone was asleep. Someone knew the secretary of the guru's personal affairs and had heard it would be Tuesday. Another person had talked to the ashram's general manager. Everyone had talked to someone who knew that she was about to leave, but no one could agree on when, and one person went so far as to presume that the misinformation was deliberately spread by the guru herself to keep us on our toes. Some lucky people were invited to go to India with her. *Sevites* would get notes slipped under their doors: "Gurumayi requests your presence to continue your *seva* in India, arrangements have been made. Please pack and be ready to leave by such-and-such day." Some would be going with the guru's entourage. Others would be leaving a few days or weeks before or after she did. The air crackled with frenzied anticipation, as though we were all roaming around with our Bingo cards, waiting for the hopper to spin and our number to be called.

I cherished my new, hard-won relationship with Gurumayi, and as much as I loved the idea of being indispensable enough to warrant an invite to India, I sensed I wouldn't be invited. I'd just gotten a new *seva* in New York. Plus, I didn't really want to go to India. I would have accepted if I'd been asked, but I sensed it was too hot, too foreign, too far. I could hardly stand in a long line for a meal without grumbling about it. How would I do in long lines in the blistering heat? And though I would never have admitted it, despite the increasing emotional distance from my parents whom I hadn't spoken to in weeks, I was comforted by the fact that they were just two hours away, as if the proximity was the only thing left keeping the connection alive.

The responses to Gurumayi's leaving were varied and fascinating. Some people got all stoic and jargon-y: *It doesn't matter to me if she is here or not, the Guru is within. It will be better without her here, there will be fewer people, it will be truly quiet and easier to go inside.* Others were deeply sad: *I will miss her sooooo much!* And some alarmingly so: *I just don't know what I'm going to do without her*!

I didn't know how to feel. I gained so much from the practices before I had engaged personally with her. Couldn't I find that connection again? Wasn't that the point? I didn't want to be so dependent on her form, even though our interactions were thrilling. I had no idea what the ashram would be like without her. I only knew that I still had growing to do, that the ashram was the best place to do it, and even though sadness and loneliness were part of my struggle, I was also still loving my ashram life. Maybe even more than before. It had become real. The struggles I was experiencing — of feeling disillusioned, of feeling powerful and important and then suddenly very, very small — were serious challenges I felt ready to take on, without the despair of my former life. I wanted to master them. My fantasies about living life as a *sanyasin*, a renunciate teacher, and focusing everything on becoming enlightened, were stoked.

One frigid evening, the whole staff was invited to a fire ceremony at the Shiva statue by the entryway to the main building. We wrote our prayers for Gurumayi's journey on a flat piece of balsa called a prayer stick and shuffled up to the fire in our winter coats to watch them burn. I loved seeing the tender faces of my fellow *sevites* illuminated by the buttery glow of the fire as they watched their sticks turn to ash. Then we trudged over to the Amrit. Outside in the main building courtyard, a caravan of black cars packed with luggage and people were all set to depart. We couldn't see who was in them, but we all knew. We were invited to gather round and wave goodbye. After the guru's entourage pulled away, we milled about the chilly Anugraha halls, drinking our *prasad*, little cups of chai and hot cocoa, commiserating with and comforting each other. Part of me felt bereft. But another part was curious. This would be a spiritual challenge.

I approached Keshavananda, who was standing alone, to see how he was doing. He was so strong and formidable, I didn't know why I felt the need.

"There is a lot of work to be done in her absence," Swami Keshavananda said. He said it again, perhaps to comfort me, perhaps for himself. Then, he added, "It's up to us to keep the spiritual energy of the ashram vital."

PART 3:
THE THINGS I CAN'T UNSEE

"You, sent out beyond your recall,
go to the limits of your longing."
—Rainer Maria Rilke

18: Correspondence

I opened the door to our near-empty room to find a "While You Were Out" memo on the floor. The switchboard delivered little piles of these memos for most of the calls I missed, although a few messages never found their way to me and caused a few friends to think I'd been ignoring them. This one, from my college ex, Alex, read, *I have some news. Call me back.*

We'd been broken up for two years but sporadically kept in touch. This was the third message in a short while from him, and when I got the first one over the holidays, I knew something was up. He wasn't a calling-to-wish-you-happy-holidays kinda guy. Every time I called him back from the claustrophobic payphone booth — I didn't have long distance in my room — I took a deep breath, closed my eyes, and prayed to Gurumayi for the phone call to go smoothly. I was excited to hear his voice but also relieved when the answering machine picked up because each call with old friends included a large patch of awkward, and I never knew if we'd get through it.

"I'm really happy. I'm just focused on spiritual practice and going within," is what I'd learned to say, when asked. Figuring out what to say and how much detail to give was tough. I got a lot of practice when I gave out my room extension in a letter to one friend, and then a bunch of old college friends started calling. I felt beloved until I realized they were checking in on me to see if, now that my hippy-dippy life choice wasn't just a summer fling, I had completely lost my mind.

When I said something like, "I had such a powerful *darshan* with Gurumayi yesterday that I felt a deep stillness for hours after," I soon realized how ridiculous I sounded to someone who hadn't had that experience. If some genuine curiosity was expressed: "What was that like?" or "What are you learning?" the call had a chance. I often had good heart-to-hearts that revealed I was not alone in being depressed after college. It was 1994, and some friends were trying a new medication called Prozac to feel better. When the medication takers were genuinely interested to see if meditation was helping me cope, it legitimized my life choices.

But more often than not, calls with old friends left me with a big hangover, feeling weighed down by their judgment and my insecurity. Silence was worse than the outright "Sooo ... you really believe that crap?" or "Is this what you're doing with your life now?" because it left me to fill in the blanks. How was it that I felt much saner and more at peace on the inside, but it didn't appear that way to others? Calls with old friends never failed to remind me that my big old ego still cared what people thought of me.

Sometimes, I wanted to make their opinions and silent concerns vanish. Instead of being polite and then getting off the phone quickly, my mouth kept moving and I found myself sharing my spiritual experiences in technicolor and trying to sell my path to them. "Maybe Siddha Yoga could help you with your work. You should try it. Come for a visit." But feeling those conversations veer off the rails didn't stop me from wanting my friends and family to wake up, receive blessings, feel the impact of the *Shakti,* and join me.

"About time!" I said upon hearing Alex's voice after a month of back and forth. "How are you?!"

Alex had been working as an assistant for a huge TV and movie producer on the 20th Century Fox lot. After leaving a spec script on his boss's desk, he and his writing partner got signed with a big-deal agent and had started production on a new sitcom.

"Can you believe it?"

"No! That is fantastic! You must be thrilled! Wow."

I played the part of Supportive Ex to a T, gathering all the details while the dahl from dinner started to percolate in my belly. I couldn't digest the fact that a man to whom I was formerly engaged — albeit marginally engaged — was now a Hollywood writer. *A TV writer! Making real money! On his way to mogul-dom!* In comparison, the biggest thing going on in my world was learning how to deal with Gurumayi's absence.

The first two weeks without Gurumayi were surprisingly difficult. It was the dead of winter. The ashram was still busier on the weekends, with many East Coast devotees showing up to do *seva* and attend evening programs, but it felt hollow and cold. I imagined the pain to be like a phantom limb. I'd turn the corner, expecting to find her bright robes billowing, only to find empty space. I'd hear laughter and be reminded of how much more of it I heard when she was around. I pushed myself to attend the practices, but the *Gita*, without the wonderful possibility of her showing up, felt far more rigorous and difficult to get up for. The emptiness surprised me, and I tried to shoo it away by filling the hole with hefty piles of vegetarian food and submerging myself in *seva*.

And as hard as it was getting through conversations with my friends, I seriously regretted giving my room extension to my mother.

"We booked a family trip to Israel in the spring. We expect you'll be joining us."

I knew it was a trap the minute the invite left her lips. The thought of being stranded in the hot desert with my family, with the weight of their contempt, expectations, and their own unprocessed "stuff" on my back, filled me with dread.

"I'll have to see if I can get the time off."

I never asked. As a full-time staff person, I knew I would have to assist with the big spring celebrations like Gurumayi's birthday. I geared myself up to deliver the news and braced myself for another call.

"Sorry, Mom, I can't go to Israel. I actually have a job here."

"You can't take a break? It seems you're too dumb to know what really matters in your life."

Silence.

"I don't understand why you're doing this to us."

"Mom, I'm not doing anything to you. I don't want to go. It's not a good time."

Then the campaign for us all to go to another "more legitimate" therapist began. "I think we need to see a professional together."

"Why, to fix me?"

"I can't talk to you anymore. Talk to your father."

I had zero desire to accommodate them by going to Israel or therapy, and each rejection of their requests brought a new attempt at coercion, as if scripted from a "How to Get Your Brainwashed Young Adult Child into Therapy" playbook. "We just want to see you and know you're okay, but in a professional setting."

I left our calls seething, wishing they would leave me alone. It took days to work my mother's nasty zingers out of my system, which I tried to do during the practices as I wrestled with all the responses to her I didn't say. Our phone calls became war zones. I decided to go back to not speaking to my parents for a while.

With Gurumayi gone, when I wasn't forcing myself to get to the practices, I allowed myself to venture out of the ashram socially. People who lived at the ashram for more than the summer often did this, and I had become one of them. Vera and I started making monthly trips to the Middletown Mall, to see popular movies like *Schindler's List* while gorging on popcorn. We strolled the brightly lit, Yankee Candle-smelling corridors, taking in the fashion and culture. An entire Madonna album had been released and, until I saw the posters spread out across the mall, I had had no idea.

The mild-mannered elders of the office, Parvati and Triveni, the people I spent the most time with, became the subject and target of my frustration, and I suppose vice versa. With the guru gone and the ashram quiet, it was time to tend to some important foundational — and boring — work for the department. Parvati named me the office manager and tasked me with creating employee and database manuals.

Triveni, the grandmother officemate, arrived in a huff one morning after an important meeting. She plopped down at her desk, the ends of her short white hair sticking out of her purple felt hat.

"Where were you?" Parvati asked.

"Since you've made Blair the head of the office, I didn't think I needed to attend the meeting," she said.

Parvati and I looked at each other in disbelief. Apparently, my being named "office manager" meant being the "head" of the office to Triveni, who was more on the front lines even though she was mostly in charge of record keeping. I was secretly glad she was the one having the outward tantrum and not me.

Triveni's grandmotherly naïveté, with behavior that seemed less mature than mine, sparked surges of rage for reasons I couldn't explain. I could see that she and Parvati were kind and harmless and young at heart. Perhaps I sensed something frail in them that brought out something primal in me, but whatever it was, I felt guilty and powerless to stop it. When teaching them how to use the computer, something I had complete authority over due to their age, I'd start off patient and kind, but after some time my irritation leaked out in *tsks* and clucks at their cluelessness. I vacillated between judging them and judging myself for being judgmental.

We also set up a series of meetings with other departments for meet-and-greets to build collegiality. In preparation for one such get-to-know-you lunch between the Dakshina and Finance departments — finance being the department that kept track of and doled out all the money we were trying to raise — I was told to pick up a floral arrangement from the Flower Department.

"Oh yes, I know your department," the head florist said. "One of your group is always hanging around, looking for scraps."

"Yeah, that's Triveni. She's always trying to make our office space brighter."

At the lunch, the Finance Department Chair commented on the lovely vase of purple anemones and yellow alstroemeria.

I agreed. "I think it's extra special because of how well acquainted the florist is with Triveni." I said it with a playful tone, explaining about her hanging around looking for scraps to add color to our office, thinking we would all laugh. But this turned out to be a Very Wrong Thing to do. Triveni excused herself.

Afterwards, Parvati scolded me for embarrassing Triveni by outing her flower poaching in front of others and told me to apologize. A cloak of guilt hung from my shoulders as I went looking for her room and knocked.

"Yes?" She uttered in a meek whimper.

"It's Blair. Can I come in?"

"Okay."

I found her lying on the floor — not even her bed — facing the window, raindrops streaming down and pinging off the windowsill. She didn't get up. She didn't turn her head. My story had literally flattened her. I closed the door and stood behind her.

"Triveni, I am so, so sorry I hurt your feelings. I thought I was joking. I didn't know what I was doing."

"It's okay," she said, feebly. "You're just being you. I have to get used to it."

All of us at the ashram were dealing with our own shame. It was so powerfully present, ready at the waiting to take us down.

My feelings of inadequacy would simmer, and I'd feel off balance, dirty, and gross for days. The practices gave temporary, if any, relief. I ate in the quiet section of the dining hall and tried to stop eating bagels in the morning.

But reliably, shortly after the thought, "I've had enough of this," entered my brain, an unexpected reminder of worth would appear. One snowy afternoon, the flakes outside the office window falling on a gentle slant, cradling the courtyard in silence, Parvati invited me to sit down. I didn't think it was going to be good, with the way a seriousness came over her, despite her intermittent smile.

"Swami Keshavananda needs someone to help write his morning speeches," she said. "I've approved it if you want to."

This was how these things worked. The head of your department owned you. If someone wanted to use you for another task, they couldn't ask you directly; they had to inquire with your *seva* head, first.

"You're asking ... me?" After the *Guru Gita*, Keshavananda brought us out of meditation and shared the weather, the schedule of important goings-on, and some spiritual thoughts for the day. They were played over the loudspeaker throughout the ashram for all the devotees to hear. Why would he need help?

"Well," she paused, looked down, and took a deep breath, as if gearing up for dramatic effect. "Gurumayi said you are an excellent writer."

Parvati watched my face scrunch in confusion. *What had I written that would make Gurumayi say that? My letters?*

"Maybe it's because of what you wrote on the Dakshina card." I had written the text for a postcard inviting people into the monthly practice of Dakshina. It was placed on little tables alongside donation boxes throughout the ashram. It was heartfelt. Apparently, it worked. "Anyway, with her being gone, he's very busy. You can write during your free time, just not while you're in the office."

I was honored. A little creative task to combat the lonely winter blues! And a chance to have some direct impact on what ideas people carried with them throughout the day. But then it sunk in that I would be writing for Keshavananda, affectionately known as "Kesh." Everyone looked up to him. I feared disappointing him.

The next morning at breakfast, I'd already been up for five hours, doing temple *seva* and making my rounds before chanting the *Gita*. Swami Keshavananda put his tray down next to mine. I still couldn't believe that not only would I be writing for Gurumayi's Number One, but he knew who I was and was willing to sit with me.

"I hear you're going to be writing for me," he said, raking his fork through a bowl of green mush known as Living Foods, a popular ashram health food delicacy made of blended veggies, nuts, and fruits not cooked above 118 degrees. "I need quotes to read at the end of the announcements and a little reflection drawing out their meaning. Baba quotes are always good."

We chatted a little, and it was nice getting to know him. Then he pushed his chair back.

"Well. See you soon. And you might want to fix your sari."

That night, I went to our little Siddha library and took out as many books written by Baba as I could find. After dinner, as the royal blue sky dimmed to dark outside the Dakshina office window, I worked alone. While others were doing dishes or chanting, meditating, or taking off to see a movie, I sat in front of the computer, beckoning the creative spirit. I gathered passages that were poetic and succinct, that had clear meaning, that one could carry in their mind's pocket throughout the day. I tried to emulate what Kesh would do and make it pop. When I was done, I submitted the speech under his door.

The first morning, after the *Gita* ended, when Swamiji brought us out of the meditation, I listened intently. The weather, the agenda for the day, and then ... he said what I had written verbatim. It was like being a playwright and hearing my words come out of the actor's mouth. It was so fun to be in the background and yet to know I had a hand in the show. As the days passed, he would sometimes shorten my reflections on the passages, but he always kept the passages I selected.

A few weeks in, I was visiting Sajjananda, who I touched base with every now and then. On my way out of her room, she said, "Oh, Swami Keshavananda was looking for you. He wants to talk with you."

I left her room with a clenched belly, and, as if it had been planned, bumped into Kesh exiting his room en route to a meeting. "You want to see me?" I asked.

"Yeah," he said, waving me over to sit down on a bench in the hallway, where not many people were passing through. He breathed deep. He shifted his weight. He moved his skull-capped head in a circular fashion, as if looking for something on the ceiling or floor. And then I realized he was struggling to talk to me. My heart opened. The formidable Kesh was human. I thought I'd help him out.

"Am I doing something wrong?"

"No, no, no," he said. "You're doing well. I just want you to get more of *my style*. First of all, you can make them shorter. Cut out anything flowery."

"Okay," I nodded quickly, relieved he didn't hate them.

"The announcements sections are so long. I am trying to tighten up the whole morning speech thing."

I nodded, waited. "That's it?"

"Yeah. You okay?"

"Yeah! Thanks for the feedback."

"Really?" he said, in an I've-just-learned-something-about-you tone.

But I had learned something about him. He was used to his feedback crushing people. He didn't want to hurt my feelings. So I had just led him through what he anticipated would be a difficult conversation. The ashram didn't teach us how to have those. I thought back on Triveni slinking away to her room. How long it took for Saj and me to get clear. In a way, with the schedule and all the rushing, things were designed so we could avoid conflict. Avoid each other.

We really weren't being taught how to relate. This bothered me. And I was just starting to catch on to how very bothered I was.

19: Righteousness

"What is anger and where does it come from? How do you manage it?"

These were the types of questions asked at the new, guru-less Saturday evening programs. They were created by the swamis for a much smaller audience and included more time for participant sharing. I missed those grand talks by the guru, with the one line or slew of truths that jolted me into a deeper awareness, but I liked the intimacy of the new program format, with a couple of hundred people sitting at the front of the massive hall. Sometimes the swamis leading the programs would ask for our reflections regarding a sacred text or *sutra*; other times, they would ask philosophical or personal development questions like the anger one. Participants raised their hands, and a hall monitor would come around with a mic.

The question about anger made me slump into my *asana*. I'd been feeling so angry that I was sick of myself. In addition to feeling triggered by my Dakshina officemates and pestered by my parents, I felt jerked around by Gab. I thought we had made up, but we frequently made appointments to talk on the phone that she wouldn't show up for. I also was eating so much that one day, instead of going to Amrit for snacks, I sat down and tried to breathe into my cravings. This time, instead of a memory from infancy, what emerged was a violent impulse of wanting to destroy something. I didn't know what or why. I tensed my jaw in frustration. Eating was easier.

Then, there was the episode with my new roommate.

For a few weeks, me and the lighting designer, who was rarely in the room, had the eight-bed room to ourselves, a new type of bliss. One day I came back to find the bed across from mine neatly made. Kevali, the head of the hall, had moved in and already unpacked and set up all her belongings in a matter of minutes. A rather stoic Polish beauty, Kevali reminded me of Meryl Streep in "Sophie's Choice." She was responsible for the entire operation of the main hall, including managing the team of hall monitors who helped meditators not only find the right seat, but also get chanting books, tissues, and cough drops when necessary.

There was usually no one in the room during the day when I popped in to get my journal or drop something off, but the next day before lunch, Kevali was lying there, clearly distressed, her hand covering her face. She looked pale and depleted.

"Are you okay?"

"No. I feel awful. And I have to be at the hall in twenty minutes." Her accent made it sound like tuh-venty.

"Kevali, you're sick."

"I know."

"You have to rest."

She erupted, possessed. "Blair, stop! I know this. The second part of the Intensive is about to begin. I *have* to go to the hall. There is no one else to do it. So just leave me alone because you don't understand."

A force rose up within me. I stood.

"I will not leave you alone. I'm telling the general manager to get you covered, and I'm going to the dining hall to get you some soup. And you are going to stay put."

Unless you were the guru, raising your voice and bossing people around was hardly considered yogic behavior, but I was out of control. The thought of her pushing herself harder than she already worked and endangering others in the process enraged me. Everyone worked too hard, and no one was speaking up about it, and I'd had it. As she began to protest, I shouted above her, "YOU NEED TO TAKE CARE OF YOURSELF. NO ONE ELSE WILL!"

She sat up, shocked, then growled at me and collapsed back down.

"All you will do if you go back there is infect everyone with your cold. Stay here."

I hardly recognized myself as I marched to the manager on duty to let him know Kevali was sick and needed to rest. *Who was this marching woman? Where had all that force come from? Was I acting like my mother?* I knew from the way I was quarantined when I had the sniffles that Gurumayi wouldn't want a sick Kevali circling the hall, but my righteousness surprised me. While I worried that I was acting out of line, part of me didn't even care that she didn't like my behavior.

Kevali would not look at me when I returned with her oranges, soup, and bread. For two days, she was in bed with her head turned away whenever I was in the room. I was worried this living situation was going to become a real problem, more *tapasya* — karma burning — but in a few days when she was back on her feet, Kevali gave me a huge, hand-on-her-heart smile.

"Thank you, Blair."

"For what?"

"I feel better. I don't know what would have happened if I didn't rest. Thank you."

I was learning that although anger was not a spiritual thing to feel, it wasn't all bad. Anger sometimes served a purpose.

Though I usually kept quiet during the programs, that night back at the hall, I wanted to learn more about anger. I raised my hand to respond to the question. Maybe all this anger I was feeling was a purifying part of my *sadhana*, and I would soon be free of it. I'd been holding it all inside, and I had the urge to share with the whole community. A hall monitor made her way towards me with a mic.

"I feel it a lot when things don't go my way," I began. My voice was always shaky when I had a mic. "And I often turn it against myself. Sometimes it's a reaction to injustice. Other times, I just feel it as heaviness in my body, and sometimes meditation, chanting, or repeating the mantra doesn't release it. I need to do something physical." I was nervous to say that last part, because it pointed to the limitations of the practices. Which were supposed to fix everything. But Kesh nodded, and Swami Durgananda, a famous journalist who became a swami, then later renounced her vows but continued to be a popular spiritual teacher, was nodding, too. Kesh asked more questions about my experiences and my thoughts, which I shared to the best of my ability.

My anger, deep and entrenched, was something that would take years to unpack. But in retrospect, it was the presence I'd developed through the practices that allowed me to begin to see it. I was strong enough to look at it and feel the discomfort of it. I'd kept it hidden, mostly for fear of becoming my mother. I didn't yet know that anger was a signal. Because if I had, I would have had to pay more attention to the boundaries that were being crossed, the work addiction, overriding my own needs to perform, and the looking outside myself for approval. All things that would have broken a spell I was still relieved to be under.

In Amrit later that evening, Durgananda approached me. She was firm, quiet, and strong. She rarely smiled. Her presence was formidable.

"I liked the way you answered those questions on the spot," she said in her breathy, no-nonsense tone. "You were articulate and thorough. That's not easy to do."

One of the program department heads, Barbara, an old-timer, popped her head into the conversation and pointed at me. "Siddha Yoga teacher! I flashed on it when she was speaking!" she exclaimed and winked at Durgananda.

I gobbled up the praise, not only because it validated my *dharma* to be a teacher and buttressed my sporadic daydreaming about becoming a monk, but also because I had developed a secret ambition to weasel my way out of boring Dakshina and into the Programming Department, where Durgananda and Barbara were key players.

As every prayer — even secret ones — seemed to be heard and answered at the ashram, my *seva* leaned in this direction. First, I got invited to be a lead chanter at programs, enabling me to take parts of different programs for free and see how they were structured and run. Then there was a note under my door inviting me to take the entire Meditation Level I course. This was a basic level meditation course, and I had no idea why, after living at the ashram for the better part of a year, I was being gifted such a simple course. *Maybe they need filler bodies. But,* I thought to myself, *beginner's mind,* meaning: never think yourself above a teaching. There's always more to learn. And the course, which was sparsely attended, did help me discover new ways to slip into meditation.

But when I was invited to take Meditation Level II, followed by the final Level III, I was confused, until after the third course it was explained that the three levels were requirements for being certified as a Siddha Yoga Meditation Instructor. I had been signed up for teacher training without knowing it. Completing the trio made me eligible for a written test that, if I passed, would authorize me to teach and emcee certain courses. I passed. My anger subsided. Things were looking up.

Shortly after my certification, a darshan girl led me into a room below the dining hall, an old ballroom that stored racks of hand-me-down clothes, so I could wear skirt suits in my new teaching role. I picked out an orange one with a Gimbels label and wore it to my first gig, emceeing a writing and meditation course.

After breakfast one early spring Saturday, the sound of water dripping everywhere as the melting snow cascaded from the windowsills and rooftops, I walked in my new, old corporate skirt suit to the children's programming trailer near Atma Nidhi for my first teaching gig, a portion of a Children's Intensive. I knew that the few adults in the room would be reporting back about my performance, and I wanted to fulfill this *dharma* of being a teacher to the best of my ability. But when I looked into the eyes of those wise, playful, boisterous Siddha youngsters, I realized much of the job was going to be a glorified babysitting job. Even though their crayon drawings of hearts, rainbows, and the guru were adorable, I was ambitious. I wanted my next experience to be teaching an Intensive with adults.

Another note slipped under my door for a mandatory staff meeting at 7:00 p.m. Staff meetings were a new thing for me. They took place in a renovated room with a view of the gardens, with banquet chairs arranged on a carpet with wide red stripes. Seeing the swamis, old-timers, and management staffers at the front of the room made me hyperaware of my rookie status. Staff meetings instructed about what was expected of us around busy times, and staff protocols, i.e., who to go to if we had problems in specific areas, etc. This particular meeting seemed sparse, and I soon realized that not all staff members were included. I wondered if we were being invited to India. I held my breath. I was ready to be with Gurumayi again and step things up a notch, maybe even get to teach in an Intensive she was at and receive personalized feedback from her. If I was invited, I'd go.

Durgananda and Kesh, who always seemed to be together, milled about at the front of the room. The swami duo announced that Gurumayi was sending a bunch of representatives from the ashram to Siddha Yoga Centers around the country to teach a course on her behalf. The notion of India evaporated as it dawned on me that I was one of those selected to go on a teaching tour. Each three-person *mandali* — the Sanskrit word for assembly — would visit three centers in three weeks, infusing the centers with a burst of *Shakti*. Teaching, travel ... It was so exciting, it was hard to wrap my head around.

It was a perfect opportunity. The harsh Catskill winter was not easily yielding to spring, and I was itching for a change of scenery. The next morning, I bounced into the office, bursting to share the news with Parvati and ready to beg her to let me go. Thank *Shiva* she already knew and had signed off on it. I rummaged through my things to pack a few weeks' worth of warmer weather clothes, and on a Thursday in late April, I got in a van with my duffle and my new travel mates to board a plane bound for Charlotte, a city I'd never visited. We would be teaching a two-day course introducing the practices called The Siddha Yoga Course. After North Carolina, we'd head to Orlando, Florida, and teach our last class in Sarasota.

Eduardo was the ringleader of our mandali. A child psychologist from Wisconsin, he reminded me physically of my gay roommate from college, although Eduardo never mentioned a partner of any gender. Salma was from Syria and worked in Registration. On the plane, the three of us talked about the trip. Eduardo, as the eldest by far, was clearly the leader and had been given the most instruction and responsibility from Programming staff. His attitude of authority brought up resentment, and I made a mental note to try to be respectful. I wished I'd felt a stronger connection to Salma, who kept quiet and to herself.

Our first stop was the lovely, granola home of Lauren, a single middle school teacher and long-time devotee. Her home had a sweet, rustic country feel, smelling of nag champa and occasional fetid wafts from the compost bin. She had a luscious backyard garden, bursting with blossoms and fruit trees. Being a city kid, I'd never seen anything like it. Despite how impressive it was to me, Lauren — and nearly everyone we met in Charlotte — mentioned what a shame it was that we had just missed the "spring bloom." After a homemade meal of baked tofu, veggies, and rice, Lauren took us to the local Ben and Jerry's for ice cream. Eduardo was in charge of our petty cash and offered to pay for our cones, but she insisted on buying. In our pre-trip training, we were told that most people would want to treat us and we should let them. It was *seva* for them to do so, but we shouldn't order expensive items.

Wanting to provide us with a spiritual experience, Lauren woke us up at 4:00 a.m. for a sunrise hike in the Blue Ridge Mountains, where we climbed a trail carrying flashlights and thermoses in the cool, pre-dawn light. The plan was to chant the *Guru Gita* on a peak ledge and then watch the sunrise. Although I'd been awake before dawn consistently throughout the past nine months, I had only seen one sunrise before in my life while tripping on mushrooms in college on the coast of Lake Michigan. After the twenty-five-minute hike up the mountain and chanting the *Guru Gita*, we waited. The waiting felt eternal as the sky brightened. We were all starting to get antsy. Just as I was sure it was too cloudy and the sun would never show itself ... bloop! The golden tip of the orb bounced above the horizon in a thrilling arrival. Sipping chai and munching on granola bars, we watched the big ball emerge and illuminate the city below. I thanked Gurumayi for all of this grace, this incredible opportunity, and we all thanked Lauren for her gracious hosting. It was a powerful start to the journey.

We spent the day pouring over the black binder on how to run the course, which we referred to religiously throughout the three weeks. It was a basic "Introduction to Siddha Yoga" course geared towards newcomers, but it was mostly old-timers, wanting a refresher and itching to reconnect with the *Shakti* in a deeper way, who signed up. We were supposed to teach a weekend course in each of the three destinations, Charlotte,

Orlando, and Sarasota, with a free orientation event on Friday nights, but by the evening, we discovered we had an attendance problem in Charlotte. Too few had signed up to make the Friday night orientation or even day one of the course worthwhile. We were welcomed instead to attend the center's regular Saturday morning *Guru Gita* program, where there was palpable tension.

The Charlotte Siddha Yoga Center was bright, warm, modern, and cozy, situated on the upper level of an old brick firehouse with big windows and a pole running right through it. Even though the floor was boarded up and covered in plush carpet, they left the pole sticking out and up to the ceiling as a representative of the spiritual fire, the *Kundalini*, which travels up the spine to the head in the process of enlightenment. Before the *Gita*, it was announced that we were attending, and while a few people came over and introduced themselves after, several devotees seemed to avoid us, rushing out of the center when the chant was over. In the Amrit, I overheard Lauren explain to Eduardo that the Center didn't promote the course well. Some Charlotte devotees resented being forced to host visitors and promote a course at their center. The mandali had not been requested by the Charlotte Center, but mandated by the ashram.

While I felt a bit stunned, Eduardo tried to explain to Lauren what most Charlotte devotees had already been told: this was the guru's wishes, and we were sent as her representatives. I wanted him to shut up. I didn't know how political it had been. I was embarrassed that I hadn't given any thought to the process of our arrival in these cities. I assumed the ashram had happily offered for three ashram-dwelling teachers to visit their centers with a course, and the centers said, "Yes! We would love to have them!" I hadn't thought about our hosts' resources or the proceeds of the course and if they were all going to the ashram, or if the local centers got to keep a percentage. And then I realized, *maybe I don't want to know*. I pushed the tainted thoughts out of my head. I was traveling. I was teaching. It was the guru's wish. And we were getting Ben and Jerry's.

But as we moved through the weekend, the icky feeling was like a bird that kept pecking at my window, demanding attention. It made sense that our presence would burden the people we were visiting with extra time and tasks like setting up, making arrangements for us, and promoting the course, leaving devotees stressed out and resentful. The three of us were suddenly in an awkward position, and I wondered what we might encounter on the rest of the tour. This once incredible blessing of a trip now seemed poisoned. A handful of Charlotte devotees, either feeling guilty or hungry for a course, signed up for one day of the two-day course. We did our job. We taught Sunday, furiously pouring over the black book to make sure we had divided up our parts correctly, each standing at the podium in our socks when it was our turn to read our parts. The one day went well, and the post-course *Shakti* feeling replaced the poisonous one. The cherry on top was getting to stay at the lovely home of the Freeds, where we each had a comfy bed, two comfy pillows, and in the morning enjoyed coffee with humongous, macaroon-shaped muffin-cookies.

At the Freeds, I discovered that being sent by Gurumayi gave us powers. People opened up to us. After dinner, Salma went to bed while Eduardo and I stayed up with our gracious hosts in their beautiful beige entertainment room, where they shared the trials of their high school senior daughter.

"We're curious about your thoughts," Mr. Freed said, mostly looking at Eduardo. "Our 16-year-old daughter — she's rebelling. She's been lying about going to parties. Lately, we think she's gotten into some pot smoking."

What a lightweight! I thought, thinking back to all the drugs I had tried by the time I was her age growing up in New York: coke, hash, LSD. I listened to Eduardo, a licensed psychologist, spew his diagnostic crap about tightening the ropes.

"You need to set firm expectations and boundaries with her. Have you talked to her about the dangers of drugs?"

"Of course," Nancy said.

They continued on, the Freed's wide-eyed gazes eating up the psychologist's advice. But I knew that his routine, by-the-book approach would backfire, making their daughter feel more estranged and rebellious. I was in the room, too. I decided to open my mouth.

"Eduardo has the degree and the experience — but being not too far out of college myself, I remember my struggles in high school, and that approach wouldn't work for me."

"Say more," Bruce said, leaning back.

"I so badly wanted my parents to be real with me, but they didn't know how. They were stuck in being parents. Did you do drugs?"

They laughed and nodded. "Of course! It was the 60s, everyone did!"

"I would share your experiences and what did and didn't work. Tell her why you're concerned. If she doesn't or won't respond to your opening up, tell her that you miss her, and that you're struggling. You just want to open the door to talking."

I could see them opening to my input, as though they were hearing a tune they hadn't heard before and were slowly shaking their heads to the beat. Eduardo tightened his lips. I didn't mean to be so competitive with him. I just felt passionately that he didn't know what the hell he was talking about. But then, did *I*? I had no formal training and had never been a parent. And yet, the theater, my own therapy, self-reflection, and the ashram's confirmation of my therapeutic skills helped me trust that my experience could be of value to them. It felt good to take them up on their bid for consultation. I was no longer a meek devotee. I was part of an envoy, spreading the teachings. I was someone who had a voice, who was worth listening to.

"I think she's onto something," Bruce said to his wife. Nancy nodded and shot her gaze towards the heavens.

Orlando was the opposite of Charlotte, and our hosts, the Sharmas, were very different from Lauren or the Freeds. This devoted American family of immigrants welcomed us at the Orlando airport with huge smiles and fresh marigold leis, as though we were the guru herself. When we entered their modest suburban home, we were welcomed first into the laundry room, which had been turned into a meditation temple, kept vital with daily practice and fresh flowers strung together, adorning a big statue of the elephant god Ganesh. Every inch of the walls was covered in framed photos of the Siddhas. There was real power in that tiny room, especially during the spin cycle.

Mr. Sharma radiated contentment. He was quiet, but always smiling, nodding his head side to side. Mrs. Sharma was spirited and funny, and made the most wonderful homemade Indian meals, served with Indian hospitality, which included offering seconds and thirds in such a persistent manner that there was no option of refusing them. When I wasn't being force-fed at the table, I adored being with the Sharmas. The love in their home was palpable: in the smells, the spices, the devotion, and the humor. The Sharmas understood their connection to Gurumayi without having to be with her. They did the practices and kept the *Shakti* alive in their hearts and home. From being around the Sharmas' innate devotion, I got a taste of what it would be like to be in India without having to be there, and that made me feel closer to Gurumayi.

Thankfully, there was a good course turnout at the Orlando Center, a light and spacious renovated storefront with a wall of windows. I could put the impact of the damning information we'd experienced in Charlotte on hold. But my sadness about leaving the warmth of the Sharma's hospitality surprised me. Gurumayi always taught us the importance of welcoming people. Until Orlando, I didn't know that to be truly welcomed is to instantly feel you belong, that you're a part of the family.

When June Bartel picked us up from the Sarasota Municipal Airport, I was still missing the Sharmas, but by the time we drove past the Sarasota Ringling Brothers Circus Museum, my mood brightened. I thought I knew Florida — I had been to Disney and visited my grandparents in Ft. Lauderdale until I was thirteen — but Sarasota was different. It was glamorous and island-like. Its turquoise shoreline and tropical vibe penetrated and filled me with delight.

Our host, June, like the town we were driving through, was sunny, vibrant, and playful. From the finely landscaped but cramped driveway entrance to her home, you wouldn't guess that behind the front door was an enormous open house with floor-to-ceiling windows, looking out over a manicured lawn extending right down to the ocean, their own private beach.

I was so excited to stay in that lap of luxury and go for a swim, enjoying a little bit of vacation. But the Bartels had a Siamese cat, and Salma was allergic. Even though Salma firmly protested, claiming that Siamese were hypoallergenic and it would be fine for us to stay as long as she didn't pet it, they had arranged for us women to stay at the Sarasota Center, which was in a private home. Salma and I piled back into June's BMW heading for Venice, FL to stay with Edith and Joe Marks.

The Marks lived in a cozy, slightly mildewy bungalow that was only twenty minutes away but practically in another world. Compared to the Bartels' modern home, theirs was stuck in the 70s. The backyard was steamy, thick with jungle flora. The small Saratoga Center where we would be running the course was in a separate studio.

Joe Marks was an artist who looked a little like Freud, and Edith was a plump retired art teacher who seemed mildly irritated by our presence. After learning in Charlotte about how our trip was a bit of a set-up for center hosts, I assumed I knew why, but Edith never let on.

We taught the course to a group of about twenty devotees. All was fine on the surface, but I started to feel a creeping sense of hypocrisy. Even as I began to feel my power as a teacher of sorts, I realized we barely knew more about how to evolve spiritually than the people we were teaching. Eduardo took the lead in answering the greater part of the questions from the crowd. I felt his answers were too attentive to the surface content of the questions, overlooking the deeper concerns participants were hiding in them. If someone asked: "Is there a time of day you shouldn't meditate?" I heard the subtext: *Is there any way to do it wrong, and if so, will something bad happen to me?* or, *Should I really make this investment in myself?* Eduardo would respond, "Mornings are best, it's a great way to start the day." Opportunity missed.

Then I tried to answer questions like "What happens if I try to meditate and nothing happens?" and discovered how hard it was to find good answers on the spot. I, too, ended up reciting stock answers from the Siddha playbook: "If you breathe and say the mantra, something *is* happening, even if you don't always perceive it that way." The best I could do was to silently acknowledge each asker for their courage. Salma had a strong, calming presence, but when presenting or answering questions, she, too, looked like a deer in headlights. We were students, not gurus.

I also noticed a sense of entitlement creeping into my behavior. We had been away from the ashram for over two weeks, spoiled silly by numerous hosts. When the Marks' brought home pizza for Salma and me — a big culinary treat for a rice-and-beans-eating vegetarian — it arrived pasty and cold. I was so disappointed, I tore it into pieces without really eating it.

"Would you mind if we put this in the oven to crisp it up a bit?" I asked.

"You want it hotter?" Edith asked.

I felt bad for asking. "Well, actually, I think it's good."

Salma kept her head down and focused on her pizza. I was ashamed of myself. When Salma and I were back in our stuffy guest room with the floral, polyester bedspread-covered twin beds, I confessed.

"I sneered at the pizza tonight, and I know they saw it. They are so generous, and I'm acting like a princess. What is wrong with me? I just can't get over the fact that we are here while Eduardo gets to stay in his own room at the beach house."

I thought Salma would correct me, keep me on the straight and narrow, remind me of how lucky and blessed we are to be here and of service. But instead, she launched into an imitation of Eduardo, with his know-it-all attitude, explaining why he was the best one to stay at the beach house. We fell on the floor laughing. Then it all poured out of us; the ugliness of the Charlotte response, the awkwardness of people paying for us everywhere we went, how we both tried and failed to hide food at the Sharma's table, how annoying Eduardo could be, and how he had set the whole Sarasota situation up to his advantage. We laughed and laughed, allowing what felt like a deep spiritual cleansing.

The last leg of the tour showcased the opulence, beauty, and bounty in the world, which made it harder to return to the austerity of the ashram and its surrounding, depressed Catskill towns. But when we arrived back home to the ashram, I was reminded of its special beauty. The grounds appeared greener and even quieter than we had left them.

The first thing we did upon returning, as instructed by a programming staff who welcomed us, was visit the temple where a hazy afternoon light streamed in through the windows. I gazed up at the statue's familiar expression: the faintest hint of a smile, his gaze looking outward and within simultaneously. *Nice to see you again, Bade Baba.* I was home, but out of sync with the ashram. I sat in the temple like a good devotee, trying to sink into my heart. My eyes were resistant to closing for meditation, so I kept them open. The road had changed me. The ashram was a source of respite, but now I knew that it had put pressure on the centers our mandali visited. I felt older, hardened by the outside world. I closed my eyes for a moment, and the sticky, gooey sensation of guilt rose up. I didn't want to feel weird about being back. This was my life now. This was my future. I had nothing else. I inhaled the elevating smell of gardenias. *Help me reconnect.*

20: Invitations

Amy, Mahadev's assistant who I adored, chatted at a dining hall table with another young woman in Hospitality, who I'd once spotted on the Amrit porch entertaining a big movie star. I felt lucky to put my tray down at their table and get to know them. But Amy and the Hospitality *sevite* were engaged in an intense conversation about popular music which I kept trying to enter, but it wasn't my subject and there was really no opening. They agreed to see a movie at the mall the following night, hardly acknowledging my presence.

Other than Vera, I still didn't have any friends, and the dark perception that I just didn't seem to fit in anywhere reinstated itself. Even though by now I knew almost all of the twenty-five or so live-in devotees in my age range, I wasn't making any traction with them. I slipped back into wondering what was wrong with me, the rejection stinging its way through my system. My mopey funk was interrupted by the arrival of mysterious notes under my door.

You are requested at a meeting: Anugraha Conference Room, Wednesday, 11:00. Parvati excused me for the rest of the morning, and I rushed into the courtyard only to realize I didn't know where to go. I stood worrying until a tall manager in business attire walked by.

"Do you know where the conference room is?"

Her eyes opened wide, as if I had asked her where the orgy was taking place. I showed her my note. "In the basement," she said, hurrying along.

What basement? Like a dream in which you keep discovering new rooms of a place you thought you knew really well, I kept discovering new areas and aspects of the ashram. A few days before I was heading out for a run around an ashram construction project, a pond that was being enlarged to a lake. An old-time devotee stopped me in a bit of a panic.

"You're going to work out, right?"

"Well, going for a run. Why?"

"Ahhhh, never mind," the man said, suddenly unsure. "I just need to find Swami Durgananda," he muttered, before walking off.

I told Vera about the strange encounter with the old-timer the next day.

"He must have thought you were headed to the gym," she said.

"The *wha*?"

After Vera's boss started returning to the Video Department in the middle of the day with wet hair, smelling faintly of chlorine, Vera figured out there was a top-secret gym with an indoor pool reserved for special staff and swamis. A vision flashed before me of one day working out in the secret gym with the swamis, but in the meantime, being invited into the conference room felt like a big deal in and of itself, if only I could figure out how to get into the basement.

Kesh suddenly appeared in the courtyard outside Swami Laundry, where I used to drop off Sajjananda's clothes, and waved me in his direction. I followed him through the laundry into a sleek dark hallway, down some stairs, and into a bunker of a boardroom with a stunning mahogany table and large leather swivel chairs. Seated in the big chairs were five other devotees in my age group, plus Kesh, the long-time devotee Barbara, and Swami Durgananda.

"We've invited you all here to brainstorm about new programming for younger people," Kesh announced. "What we want to know is, what people your age and slightly younger are looking for."

"How could Siddha Yoga help them?" Durgananda added.

I stayed quiet and listened to a number of my peers jump in with ideas. I couldn't believe I was in the ashram boardroom, included in the behind-the-scenes programming.

I tried to remember how I felt only a few years ago in college. I wasn't able to meditate. It was too hard. I thought about my college theater friends, smoking, drinking, and getting high in their dorms and houses. I thought about all the people in the Greek system, sorority sisters and frat boys. I couldn't see any of them being interested in meditation or chanting, even though it might have helped them in a number of ways. As I listened to the ideas being tossed around — "a course on discipline!" "feeling the divine love of the *Shakti*," it all sounded like BS. Barbara took furious notes. I decided to stay quiet.

Keshavananda called me out. "Blair? Do you have anything to add?"

I hesitated. I looked at my peers. I tried to think of something constructive and palatable to say. "Isn't the discipline of the yogic path opposite of what most young people are looking for?"

"Maybe," Kesh said.

"I think young people are focused on freedom and partying. How would we draw them in?"

"The *Shakti* will draw them in," the young woman from Hospitality said.

I winced.

"Maybe they need help with concentration." I suggested, trying to be positive. "Or with having enough self-esteem to make healthier choices."

Matthew, an attractive, sandy-haired Brit, jumped in. "That's precisely *why* they need the practices! To make better choices."

The six of us younger folk started thinking of ways to tailor the practices to college life and emerged from the meeting as the College Student Course Committee, tasked with creating a weekend course that focused on the practices and contemplation while navigating a mindful college life. We had two weeks to develop the outline for the course and submit it for review. If it was accepted, it would go on the summer course schedule and we would facilitate it with the aid of a swami just before the college kids went back to school. It was a hopeful evolution for the new season. I was going to meet regularly with people my age. I was creating a course that could help people with wisdom from my actual experience! And I would be teaching it, too. I still officially served in the Dakshina Committee office, but I had finally entered Programming.

Gurumayi always said we should practice seeing God in each other, and whenever Mahadev, the wise man with MS greeted me, it was easy to do. His smile made me feel special and welcome. He was wheeling his way through the lobby when I bumped into him en route to the dining hall.

"Mahadev, how are you?"

"Well, I've been in a little physical pain lately. So, not so good," he surprised me with his honesty. "And my two assistants aren't helping. They're at war. I don't know what to do. All they do is argue."

"I'm sorry."

"Come to think of it, I hear you're good with people. Do you think you could help Amy and David work out their problems?"

I felt honored. But I had never done this emotional support thing with a couple.

"Come, meet us for dinner. We'll be in the dining hall tomorrow at six."

It all happened so fast, I agreed. What if I made it worse between them?

At dinner I approached the three of them, sitting at one of the big round tables with the floral plastic tablecloths. The strong smell of curry wafted through the wooded hall, which was aglow with the early evening spring sunlight. My chest was pumping.

"Here she is!" Mahadev exclaimed. Amy smiled and nodded, and David sat on the other side of the table with his arms crossed and head cocked to one side. The pressure was on.

I searched for words, but no small talk or intro presented itself, so I decided to just get to the point. "Mahadev told me you two have been struggling."

"We're not communicating," Amy launched in. "I end up doing so many things myself because he's not there at the times he should be."

"We communicate," David rebutted. "She's just negative and judgmental."

"Are you kidding me?" Amy said. "I work *way* overtime. We need to divide the work and then stick to what we decide!"

This was way out of my league.

"There you go," David said with a callous edge. "Inserting your negativity. You need to have faith that everything is all right," David said, borrowing from the Guru's yearly message.

Ugh. I felt like I was in the middle of a lover's spat, and I felt sorry for Amy. David's know-it-all tone was nauseating. The dynamic was clear to me. David was warding Amy off, refusing to hear her.

How was it that I could see people's issues, and yet I had so much trouble making friends? It didn't make sense, but I didn't have time to look for the answers. I needed to find a way to talk to David that might help. I took a breath, and an opening presented itself.

"Sounds like you're trying to be her spiritual teacher," I challenged him.

"YEAH!" exclaimed Amy. "I have a spiritual teacher. I just need you to work with me."

I invited Amy to tell David exactly what she wanted in a calm tone. She took a deep breath and obliged. "I can't do this all by myself. We need to divvy up the work, and I need you to show up when you say you're going to."

I could see him stiffen up, but finding my footing in this new therapist role, I intervened. "Before you fight her, David, just *listen* to her."

He moved in a jerky motion, fighting with his impulse to fight her. Then, he softened.

"Wow," he said, awash in realization. "I haven't been hearing you. I've just been fighting."

With one fierce nod, Amy said, "Yes."

"I'm so, so sorry. I've just been in my head over here." David promised to go to the temple later that evening to reflect on why he'd been shutting her down. He felt awful, but I felt like a million bucks. Breakthrough accomplished.

Mahadev wheeled beside me as we left the dining hall. "I can't tell you how much I appreciate your help. And how much I enjoyed watching you work. I really hope they've got it now."

Watching me *work*. While he felt hopeful about the future, I felt like I was stepping into mine.

WHILE YOU WERE OUT *Your mother called 6:53 p.m. Your mother called 12:30. Your father called, call him back.* I waited for a time when my roommates would be out and used the collect call trick to reach them.

"Blair, we're worried about you," my father pleaded. "I really think we need to see a professional, as a family."

"We already went to therapy, Dad," I said, reminding him of the session I'd agreed to when I'd gotten accepted to the ashram and the therapist said I was old enough to make my own life choices.

"We think you should give it one more try, for the sake of the family."

Hearing desperation in my father's voice disarmed me. I hated disappointing him, and I couldn't live with the idea that I was causing him such pain. My mother must have been driving him nuts.

And so, while I was busy playing therapist, my family corralled me into seeing one.

But this left me in a tizzy. I hung up the phone feeling enraged and confused. It wasn't my job to make them feel better and I didn't want to do their work for them. I could still cancel the appointment. I went to the temple to try to calm down and to ask Bade Baba.

I heard a voice that said, "Go." And for the first time, I wondered: Was it *his* voice? *My* voice?

Does it matter?

Another note: *You are invited to a special dinner at Anugraha Amrit Saturday night before the program. Arrive at 6 p.m.* Dinner? A "special dinner?" This was new. Was it a dinner to discuss living in India? I hoped.

I showed up in Amrit on time, but all I saw was a table set for ten on a closed-in section of the porch. Finally, Barbara strolled in, followed by a few other devotees that I knew but not well. It was a random grouping that I couldn't classify by department, age, or time spent in Siddha Yoga. Then I saw Maya, Gurumayi's long-time senior aide who had been in the private *darshan* with Leon. *This must be related to Gurumayi,* I thought. Maya announced that the dinner was in honor of Rabbi Gelberman, the head of the Interfaith Seminary training in the city, who had come for a visit.

The rabbi, in his 70s, with Einstein-like hair and a Groucho Marx sense of humor, loved Gurumayi and often made special trips to the Catskills to see her. He had come to discuss some official business with her secretaries.

He entered boisterously, with a young female assistant in tow. A few kitchen *sevites* brought bowls of food to the table, which felt weird — being served while seated. As we ate, he entertained us with stories about Baba, Martin Luther King, and other luminaries he had mingled with. At the end of dinner, he even did a few magic tricks and then invited us all to pick an angel card, a small deck with an angel on one side and a spiritual word like "peace" on the other. I picked "creativity," and he told me he could sense I had some creative passions that I wasn't fully utilizing. Maya raised her eyebrows at me, and I was grateful for the sarcasm in the gesture, knowing that I wasn't the only one rolling my inner eyes.

I watched the young assistant gaze lovingly at the rabbi. She had a certain buoyancy about her and, with her slight Long Island accent, reminded me of some long-ago friends from summer camp. While trying to savor the sponge cake, a special *prasad* for the occasion, I asked her what her connection to the rabbi was. "I'm his wife!" she replied. I nodded and smiled as though there was no part of me screaming, *You're kidding, right?* There was close to a fifty-year difference between them.

They turned towards each other and looked very happy.

Finally, it dawned on me that I was there — like everyone else at the table — because I was Jewish. I felt *jada* for not getting it sooner. Although his Interfaith Seminary was for the instruction and celebration of all faiths, because he was a rabbi, Gurumayi had gathered up a bunch of us Siddha Jews to welcome him and make him feel at home. The realization left me with a mix of sensations: proud of my heritage, honored to be selected, but also corralled and branded. Being on the path did not erase my Jewishness. My mother's words, "it's a race *and* a religion," echoed in my head. While it was nice to be included in a special event, the only spiritual leader I really wanted to have dinner with was Gurumayi.

But it also was another reminder that I wasn't just on a path. I was part of an organization. A month later, I discovered that Gelberman had come that night to personally present Gurumayi with an award for her spiritual leadership, which would be officially given in a few weeks at the graduation ceremony of Interfaith students at the majestic St. John's Cathedral in Manhattan. Since she would not be able to attend, I, along with Jewish

Maya and non-Jewish Swami Keshavananda, were invited to do so in her stead. It was an incredible honor.

Sitting in the grandeur of St. John's Cathedral, witnessing a beautiful cohort of new Interfaith ministers graduate, I relished my role as a Jewish Ambassador. It made me feel special, included in Gurumayi's thoughts, and proud of my heritage. But an upcoming appointment with my parents — at the Jewish Board of Family Services no less — evoked my inner OY.

21: The Doctors

Parvati gave me permission to leave the Dakshina Office early one Wednesday to take a van to the city for family therapy. Archie, our short, bald psychologist, shook our hands and walked my mother, father, and me down the hall to the stuffy beige room he worked in. My sister was spared.

"Blair has made it very clear she doesn't want to have much to do with us," my mother started in. My father took the baton and continued, "Meditation is fine, but we don't understand why Blair is making these life choices to live at an ashram. Naturally we're worried about her, and we think maybe she is at the ashram to punish us because she's angry."

I didn't respond, but I watched myself sitting with my arms crossed and my jaw set, like a sullen character in a John Hughes movie.

"Well, what *is* she doing at the ashram?" the therapist asked my dad.

"A lot of meditating, I guess? I don't know."

"Ask her."

I shared about the Dakshina department admin work and some of the skills I was building. "I'm good with people. And I'm writing. And I'm getting calmer, more thoughtful."

"I don't understand why you have to live there to get that," my mother said in that hostile tone of hers with the little darts coming out of her mouth. I tried to enlist Archie to my side.

"See? That doesn't make me want to talk to them or be near them much."

At the session's end, Archie assessed that the real tension was between my mother and me and thought we could make progress if she and I agreed to continue the therapy for a while.

I was not overly impressed with Archie. He lacked Kate's charm, humor, and emotional availability. But he was trained and traditional. He asked the right questions and listened to the answers. As resentful as I felt being there with my parents, their relief and gratitude that I showed up, though I'd never admit it out loud, almost made the whole thing worth it. I was sick of avoiding their phone calls and the tension when we did speak. I wanted to work it out, even though I doubted we could.

Summer, my favorite season, seemed muted without the thrill of knowing I could bump into Gurumayi at any moment and receive a teaching or blessing that could change my state of mind for days. Despite there being no orange flag flapping above the main building, there was lots to do to accommodate the influx of devotees on the weekends, and we were kept busy, even though most of the courses and Intensives were only half-filled. One morning, the temperature in the Dakshina office rose, and sweat trickled down the back of my neck.

"Do you think we could get a fan in here?" I asked Parvati while staring at the computer screen in our hot office.

Triveni said she noticed extra fans lined up outside the manager's office. Maybe we could get one from there. She always knew about stuff like that, and I appreciated her for it. I wanted to get out of the office, so I volunteered.

"I'll go check it out. Anyone want an iced chai while I'm out?"

"No thanks," Triveni responded. "Dr. Jorge has me off sugar."

Dr. Jorge was a naturopath frequented by ashram staff. She got rave reviews. Triveni once came into the office with a mountain of fresh pineapple chunks, saying, "Dr. Jorge says pineapple is good for the liver." Jorge patients brought jars of supplements and blue bottles with droppers to dining hall meals. Vans left the ashram weekly for the half-hour trek to her home office in Napanoch.

Maybe it was the heat or the feeling of missing Gurumayi, but as I stood staring at a line of old fans, I wondered if Dr. Jorge could help me heal my old sluggishness, which was creeping back. After the *Gita* in the morning, that post-chant feeling of effervescence was less reliable, so like many full-time staffers, I stopped getting up for it and went straight to work. I was finally getting that spiritual practices were not the solution to life. They were a tool. And not always as reliable as advertised. I decided to see Dr. Jorge.

A van full of devotees arrived at her cozy, bucolic home in the early evening. A few sat on the couch while the rest of us sat on the floor in the living room, waiting our turn. Supplements were lined up on a set of white, curly wrought-iron shelving units in her living room. One by one, each person would have their appointment and emerge fortified with a list of unique holistic prescriptions and dietary restrictions: drink sour cherry juice, don't eat sugar, eat sour cream, don't eat bread, etc. The bottles and the supplements and the restrictions held the promise of healing. I hoped my health protocol would include lots of supplements and a massive list of dos and don'ts to guide me back to feeling good.

"You're too pretty to be tired," Dr. Jorge said on my first visit, in a rough New York accent. The accent and the compliment warmed me to her immediately. Jorge practiced kinesiology, lifting my arm, having me hold it there, asking questions, and pushing down on my arm to get a "read" on what was going on.

"Did you ever smoke? Do hardcore drugs? You know, hallucinogens, cocaine, things like that? Did you live in a city?" She placed her other hand in front of the regions where my organs lived in my body. I responded "yes" to all her questions.

She diagnosed me with toxic liver syndrome, which she said sounded much worse than it was, adding that it was probably due to the hardcore drugs. She gave me only one tincture to take, no dietary adjustments. "Just drink more water. You're pretty healthy."

I was disappointed. In some twisted logic, I'd equated the need for healing protocols with being special. I hadn't realized how attached I'd become to the part of me that believed I needed fixing. I got on the van with my one tincture, envying those who cradled brown bags stuffed with vitamins and teas on their laps.

I sat cross-legged in the tinkling temple silence, looking up at Bade Baba, a streak of summer sun kissing his bronze cheek. I felt my heart swell. I loved having this moment to myself in the empty temple on a Wednesday afternoon. A wave of affection for the ashram and my posse of living and dead teachers rolled into my lap. My eyes moistened and tears streamed down. *Bade Baba, how can I carry this love with me to see my mother in the city? Please help us heal.* I *pranamed,* placing my head to the floor, and walked meditatively around the statue, past the car-sized crystal, feeling buoyed by hope and peace.

Parvati was going to the city to have dinner with some big ashram donors — whoops, we didn't call them that — *people who give generous gifts,* so she decided to drive me down to the city later that afternoon for my third therapy session with Archie and my mother. I wasn't sure we were making progress. On the drive down, I replayed key moments from our second session, when I had told Archie of the impact of my mother's temper.

"You were abusive," I said to my mother.

"Abusive? Are you *kidding* me? You're deranged. I lost my temper sometimes, but who doesn't? I wasn't abusive."

"See — calling me deranged — it's mean!"

My mother balked, and Archie seemed not to know what to do with us.

As the car slowed down in city traffic, I was dreading another evening of it. I tried to recall the peace I felt earlier in the temple.

"Good luck. Pick you up at eight," Parvati said, like a sweet mom dropping me off at the mall, leaving me on the corner of 90th and Third.

"Mom," I picked up on our usual refrain in Archie's office. "Just because I decided not to go to Israel doesn't mean I don't want to be a part of this family. I come home for visits. No one is pressuring me to stay at the ashram. At least Dad understands that I'm happy. Why can't you?"

Archie's bald head was shiny with sweat. He wore a short-sleeved button-down and tie. He looked at her.

"Well, it's hard for me to see how you're happy, but okay."

"This relationship is not going to work if you don't understand that I don't like everything you do. I'm different."

"I can accept that. As long as you come home and you're a part of the family. But acceptance needs to go both ways. You have to stop trying to convince everyone in the family to be a part of it. That's the thing that worries me the most. I feel like we've lost you."

I recalled a moment in the car with my parents, asking them to play a tape of one of Gurumayi's talks, which they begrudgingly did but then didn't get it. And then another, telling my mother how meditating without having a guru (which she did regularly) is flat, you need a teacher to awaken and guide the sacred energy. And then that awful moment, passing around Gurumayi's chocolate *prasad* after dinner, telling my parents it carries blessings and watching their eyes meet with concern.

Her words, spoken without her usual darts, shocked me into a moment of seeing my entire Siddha Yoga experience as a violent cliché. I hadn't realized the extent to which I talked about Gurumayi in their presence and tried to bring them onboard. I felt deeply embarrassed. As all the conversations in which I had tried to convince anyone, not just my family, flashed before me, the humiliation intensified.

After a long pause, Archie asked, "Blair, do you know why you try to get your family involved?"

The room tilted a little. The answer was so obvious. If they valued spiritual growth, we could find common ground. If we could talk about things that felt meaningful, not just gossip, cultural events, and what was wrong with me, then maybe, maybe, we could feel truly close as people, not just because we're supposed to. "I feel lonely when I'm with them."

After another silent pause, Archie asked my mother, "Why do you think Blair's so lonely?"

She took her time in answering. "You know. Her sister, three-and-a-half years younger, really took it out of me. She was very sensitive, and Blair seemed naturally independent, happy, able to fend for herself. I guess when she was younger, I really just let her be. My hands were full."

As she continued to speak, the isolated little girl that had been frozen in a bubble for twenty-plus years appeared to me, and as I touched her loneliness — a feeling so old, so deep, so heretofore totally eclipsed — I fell into what felt like an infinity pool of grief. I suddenly recognized the pain for what it was: loneliness. And the loneliness of those young years, of high school, of college, of living at the ashram, poured out of me in uncontrollable sobs. My mother had no idea what to do. She tried to say something to make me feel better, but the therapist guided her to simply put her arms around me, an awkward gesture that long ago I had unknowingly and chronically ached for.

I got into Parvati's car, a haven from the assault of the city streets, rawness pulsating, my face swollen and streaked. She looked at me with compassion. I could see her managing her curiosity like a puppy on a leash, but I couldn't utter a word. We silently cruised along the thruway into the dark night, heading home.

In my follow-up visit with Dr. Jorge, she asked me about the fatigue.

"I feel much better. I can breathe more freely," I said. Maybe it was the tincture. Maybe it was the relief of bottled-up years of loneliness uncorked.

"Good," she said, while lifting my arm and pressing, testing my body and organs for weakness. "Okay then, feel good."

That was it? I was done? One visit. Dr. Jorge never told people they were done in one visit! As I was gathering my things to go, she added, "And you should go back to the religion you were born in. This ashram stuff is not good for you. You people get stressed out waking up so early, working so hard, not eating enough protein. Everyone's tired."

My gratitude towards her immediately soured. *Who asked you?!* I trusted her with my health, and she piled on a load of judgment about my life choices. I was used to it from my family, *but from my healer?*

On the ride home, staring out the van window at the sun resting on the horizon, its orange rays illuminating the lush rural landscape, the shock and outrage gave way to a little curiosity. I considered if there was any truth in Jorge's words. Go back to Judaism? Not a chance. That felt like stuffing myself into a shoebox. I had no calling to study or immerse myself in it.

But I hadn't forgotten my true childhood religion or that moment at *The Fantasticks,* when the electricity of the performance moved up and down my spine. I thought about how far I felt from my passion for performing. What had happened to my love for rich characters, transformative stories, soul-stirring performances? Could I still sing if I wasn't chanting? *Was I a singer?*

Could it be my search for God was nudging me back to the theater?

Shortly after my visit with Jorge, I worked up the courage to visit the *Seva* office and officially request moving to the Programming Department, the *seva* that would best accommodate my creative and performative inclinations. The *Seva* director, with arms crossed and a skeptical eye, listened to my case, including my frustrations with feeling futile in the Dakshina office. She told me to continue along with what I was doing: serving full-time in Dakshina and part-time with my extra *seva* in Programming. It was anticlimactic, but at least I was advocating for my needs.

As the summer wore on, some courses were only a quarter-filled. I asked Swami Keshavananda why we had so many courses if people weren't taking them.

"Gurumayi likes it that way," he said. "The Intensives, filled or not, keep the *Shakti* flowing."

I understood. Keeping the *Shakti* flowing was a constant effort.

One that was making me tired.

22: The New Yorker

I awoke at 3:00 a.m. from a dream with Gurumayi. We were sitting across a wooden picnic table, with lots of young people milling about around us. Like a bionic woman, she pulled back a piece of flesh on her forearm to reveal an exquisitely smooth, muscular mahogany bone. "This is how strong you need to be inside," she said, and as I peered into the darkness of her wooden bones, I noticed they were engraved with Baba's name.

Ever since the "let's-look-for-you dream," I'd taken dreams with Gurumayi seriously, believing they contained messages about direction for my soul. Even though the practices were showing their limitations, I still wanted to be that strong. I wanted to carve my devotion into my bones. I wanted to cultivate stillness on a more regular basis. But I also wanted to expand into the playfulness of summer. I polled a few old-time ashram residents for swimming holes, but in a depressed rural town with a large population of Hasidic Jews, finding a place to swim was not easy. I took more walks off ashram grounds, frequently visiting the Mountain Market with Vera for shopping, snacks, and escape.

The Mountain Market was an everything store that sat adjacent to the ashram grounds. It had a small grill for veggie sandwiches and a freezer for old-fashioned, Good Humor ice-cream pops and the newer, healthier Frozefruit popsicles. It even sold Indian clothes and incense. One time, roaming the aisles and looking at random, cheap plastic toys, Vera and I came upon

Kesh sitting at a table in the back, spread-legged in his robes, popping potato chips and gazing up at a basketball game on a corner-mounted TV. Swamis were supposed to meditate and spend every waking moment being devoted to God, and yet here he was in a clandestine moment, behaving like a regular guy. I don't think he was drinking a beer, but he might as well have been. I wondered if he ever felt trapped or depressed about being a swami. I wondered if he, too, felt dry, rudderless, and antsy without having the physical guru around to act as a focal point. I wondered if he carved Gurumayi's name into his bones, and if sneaking some TV had any effect on the strength of his devotion, or if he needed breathing space to be a person in the world.

One mid-summer day, as I walked alone on the long, dusty road connecting the store to the main building, I took off my shoes to feel the coolness of the earth. I was wearing a button-down rayon dress that billowed in the breeze, alternately puffing up in the front and then behind me like a parachute. I felt so alive, and with the sun beaming down and warming my hair, which danced around my face as the wind gently teased it, I felt a new side of me emerge, an Earth Mother side, all fertile and serene. I felt distinctly more woman than girl.

It was an evolutionary moment, but as it turns out, not a private one. Swami Keshavananda was holding court in the courtyard. As I approached, he waved me towards him. I put on my shoes and attended to him.

"I was just thinking as I saw you approach. I have a nephew in DC who you would be perfect for. "

Stomach flip. *Is this really happening*? Through his seemingly generous offer to connect me with a suitable partner, Kesh was seeing me as a sexual being. Kesh, the number two spiritual head of the ashram, who occasionally took off to eat chips and watch basketball, was pawning my sexuality off to his nephew. It was inappropriate, thoughtful, and titillating all at once. What I had just experienced inside myself on my walk actually transmitted to another person who could perceive it. It revealed another dimension of my power, even though it was a type of power we didn't talk about and were supposed to suppress in the strict, dogmatic environment.

And then, like a colorful instruction manual opening before my eyes, the limitations of monkhood crystallized. Robes were not enough to conceal our humanity. Being a swami was an exalted role but, at the same time, so rigid and contained that it inevitably led to all our humanity leaking out. Underneath the robes, the flesh remained.

I left Kesh's side to get a cool drink at the Amrit. I nearly bumped into Bo, a gorgeous, tall blonde model-turned-massage therapist. Gabby knew him from the city and had introduced us a while back. He invited me to sit with him and his small group of New York friends. I felt a little insecure, which he saw, and commenting that I looked a bit tense, asked if I wanted a shoulder massage. I cringed at how much I wanted to feel his hands on me. And he was a very good masseur. I could have sat there all afternoon. With waves of relaxation and the long-lost stimulation of touch streaming through me, I stepped into a forgotten type of bliss. I felt grateful I was not a swami.

The next morning, I awoke from a dream in which I was in Gurumayi's bedroom, a sacred place very few people get to hang out, but I was wearing sneakers so I was asked to leave. Then, I heard she had taken *mahasamadhi* and died. I was so angry with her for leaving me. Bo was her successor. He didn't have the *Shakti* that she had, but we were all supposed to follow him.

The massage and the message in the dream roiled inside me. The fantasy of monkhood was slipping away. A new kind of longing was creeping into its place. It terrified me. I had to stop it before it destroyed me and everything I had been working towards.

Another note under my door. *What would the mandatory staff meeting reveal this time?* A message from the guru, a major change in the way we do things, a new adventure within or without — all was possible, and the possibilities were always interesting. This meeting turned out to be none, and, in some ways, all of the above.

A few swamis and the head of the PR department — responsible for managing the ashram's image and interactions with the public — were milling about at the front of the room, and all 150 or so of us full-time *sevites* shuffled in. They got to the point quickly. *The New Yorker* magazine was working on an expose on the ashram, and they'd gone digging for dirt with former devotees who had a bone to pick, people who'd told some pretty horrific lies.

I was partly intrigued, like watching a soap opera, and at the same time, incredibly nervous about what we were about to hear. I remembered the first time I saw people chanting and found it silly, thinking it belonged in a movie, and now I was afraid of feeling exposed and ridiculed by what *The New Yorker* would say about the place I loved. Plus, I'd mostly ignored the ashram dirt that I had occasionally gotten whiffs of, which was easy to do because there was a distinct hush-hush vibe whenever it came up: Gurumayi had a brother who was initiated as a co-guru and, because he liked women and motorcycles, was asked to step down and was never heard from again. Without the full picture of what went down, I made up a story in my mind that Gurumayi, who had served as Baba's English translator, was really the only true guru, but India was not ready for a female guru, so Baba had succeeded the power to both of them.

"Many of you already know the story of Gurumayi's brother. Some of you were around for the initiation and saw the whole thing unfold in action," a friendly teaching swami in charge of breaking the news said. "Before Baba died, he initiated both Gurumayi, who was very beloved and visible as Muktananda's translator, and her brother, Swami Nityananda, with the power of the guru. However, the young Nityananda didn't seem so interested in being a guru. Due to the repeated breaking of his guru *dharma*, he eventually was asked to step down."

When I had heard other devotees tell the story, they added that there were way more people lined up in front of Gurumayi's chair during *darshan* anyway.

"*The New Yorker* has gotten Nityananda to tell his side of the story, and it's not good, nor is it true. They say he was forced by Gurumayi to resign and permanently leave. *The New Yorker* has interviewed Nityananda, some of his followers, as well as a group of other devotees of Baba's who were misbehaving on ashram grounds and asked to leave. They're spreading some nasty lies about Baba to get revenge."

I was afraid to hear rumors about Baba because I loved him.

"Baba. Baba, Baba, Baba," the swami at the head of the room uttered, repeating his name perhaps as a stalling effect. "Well. There's no way to say this gently. The article accuses him of molesting several young devotees."

Oof.

We were being given a heads-up so that if the article came out, which it probably would in two or three months' time, we were not shocked, and as staff members, we could begin to prepare to handle and answer questions. The head of PR warned us that while the ashram would try to fight it, the article would likely be released, and it was going to be very challenging. The staff would have to act as community leaders in dealing with the fallout.

The party line: it's not true.

I tried to keep my mouth from hanging open. I couldn't tell my stomach from my bowels. I somehow knew, aggrieved ex-yogis and all, that the accusations about Baba were true. It must have read on my face because after the meeting, Barbara, the dear and faithful old-timer from Programming, grabbed me by the arm.

"Blair, I knew and lived with Baba for years. What they're saying isn't true. There's no way. He was so full, so happy. There would have been no need for him to do that. I tell you, I spent a lot of time with Baba. A lot of time." She lowered her eyes and shook her head in dismay.

I watched her try to convince me, but I felt that she was trying to convince herself. The news caused a separation within me. But people spread nasty rumors all the time. Why was I so willing to believe the accusers?

I spent the next few days wandering around with a cloud hanging over me. I couldn't breathe. I couldn't get the accusations out of my mind. I skipped the practices. The ashram schedule was mostly designed by Baba, and somehow I felt they were tainted.

In the room alone, I stared at Baba's autobiography, a book I had read three times. I believed his journey, his strict devotion, his willingness to immolate himself in the spiritual fire. Why was I so willing to dishonor his enlightenment so quickly?

The answer came when I was fetal on my bed, writing in a journal. I bumped into a secret I'd never shared, of my charming musical theater teacher in high school, a man who, like Baba, had a beard and was adored for his cool relatability and humor.

I was assistant directing the musical *Follies* with him, and we met alone in school on a Saturday to go over blocking. He asked me how old I was.

"Sixteen," I said, tensing up. "Why?"

"Because I'm forty-two, and we're coming on to each other."

I did my best imitation of a wax statue, and he backed off. I was spared.

I adored him, yes. I liked being around him and having him to myself, true. But I knew I wasn't coming on to him, and his suggestion repelled me. I didn't tell any adults. I didn't want to get him in trouble, and sadly, I didn't want to lose what I had received from the abuse of power: the confirmation that I was desirable. I put the interaction in a bubble so we could move on — get on with the show, to be literal about it. I was heart-achingly disappointed in him, but I didn't consider then that this was how he was wired, and that others might not be spared from physical harm as I had been.

That was my first experience of the shadow side of seemingly good men, and from there on, I learned more about it from the sexual abuse and incest stories of my friends, from Kate, and on Oprah. Healing from buried sexual abuse had become so popular, some therapists were accused of provoking their clients into having false memories. Sexual abuse was something Kate knew about firsthand from her father. She had done so much personal healing work and helped others heal from it. She had comfort with the topic. She had insight. I knew she would be a safe place for me to turn with this new information. I sought out a moment to call her on a break, when few people were roaming the halls.

"Kate, thanks so much for returning my call," I began, double-checking to make sure the phone booth door was shut tight. I braced for her judgment as I launched in. "I recently found out that Gurumayi's teacher, Baba, has been accused of molesting women and young girls. It's supposedly rumors. But I don't know."

She was silent.

"I don't know what to do."

The silence was torturous.

"I am so grossed out. I feel so ... so shocked. I feel ... betrayed." That was the word. *Betrayed*.

"Yes," she said, cut short by the sharp inhale of her cigarette. "You betrayed yourself."

Now the silence was mine. There wasn't much to say after that.

I thought about that statement for a long, hard time. The Siddhas were supposed to be ascended masters, who lived in a permanent state of Nirvana. *Siddha* means "perfect" in Sanskrit. Remembering Kate's one-time ironic nickname for me, "the queen of perfection," I realized: perfection *hurt*. And yet, I had committed to a spiritual practice which was based on following *Siddhas*, "perfected beings." Had I betrayed myself for believing someone else could be a perfect human, that someone else had the key to life? Had I betrayed myself for trying to be perfect like them, trying to squeeze out all that was unloveable within me and lay it at their perfect feet? I didn't know what to believe anymore about anything. I didn't know how to accept that Baba had done some truly horrible things that caused damage to people whose lives he was supposed to be saving, or at least improving. If it was true, then spiritual power did not prevent, but instead *allowed* Baba to perform heinous and distorted actions towards others.

As horrible as the realization that someone who had done so much to uplift people had also done the most destructive thing imaginable, there was something brewing that I found even harder to swallow, a relentless restlessness that even meditation couldn't quell.

23: Velvet Air

One late-summer evening, Vera and I walked several miles, by the modest houses and colonies of bungalows, to the nearest restaurant, an Italian cafe with sugary tomato sauce and rubbery bread. We enjoyed it for its novelty, but after eating the pure food at the ashram, it made us a little queasy. We were silent on the long stretch of country road back towards the ashram, all talked out, bellies distended, bewitched by the cacophony of cicadas and crickets. It was so beautiful, I couldn't imagine why, just a few days ago, I'd wanted to leave or where I'd go next. In fact, maybe *The New Yorker* information was bogus, and my feelings of wanting to leave the ashram were temporary.

At the edge of the ashram grounds was a large stream with a waterfall. We came across a huge gray-blue bird perched on a fallen branch spanning the banks. The bird, looking like a T-Rex and pelican combo, stared at us before taking off. I'd never seen anything like it.

"Heron. They're prehistoric," Vera said.

It was my first heron sighting. We felt blessed, as though we had had heron *darshan*. As we were parting, she tossed out:

"Didn't you say your ex-fiancé or boyfriend was a TV writer working on a new show about people in their 20s?"

"Yes. Why?"

"Because there's this new show called *Friends*. It's about people in their

20s. It's getting really good reviews. Is that his show?"

I felt the stirring of a tsunami start to crest inside me. But first I had to deal with the culture shock.

"Wait. How do you even know what's on TV?"

"Well, errrr …" Vera scanned her internal world to see if it was okay to let me in on her secret. "Sometimes I watch TV in the video department."

"You sneak! TV?!" I joked. Leaving to see a movie was one thing, but watching TV on ashram grounds seemed really taboo. I didn't know the name of Alex's show, but the scenario sounded familiar.

"Come over to the video department tomorrow night, and we'll watch it!"

I spent dinner excited and nervous about what I might see on TV. *What if the show sucked? What if it was great?* And even though I was pretty sure we wouldn't get caught, I felt guilty about sneaking, going behind the guru's back, and watching TV in her house. I'd had enough impure thoughts rolling around in my head. Watching this show was sure to add to them.

I met Vera in the Anugraha courtyard, and we surreptitiously made our way to the video department — also in the basement — where Vera edited video footage of the guru's talks for worldwide distribution. The space was clean and modern, with high-level equipment, newly carpeted floors, and the faint smell of incense. It was much nicer than the Dakshina Office.

At one of the editing consoles was a monitor and a cable box. I hadn't seen one of those in a long while. There was a good chance that this was the only cable box in the entire ashram. Then, I saw not only Alex's name flash across that little screen in the opening credits, but his writing partner, also a good friend from college. It didn't stop there. Jennifer Aniston, an actress from my high school, lit up the screen. We'd both worn chunky boots and our curly hair in blown-out bobs, and once someone had tapped me from behind, mistaking me for her. And then there was David Schwimmer, also a Northwestern alum whom I'd met numerous times at college parties hosted by the coolest of the cutting-edge, avant-garde theater crowd. He always looked past me, having already decided that our meeting was of no consequence.

There they were. And here I was. In an ashram in a partially renovated Borscht Belt hotel with probably only one cable box, watching what would soon become a TV classic.

I was a flip-flopping mess. Minutes ago, I'd been content with ashram living. Then I saw this new funny show in which people I knew were out there "making it," successfully navigating a world that felt harsh and terrifying to me, and I felt smaller than small. It was hard to wrap my brain around this difference in paths.

Lying in bed that night after the show, I stared at the springs on the bunk above. *Go back to your religion of origin*, Dr. Jorge had said. If I could feel this jealous, this provoked, had I ever really left it?

And why was I so busy comparing? Had I not learned anything? My jealousy was compounded by the realization that, after so many hours spent in contemplation and practice, my ego still ruled the roost. *Had my pursuit of spiritual life been a failure, a waste of my talent? What if my time at the ashram had simply been an avoidance of life, running away and not towards?*

Many devotees owned houses near the ashram, sweet little fixed-up bungalows, some with hot tubs in the back, or new, fancy houses that they built nearby. Giuliana, a dear, older Italian devotee, invited me to her friend Roseanne's house to 'hang out' on a Sunday afternoon. Roseanne was a sassy brunette, an unmarried PR agent living in the city, and a sometime musician who had a country house with a piano. Just a year ago, I wouldn't have wanted to spend an entire afternoon chilling off campus, but I was delighted to have a social reason to leave.

Roseanne had a small country kitchen with sweet yellow curtains and a plate of cookies on the table. The September sun had lost its oomph, and her house felt cozy. After tea and cookies, Roseanne sat down to play the piano. Pretty soon, the three of us were gathered round the upright belting out folk tunes and theater songs, a few by James Taylor, a few from *A Chorus Line*, even a Gershwin tune: *They Can't Take That Away from Me.* Eventually I belted out a solo, Bette Midler's "The Rose."

Some say love, it is a hunger, an endless aching need.

I connected with the notes inside my body before releasing them out into the air, and they landed effortlessly on key. All that chanting had kept my voice in shape. The women were impressed. I felt fantastic.

I felt like I was a singer.

Then I returned to my room alone. Once I coveted being alone in the room. Now it felt claustrophobic. I paced. I wrote furiously in my journal. I couldn't deny that I wanted more of what I had just come from — hanging out with people, being out in the world, and sharing my talent.

I had watched various emcees — great scholars, famous authors, and activists — speak at programs and Intensives at the head of the hall and often thought that, with my acting training, I could do that. As my experience teaching grew, I wanted to. But it seemed as far away as getting a part in a TV show. Very few people were selected to be speakers at that level. And then a new note under my door: an invite to give a talk at an Intensive. Gurumayi wouldn't be part of the Intensive I was speaking at, but if I did well, who knows, maybe one day she would be.

But while I showed up to the Dakshina office during the days, met with my speaking tutor in the afternoons and with the College Course Committee at night, I was half in what I was doing and half in a cyclical inner dialogue about leaving. I fantasized about living in Manhattan and starting a new life out in the world, with its panoply of food options and park walks and shoe styles. But, the counter-voice argued, if I could hang in there and stay on the ashram path, I would pass through those worldly desires and enter into a deeper immersion of tranquility. My insides spasmed like a fish out of water.

Then there was the question of faith. I had put my faith in this path. It had taken me so long to do. The path had given me a way of seeing, being, and the space to evolve. The question I needed to answer was if I was ready to put my faith in myself. The split existence plagued me.

Gurumayi, please help me to know if the spiritual fire is getting too hot and I am jumping off the path before it's time. I wrote and rewrote a letter to her fifty times, scared to send it. I wanted to kill off the voice in me that was becoming clearer. It whispered as I roamed the ashram halls. It spoke boldly while I chanted the *Gita*. It said, *You can go now.*

With a budding conviction, I wrote my letter asking for blessings to leave the ashram and again try my hand as an actress and a singer. I placed it in the plastic white Staff Mail tub that went to Ganeshpuri daily, via courier or devotees traveling back and forth. I moved through the days, between the buildings, between the summer and fall, between the pros and cons of staying and going. *Gurumayi, please help me to understand my next moves. You said that the ashram was a school. How do you know when you are ready to graduate?*

Thankfully, teaching the College Course got my mind off of waiting for her reply. Only twelve people signed up. It was a small course held in a small conference room, but the students were engaged. I delivered the talk I wrote about time management, teaching how to divvy up time to meet all your needs and not beat up on yourself when you don't follow through on your original intentions. Somehow, I sensed the information would come in handy in the next phase of my life. I looked into those collegiate kids' eyes. They seemed so young, and yet I was really only a few years older. I felt like my college experience was worlds away from who I had become, but once again, I was graduating.

After the course ended, Kesh congratulated us.

"Can't wait to see what's next from you all," he said, his eyes landing on me. I hugged my meditation pillow to my chest along with my secret desire to leave.

Two weeks later I received a note back from Swami Kripananda. The kind, elder swami who had sent me the first response I ever received from Gurumayi was the same one to send me my last, only this time we knew each other personally. After the brief opening describing the peaceful mornings in the Ganeshpuri courtyard where devotees gathered at Gurumayi's feet for *darshan*, the fateful words appeared:

"As for your inquiry about leaving the ashram, Gurumayi says that's fine. Blessings for the next leg of your journey."

She let me go.

Underneath the blessings in the letter, I felt a chill, and I worried that in my excitement to leave I had acted ungratefully. *What if I had let Gurumayi down? What if I was supposed to be a* Siddha *teacher, not just a teacher? What if I just couldn't stand the heat?* My heart raced. I panicked. I doubted. I went to the meditation cave, that dark, noiseless room I hadn't been to in months. I couldn't slide into meditation. My mind swirled.

Would I return to my stuck, single self outside the ashram? Or had I gathered the strength to put myself out there and not collapse in on myself or crumble for weeks on end when I blew an audition and the casting agents didn't even lift their eyes from their pile of headshots? Was I throwing away all the advancement I had made in my ashram career? Or was it time to be massaged by a man without breaking the rules, time not to simply stand by while blindfolded players swiped at the piñata of life, but to become an active hitter, jerky swings and all?

Sitting there in all that spinning and agitation, I decided I'd had enough. I'd spent so much of my ashram experience in an inner swirl. The content had just shifted from figuring out how to stay to figuring out how to leave. I decided: if the whole point of Siddha Yoga was "God dwells within you, *as you*," then my wish to leave was divine inspiration. I left the cave fortified, and for a little while, the nagging doubts all but subsided.

Now that I had received the official OK, I could let the cat out of the bag.

"Well, I can't tell you how glad we are to hear it," my mother said. I didn't have time to gripe at any smugness on her part because I had exactly $235.00 to my name and needed their help.

Triveni was on vacation, so I was able to break the news to Parvati in private.

"Oooh, this sounds serious," she said on the Monday morning I approached her. She swiveled her chair around to blink at me.

"It is," I shrugged.

A gust of wind agitated the trees outside. The autumn light poured into the office windows from the courtyard, the only time of day it would before it moseyed to the other side of the building. I realized I wouldn't be in this office much longer. What a relief.

"I'm leaving in a few weeks, after my talk at the October Intensive. I'm ready to go back out there." I told her about wanting to try to make it in the world. That I felt strong enough to give my acting and singing a go.

"I don't understand," she shook her head, as if she was saying *kids these days*. "You're doing so well here! You're teaching, you're writing courses, you're *respected*. Why would you want to *leave?*" She looked at me and beyond me at the same time, like the therapist she had been before the ashram, struggling to form an analysis. At first, I was irritated. I wanted her to be just a little happy for me that I had made a decision and felt strong enough to return to the world. But that wasn't her worldview. "I don't understand," she repeated. "This is where everyone wants to be."

I understood that she needed me to want to stay to validate her life choices, and I felt sorry for her at that moment. The ashram was her job, her *raison d'être,* as mine had been just a few months ago. There was no space for another way of being on the path.

But my spell of clarity was, in a few hours' time, infected with doubt.

Parvati was right. You're giving up on something really special. Maybe your problem is with completion. Or success.

This is what groupthink does. When you try to break free or individuate, it lassoes you back into the certainty of its distorted logic. It seeks to concentrate power in one or the whole, not distribute it amongst its parts. It pulls you into the stability of the known, not the chaos of curiosity. Spiritual groups may teach you to seek knowledge within yourself, but they want that knowledge to fit the mold.

I needed help figuring it out, and I didn't trust anyone in the ashram to be the right person. On a jaunt down to the city to search for apartments, I popped in for a paid visit with Kate to make sure I had my head screwed on straight.

I felt a little sad as I buzzed up to her apartment. Waiting for the rickety elevator, a cruel irony presented itself. Years of going within, investing in my spiritual development, did not stop me from needing outward guidance and assurance. In many moments at the ashram, I felt at one with all-that-is, deeply connected to sacred stillness. And yet I was still a confused young woman in my twenties, seeking direction for my life.

I told Kate about my plans to move back to New York.

"A few people, including my *seva* boss, have asked me how I could give up on living in bliss now that I've become a valued community member, and I've started to doubt myself. I *am* doing well there. Am I crazy?"

"Isn't the point of the whole thing to know that bliss is inside you, not attached to the place? Otherwise, you'll be enslaved to the place forever."

Enslaved. Predictably, Kate provided the words and wisdom I needed. And at the evening program that week, the ashram replayed the video of the *Gurukula* talk, the one I'd heard live the summer before, in which Gurumayi described an ashram as a temporary place of discipline and intense study, not a place for work, career advancement, or relationships. That replay validated my entire decision to leave, and I was glad it came from her.

But against all conditioning, I started to think more critically of my guru. The thoughts sloshed against the sides of my brain, causing mild headaches. I still believed in the spiritual value of the *Shakti* that had been transmitted to me through Gurumayi. But was she *enlightened* — living permanently connected to the divine? If she was beyond fear, why did she appear to be operating from it by not talking openly about the problems in the organization? Why did I have to hear about them through *The New Yorker*?

For the first time since she'd left, I was glad she wasn't here. I wouldn't have known how to face her.

My second birthday at the ashram arrived. I was turning twenty-five. As I went around giving out Hershey's kisses, as was custom to offer a little *prasad* to others on your birthday, I said goodbye to those who hadn't heard the news. It was refreshing to have big congratulations from people like Giuliana and even Swami Keshavananda, who really boosted my ego when he said, "Well, we can say we knew you when."

Vera's eyes welled up when I told her. I was touched by this but felt regret when she iced me out for my remaining weeks, the chill of her weak smile nipping at me as she got up from the breakfast table just as I sat down. I tried to imagine my birthday next year, celebrating with friends out somewhere in the city, and returning to an apartment of my own. I wondered what I would wear and who those friends would be.

I had to steel myself to focus on preparing for my talk at the Intensive in the main meditation hall. My talk was the final talk of the Intensive, a personal story about that momentous chanting experience in Los Angeles when I was so depressed, I was going to do something drastic but instead decided to sit down and remember the chant I had heard at the newcomers *satsang* at the Chicago center. I wasn't exaggerating when I wrote, *Chanting saved my life.*

After I handed the draft to someone at Programming, who handed it off to someone in the PR department, I was asked to edit out the stark details of my depression at that time.

At first, I took offense. "But that's how it really was."

"Yes," said the head of PR. "But the point of your talk is to inspire, not to frighten people. Plus, your experience was unique. We don't want to make false promises about what chanting will do for everyone."

False promises. The phrase echoed in my head. No, I didn't want to give those either.

After a few rounds of editing, my story was approved in a meeting with one of the Intensive's swamis and a Program officer, and I practiced it on my trips to the city, in the frantic search for a new apartment. I zig-zagged between the ashram and Manhattan, going down and back in one day, and sometimes staying over with Gabby in her room, clearing my final belongings out of what used to be our place. The jolt of moving between the secular and the sacred worlds in such a short time left me with a sort of spiritual whiplash. When I wasn't excited about the impending move, I was fretting about how I was going to stay calm in the face of all that city chaos.

One thing was clear. I had no need to live near the Manhattan ashram anymore. I wanted to be where the action was happening. I scoured the real estate ads for Greenwich Village studio apartments in my price range, buying the *Times* for the real estate section at the Mountain Market. It was at the height of a hot rental market. The New York University college kids had gobbled up all the small, affordable studios.

I reacted to each apartment possibility as if my life depended on it. In a way, to my post-adolescent brain, it did. I had already given notice at the ashram and if I didn't find a place by mid-month, I would have to live with my parents, a deadening prospect given that they had moved into a one-bedroom apartment and our relationship, though much improved, was still strained. After looking at five or so places and feeling that I didn't want to live in a decrepit claustrophobic box with a tub in the kitchen and one window facing a wall, my parents' friend's daughter was moving out of a village apartment, not far from my Siddha friend, Menake Deb. It was a charmless, renovated, cookie-cutter studio, its only hip feature a brick wall. It reminded me a bit of a college dorm, an apartment that said, *I'm imitating a downtown artist's life rather than living one.* I had a three-day deadline to decide on it, while the rest of the Village inventory of affordable studios was dwindling to zero. On the last day of that window, accepting my likely fate at the brick wall apartment, I ran down to the city to view the sweetest pre-war studio on Jones Street, a 400-square-foot room with crooked hardwood floors, a kitchen-breakfast bar, a non-working fireplace mantle, and a wall of three tall, gothic-crested windows overlooking the quaint street. I saw my life there, sitting by the windows, meditating, drinking coffee, inviting people over, getting dressed up. I looked forward to being a girl — wearing sexy outfits and flirting again, maybe a little like the young people in *Friends*.

However, not having a job yet meant that I had to ask my father to co-sign the lease. "It's not as nice as the one you and Mom discovered. But it's cheaper, and it's the one that really suits me."

"Okay," he said. "But you've gotta get a job."

One big challenge accomplished. One to go.

On the day of my talk, a few days before my departure, I was invited to take the afternoon portion of the Intensive, but I spent the time nervously packing instead. Gabby had signed up for the Intensive. Having someone in the audience I knew who had seen me perform all the way back in college would be comforting and risky, simultaneously lowering and raising the stakes. Her opinion mattered.

Before every *seva*, it was customary to chant a short prayer about surrendering the fruits of your actions to God and getting your ego out of the way. I must have sung this prayer ten times. My legs were shaking. I felt wobbly as I entered the hall at the final break. When it was time, I did what I'd seen so many others do: rise carefully from my meditation cushion up in the front and walk slowly to the lectern. I took a breath and looked out. The hall was only a quarter-full, but that was still a lot of people. After so many *Gitas*, evening programs, and courses, I finally got to see what the hall looked like from this angle.

I buzzed with *Shakti* and nerves as I began. The talk went fine, no major flubs or slip-ups. But I really couldn't be sure how it landed with the audience.

I joined the stream of people leaving the hall and heading to Atma Nidhi for dinner. A few people, one I knew and two I didn't, said they enjoyed my talk as they passed. But Gabby's reflections, as my friend and the person who'd walked this path with me from the start, mattered the most. We were supposed to have dinner together after the Intensive, before she headed back to the city for the work week, but I couldn't find her. She knew what a big deal this was for me. Why hadn't she made it a point to come find me and congratulate me?

As I stepped onto the wooded path between the buildings, the air thickened. Leaves carpeted the forest floor, forming a speckled gold and orange path. The sky was white, and an evening chill descended. I finally spotted her at the end of the path, her red shawl draped neatly over her shoulders, walking with some devotees from the Intensive. We hugged and made our way into the dining hall. We talked about her experience at the Intensive, about our summers, my new apartment, and her new roommate. She was happy I was returning to the city, but let me know she was still upset with me for leaving. I thought we were finally getting over my abandonment of our life, but there was still more. Sigh. She didn't say a thing about the talk.

Finally, I took the bait. "So, what did you think?"

"About what?"

I wanted to shake her. "My talk."

"You were good," she said ambivalently.

"Thanks," I said, feeling enraged, exposed, and impotent. My heart curled up into my chest. When we parted that evening, I had a sense that Gab would not be one of the friends I relied on when I moved back into secular life. The rift had grown too big and gotten moldy.

In my final two weeks at the ashram, as I said my last goodbyes and tied up loose strings at the Dakshina Committee office, the trees exploded into their fiery show, and the air was often pregnant with moisture, giving it a smooth texture, like breathing velvet. On the morning of my last *Guru Gita*, various shades of blue-gray streaked the sky. I knew I wouldn't continue to get up before the sun in my new life. I would miss the intimacy and silence of this time of day. I took a gulp of that thick air, bringing the crisp moisture deep into my lungs.

After the *Gita*, a group of us stood in silence, waiting for the shuttle to the main building for breakfast. I looked out at the low clouds, at the red, gold, and purple hues of the trees, the smell of decomposing leaves infusing the air around us. A wave of peace ran through me.

Wow. I am really going to miss this.

I closed my eyes, the velvety air flowing in and out. I had given everything of myself to this path. I had a year and change of having all my meals and rent taken care of, like a do-over of childhood, so that I could build strength, go within, and know myself. I felt so much older than when I arrived, and not just because Gurumayi had joked that I was sixty. My self-perception had emerged into an understanding that I was unique, that my uniqueness had value, and no matter how many times I confused it for damage, the correct understanding was indelible.

I felt totally blessed. I almost wanted to cry, to fall to my knees in gratitude right there, waiting for the shuttle. The big yellow school bus arrived. I hopped on and landed in a seat in the back, hoisting my knees against the seat back in front of me. I looked out at the ashram grounds, moving quickly out of focus as we pulled onto the road. My very next thought: *I can't wait to start my new life.*

24: A Trail of Equipoise

As I emerged from the subway, a waft of spicy, hot air from the restaurant vent assaulted me. My legs were burning from climbing the subway stairs, but I liked how they looked in the Nine West boots I bought on sale for my new job as a data manager for the online version of *Playbill*. I reached into my backpack and pulled out my keys.

This was the week. On the three block walk to my apartment, I knew I would pass a newsstand where it waited.

So much happened in the span of just four weeks, like I'd been living in a video on fast forward. I filled the Jones Street apartment with a few pieces of extra furniture from the storage bin at my parents' apartment building, scrambled to get a job, and commute to and from midtown every day. Walking home from the subway was new and disorienting. Every time I approached my four-story walk up and fumbled with the keys, relishing the sweet sound of the jingle — *my own keys!* — I felt excitement about life's possibilities.

I was thrilled to get a job so quickly, and one connected to theater, writing, and this amazing new thing called the Internet. During my interview at *Playbill*, after the secretary buzzed me in, I walked past the cubicles and heard for the first time a crackly, multi-toned buzz — the workings of a dial-up modem — followed by a cheerful man's voice alerting: "You've got mail." When I got my own email address, I searched the America Online

(AOL) database for other contacts who had one, too. I sent a brief note to Alex and felt somewhat hip and savvy, for a change, in being able to do so.

Most days, I felt focused and noticeably not shrouded in my old heaviness. Other than the siren song of the donut shop around the corner, which got louder when the pang of loneliness hit me at night and on weekends, there was a solidness to the enthusiasm about my new life. At lunch, I took my Styrofoam square of steamtable veggies back to my desk and ate while flipping through the theater trade mag, *Backstage*. In the latest edition, I circled three interesting, affordable acting classes and one jazz pianist who was looking to partner with a singer. I'd been fantasizing about singing in a club and getting a part in a play.

As I walked towards the newsstand, the chatter in my head focused on what I would read and how it would affect me.

There it hung in the newsstand window, *The New Yorker*, with its title "O Guru, Guru, Guru" pasted boldly on the front. The cover story was about *my* guru. Protectiveness and intrigue jockeyed for position within. I ordered vegetarian take-out from the falafel place two doors down and sat down to read.

It was awful. The article accused Gurumayi's followers of carrying guns and threatening violence to her brother on her behalf. She was painted as a power-hungry abuser of her brother. Women who were sexually abused by Baba shared their memories. The accusations were no longer rumors that I sensed were true, but real people's words, printed in ink in a venerated publication. The article's author was aghast at the ghoulishness of the ashram, but I didn't recognize the Disney-esque place she described. I still thought it was beautiful. And when she quoted Gurumayi telling her mother to go jump in a lake, I knew how cruel it seemed. But in my mind, I could see her saying it, hear the tone she used at the ashram when she play-acted anger to make a point. Oddly, it made me smile.

I reflected on being both afraid of and thrilled by Gurumayi's anger, fearing I might be scorched by it but never was. She would raise her voice and scrunch her brow in this exaggerated way that signaled she was overdoing it to make a point. "What do you think an ashram is?" I remembered her yelling to a group of devotees hanging out at Amrit in the middle of the day. "A place to eat vegetarian food and fart?!" She seemed more to me in that moment like Jesus in the temple than abusive. I remembered asking Kesh how it felt when she criticized him in front of thousands of people. I thought he was telling the truth when he said that while it looked bad, on the inside she was blasting him with *Shakti* so strong, he couldn't hold his head up. That was why he always had to put his head to the floor.

But the article implied that she was really mean to real people. I'm flummoxed in reconsidering everything.

The phone rang. Sweet music. The sound was so soothing, so full of promise. I was not alone. Someone cared about me. Someone wanted to connect.

"Ah, hello, is Blair Glaser there?"

"This is she." I recognized his voice but hardly believed a Siddha swami was calling me at home.

"Blair, it's Swami Keshavananda. How are you doing?"

I was happy to hear his voice, and yet, it was so awkward.

"Good." I said, wanting to tell him I was just thinking about him but more curious as to why he was calling. "How are you?"

"Well. I suppose you know the article came out. I wanted to check in on you. Did you read it?"

It was splayed open on the counter, decorated with tahini smudges from my falafel takeout. "Yeah."

I was touched. He still cared, even though I'd left. Someone over there was thinking that I might be here alone reading this shit show and it might be affecting me and I might need a friend.

"You okay?" Kesh asked.

"Yes. I'm okay." I didn't know how I would continue on the path, but I hadn't abandoned it yet, just downgraded to a layperson's approach. I didn't tell him that I understood even more how putting anyone on a pedestal is dangerous, that real hurt was caused and it disgusted me, that one month into creating a different life I was forgiving myself for my own self-betrayal. I couldn't think of anything to say to him, so I just said, "Thank you." He checked in one more time, hardly believing that I was okay. We managed to muddle through a brief catch-up and hang up.

A few weeks after I left, several friends in my age group, including Vera, also returned to the city. The ashram had nudged them out. I patched together a loose network of old friends and devotees from Siddha Yoga and saw a lot of great shows through my job. Instead of a raucous and rollicking New Year's Eve, Gabby and I, still loosely connected to one another and creatures of habit, felt the pull of nostalgia, and despite the fact that the bubble had burst, we got a ride to the ashram.

The hall was packed, and the lights were low for the 24-hour chant that would peak at midnight. Kevali hugged me as we entered and escorted Gab and me to two seats near the front of the hall, which was still an honor even though Gurumayi was in India. It was so weird to be back and not be on the inside, like going home after you've moved out and your room is now your mom's office, but I was clear that I wouldn't have it any other way. Chanting wildly towards the New Year, I vacillated between feeling connected to the chant and over it.

On New Year's Day, we listened to an audio stream of Gurumayi's New Year's talk piped in from Ganeshpuri with her New Year's Message, a guideline to live by for 1995. The message was *Blaze a Trail of Equipoise*.

I mean, with all the doubts about the path, the message — with two key words from my whole ashram journey, *blaze* and *equipoise* — was a beautiful send-off. *Blaze a Trail of Equipoise* was the beginning and the end, the full circle message I could sink my teeth into. It was as if I'd received her blessings to move on even as I was breaking free of the Siddha Yoga playbook.

That was the last ashram celebration I ever attended. I visited the ashram just twice more over the next six years, to show my serious boyfriends where I'd spent the most transformative year of my life. After the devastating accusations came out in *The New Yorker*'s article, devotees left in droves, and the ashram eventually closed its doors to day visitors sometime in the Aughts.

Epilogue: Reckoning

More than thirty years after leaving the ashram, I find no shortage of streaming documentaries about transformational groups gone haywire with scandal, distorted beliefs, and abusive leadership. I spent much of the COVID pandemic watching them. They all bring my Siddha Yoga experience into question, forcing me to see it from new angles. The Netflix documentary *Wild, Wild Country*, about the '80s Utopian cult that took over an entire town in Oregon, was the first to push my buttons. That organization's attempts to preserve itself supposedly resulted in murder. Towards the end, one of the main characters, a lawyer, shares his love, respect, and appreciation for his (obvious to us viewers) corrupt and drug-addicted guru, Rajneesh / Osho. One part of me wants to shout, "You're a lawyer! You've got a brain. Open your eyes!" Naturally, another part of me relates to him.

Maybe the lawyer had mystical experiences of synchronicity with his teacher that made him feel loved and known, experiences like mine that are difficult to make sense of because they *feel* so personal. Maybe he felt giddy inside whenever his teacher was around, as one might with their favorite pop star, and that feeling blinded him to his teacher's true character. Maybe his own hidden talents were revealed in his teacher's presence, talents that helped him excel, filling him with unspeakable gratitude.

Daniel Shaw, a former Siddha Yogi, psychotherapist and author, pops up on Netflix's *Cults, Explained*. In the late '90s, Shaw, a crusader against the trauma caused by narcissistic leaders, helped establish a website that catalogs all the tragically distorted and unethical aspects of the SYDA (Siddha Yoga Dham America) ashrams. On this site, people openly discuss the impact of Baba's sexual predation, Gurumayi's power-hungry behavior, and more. Many former devotees report being seriously hurt by Siddha gurus, their hearts and lives broken, their ability to trust shattered. I believe every one of these tragic stories. On a popular podcast, "A Little Bit Culty," hosted by ex-members of the famed NVXM cult, Shaw shares several stories of Gurumayi's sadistic abuse. One reveals how she commanded a group of devotees to turn on another student without explanation. It's sickening to hear how she set people up to endure incredible pain, in theory for their spiritual growth, but seemingly for her own enjoyment. Maybe Gurumayi *had* been laughing at — not with — me, to my face.

And still. That possibility doesn't cancel out the usefulness of my time with her.

My story is not a tragedy.

I was lucky to go into my Siddha Yoga experience after having encountered some good psychotherapy. I was lucky that the groupthink of the ashram didn't bar me from seeing family members, and I was lucky to have family members whose imperfect but dogged love was a part of my healing process. And I was lucky that, despite all its rigidity and dogma, the practices helped me develop the skills for contemplation. The ability to cultivate space between my awareness and swirling mind in order to hear what my inner self was really saying played an instrumental role in my leaving.

Holding these two truths — the cultish abuses of the organization and its personal value to me — is perilous. If I stand only in solidarity with the victims and make the entire organization bad, then I must reject the many good things I gained. I must deny my own gratitude. If I only honor my experience, I act as Osho's foolish lawyer, blind to the searing injustices caused by Siddha Yoga. It is a complexity I live with.

Shortly after leaving the ashram, I realized that I could merge my two passions, healing and theater, into a profession. I thought I invented *drama therapy*, the use of theater techniques to heal and solve problems, until I discovered it was a real modality I could get a Master's degree in. I led popular workshops for women and loved working as a psychotherapist, largely with women who suffered sexual abuse. But after twenty years, I started studying the intricacies of leadership and the relationship between leaders and followers. These days, when I'm not writing, I work as an executive leadership coach, consulting with leaders and their teams.

The impact leaders have on their followers and companies is multifaceted and compelling. Most leaders have little awareness of how they are being perceived and internalized by the people they lead, all of whom have a wide variety of backgrounds and life experiences. I help mission-driven leaders make sense of these multi-layered machinations and build bridges to those they need to influence. My clients tend to be passionate people who are interested in creating equitable company cultures and are willing to explore the impact of their behavior on their organizations. They tend to err on the side of holding back from leading because they are sensitive to power dynamics and don't want to overstep. I'm often nudging them to step more fully into the authority of the role so they can carry out the tasks of leading and earn the trust of their staff. But, I will often remind them, *it is the role* that holds the power. *Their* power lies in being able to play the role with as much authenticity as possible and with accountability for the inevitable mistakes that all leaders will make. Leaders who model accountability show their followers that being human — not *perfect* — is what is required, and can establish more creative, risk-taking environments.

Gurumayi betrayed her followers primarily by propagating a deferential system where there were no checks on her power. She has failed to acknowledge Baba's predation and engage the victims and the community in an open and healing forum. Her inability to hold space for the victims and be accountable for the legacy of his wrongdoing is another devastating impact of the power differential that comes from idolization and the need to uphold a perfect image.

I can't stop trying to make sense of my time involved in Siddha Yoga, but in truth, it remains a mystery. After years of distance and retroactive suspicion, and of reckoning with the dangers and benefits of my spiritual practice, something inexplicable about my connection with Gurumayi resurfaces from time to time.

A few years after the uncanny "visit" that day in Soul Dog, she appeared at another vulnerable time. Still single and without children at thirty-six, I wanted to put down roots. I took up a grueling search for an affordable home, starting in New York City and eventually looking at more than eighty houses upstate. When I finally found The One in the gorgeous hamlet of Woodstock, New York, on the other side of the Catskills from the ashram, it had holes in the floor and appliances from 1975. I'd heard horror stories about renovations — long waits, money bleeds, shady contractors — and being single made me feel prone to being taken advantage of. But I took the risk. After the first day of interior demolition, I went to check on progress. The house was all bones, a cavernous shell. A workstation in the living room showcased a bulletin board propped up on a chair, hosting nothing but a paper pinwheel and a picture of Gurumayi.

I did a double-take. "Why is there a picture of Gurumayi on the board?" I yelled out to the men somewhere around the house.

"Who?" asked my contractor, appearing from nowhere.

I pointed to the board.

"Oh, we found her underneath the stove, and the pinwheel in the wall. We put them up there for good luck."

They had no idea who she was or what she had meant to me or how many houses I had looked at before finding this one. I smiled, shook my head, and muttered to myself throughout the day. The renovations went off without a hitch. Another serendipitous mystery.

After all the betrayals spawned by my own gurus and many teachers far and wide, I still believe in the power of growth and community, of gathering with like-minded people to practice something that lifts us out of the weeds of our daily existence, towards awareness, expansion, and self-betterment. Spiritual practice can be a terrific way to grow, and teachers can provide wonderful, lifesaving guidance.

In *Cults, Explained*, ex-Siddha psychologist Shaw recalls feeling "wave after wave of love and connectedness" when he first joined Siddha Yoga. Later, he realized it was all a delusion, a part of getting sucked in. For me, today, with a little time and effort, I can still access the stillness and ecstasy I felt within myself at the ashram.

Just before the pandemic — irony of ironies — my husband and I relocated to LA. The isolation of quarantine was hard on us, and a good friend on the East Coast introduced me to her LA friend, Linda. Linda and I discovered that in addition to both being writers, we were ex-Siddha devotees and also, in need of some inner equipoise. We now meet on alternate Sundays with Rhoda, another ex-devotee, to chant and meditate and enjoy a homemade lunch.

No guru. No groupthink. No lofty goals of enlightenment. Just the practices and good company. It is deeply rewarding.

Author Bio

Blair Glaser is a leadership consultant and creator of the HI (Human Intelligence) Substack. Her essays have appeared in Longreads, Oldster, Quartz, HuffPost, Inside Higher Ed, Dorothy Parker's Ashes, and others, as well as in literary magazines such as Brevity, In Short, and The Mantlepiece. She's read stories live at events such as Writer's Read, Generation Women, and The Woodstock Bookfest. Blair lives with her husband and dog-ter, Vanna White, in Venice, CA. More can be found at www.blairglaser.com.

photo © Kim Fox Photography

Acknowledgments

Firstly, I would like to thank Naomi Dunford for coming up with an affordable three-month course called Write a Book with Me, which I took thinking I would outline a leadership book for my website. Ha ha. That course set me on the path to write TIL and began my foray into narrative nonfiction, for which I needed a lot of help and encouragement early on. Deepest gratitude to Martha Frankel, Susanna Einstein, and Kathleen Harris for providing it. To Kristin Noel for publishing my first ashram-related essay in Best Health. And to all my earlier draft readers: Sarah Patterson, Jill Leigh, Laurice Adams, Deb Blossom, Linda Schreyer, Aileen Weintraub, Mindy Johnson, Rhoda Pregerson, Deirdre Day, and Amy Ferris for their time, and for their kind and useful reflections.

Thank you to my incredibly sensitive developmental editor, Elizabeth Gassman, who taught me how to shape the story with more depth and layers. To Allison Williams for normalizing Seven Drafts in her book of the same name — I ended up with nine. To my online forum of writers that outlined all the necessary evils involved in publishing a memoir in this day and age, and for being a safe space to share and vent. To my writing group, since 2022 — who have at times included Lea Page, Barbie Beaton, Kate Kaiser, Sandra Eliason, Diahann Reyes-Lane, Jennifer Berney, and Jacque Gorlick — thank you for your diligent eyes, your patience, belief in my writing, and offering the tough reflections that make me a better writer. And deepest thanks to Lea Page, for being an insanely generous companion and book midwife.

Thank you to those who agreed to read and provide public feedback: Jeffrey Davis, Kaitlyn Herman, Oliver Radclyffe, Sasha Cagen, and especially Sari Botton, who offhandedly agreed to pass the manuscript on to Naomi at Heliotrope. Thank you, Naomi, for your kind and visionary partnership in bringing *TIL* off my desktop and into the world. Extra thanks to Ray Kuntz for the extra protection.

Thank you to my friends. Too many to name here, but you know who you are and how much I love and depend on you. And to Richard Nodell for your soulful insight and sophisticated guidance over the years.

Thank you to my amazing graphic designer, Joanna Holden. And to Rick Simner, for providing a cover that thrills me, and for being a brother even though we're technically cousins. And to Alexis Silver for your love and things too many and complex to name here. I love you both.

Thank you to my beautiful parents. A home with regularity, routine, and love is a privilege that can set the stage for success later in life. I am so grateful for you, your hard work, and support over the years.

Finally, I would like to thank my husband, Aaron. Prior to this book, I attempted to write four others, but was not able to complete them in large part because I couldn't tolerate the loneliness of writing. As a result of your tender presence and companionship, your belief in my story, and generosity of heart, the writing of this book was possible.

www.ingramcontent.com/pod-product-compliance
Lightning Source LLC
Chambersburg PA
CBHW031316160426
43196CB00007B/560